Paradise Restored

The Social Ethics of Francis of Assisi

A COMMENTARY ON HIS "SALUTATION OF THE VIRTUES"

J. Hoeberichts

PARADISE RESTORED: The Social Ethics of Francis of Assisi – A Commentary on Francis' "Salutation of the Virtues"
J. Hoeberichts

Franciscan Press
Quincy University
1800 College Avenue
Quincy, Illinois 62301-2699
Ph. 217-228-5670
Fax 217-228-5672
www.francisanpress.com

©2004 Franciscan Press

All rights reserved

Book design and typesetting by Laurel Fitch, Chicago, Illinois
Cover design by Terrence Riddell and Sharon Barnett
Cover art by Terrence Riddell

Printed in the United States of America
First Edition: 2004
First Printing: 2004
9 0

Library of Congress Cataloging-in-Publication Data

Hoeberichts, J., 1929-
Paradise restored : the social ethics of Francis of Assisi : a commentary on his "Salutation of the virtues" / J. Hoeberichts. – 1st ed. p.cm.
Includes bibliographica references.
ISBN 0-8199-1008-2
1. Francis, of Assisi, Saint, 1182-1226. Saluto alle virtiá. 2. Christian ethics–Catholic authors–History–To 1500. 3. Sociology, Christian (Catholic)–History–To 1500. 4. Social ethics–History–To1500. 5. Virtues–History–To 1500 I. Title.

BJ15249.H574.2003
241'.,42–dc21

Contents

ABBREVIATIONS vii

PREFACE ix

PROLOGUE: SYNOPSIS 1

CHAPTER I: INTRODUCTORY QUESTIONS 5

AUTHENTICITY

LITERARY GENRE

Song of praise

Didactic poem or penitential song

Play

Song of victory

Scheme for a sermon

Prayer

Reminder

SITZ IM LEBEN

Itinerant preaching

The everyday life of the first brothers

The crisis of obedience during the last years of Francis' life

Francis' depression

The conflict with the learned brothers

DATE

STRUCTURE

Lehmann

Reijsbergen

Zweerman

v.d.Goorbergh-Zweerman

TARGET GROUP

CONCLUSION

CHAPTER II: SALUTATION OF THE VIRTUES AND PRAYER FOR THEIR SALVATION (VV. 1-4) *37*

TEXT

GENERAL OBSERVATIONS

Queen. Lady, sister

The Lord save you

Holy, most holy

The number of virtues, their selection and relationship

DETAILED EXEGESIS

Ave--Hail

Queen Wisdom

With your sister, holy pure Simplicity (v.1)

Lady, holy Poverty

With your sister, holy Humility (v.2)

Lady, holy Charity

With your sister, holy Obedience (v.3)

Most holy virtues, the Lord save you all (v.4)

CHAPTER III: THE ACQUISTION AND POSSESSION OF THE VIRTUES (VV. 5-8) *153*

TEXT

DETAILED EXEGESIS

There is no one at all in the whole world

Unless he first dies (v.5)

Whoever possesses one, possesses all (v.6)

Whoever offends one, offends all (v.7)

And each one confounds vices and sins (v.8)

CHAPTER IV: THE EFFECTS OF EACH INDIVIDUAL VIRTUE (VV. 9-14) *173*

TEXT

DETAILED EXEGESIS

Holy Wisdom confounds Satan

And all his malice (v.9)

Pure holy Simplicity confounds all the wisdom of this world

And the wisdom of the body (v.10)

Holy Poverty confounds all covetousness and avarice

And the cares of this age (v.11)

Holy Humility confounds pride
And all the people who are in the world and
All the things that are in the world (v.12)
Holy Charity confounds all the temptations of the devil and the flesh
And all carnal fears (v.13)
Holy Obedience confounds all wishes of the body
And all wishes of the flesh (v.14)

CHAPTER V: THE OBEDIENT BROTHER (VV. 15-18) *233*
TEXT
GENERAL OBSERVATIONS
Parallel texts
Structure
DETAILED EXEGESIS
And [the obedient brother] has his body mortified
To obedience of the Spirit
And to obedience of his brother (v.15)
And he is subject and submissive to all the people who are in the world (v.16)
And not to people only but even to all beasts and wild animals (v.17)
So that they may do with them whatever they want, insofar as it has been given them from above by the Lord (v.18)

CONCLUSION *259*
BIBLIOGRAPHY *273*

Abbreviations

Writings of Francis

Adm	Admonitions
ExpOurFather	Prayer Inspired by the Our Father
LetCler	Letter to the Clergy
1 LetCust	First Letter to the Custodians
1 LetFaith	First Version of the Letter to the Faithful or Earlier Exhortation to the Brothers and Sisters of Penance
2 LetFaith	Second Version of the Letter to the Faithful or Later Admonition and Exhortation to the Brothers and Sisters of Penance
LetLeo	Letter to Brother Leo
LetMin	Letter to a Minister
LetOrder	Letter to the Entire Order
LetRulers	Letter to the Rulers of the Peoples
OffPass	Office of the Passion
PrGod	Praises of God
PrHours	Praises to Be Said at All the Hours
RegB	Later Rule (1223)
RegNB	Earlier Rule (1221)
SalBVM	Salutation of the Blessed Virgin Mary
SalVirt	Salutation of the Virtues
Test	Testament
True Joy	True Joy

SOURCES FOR THE LIFE OF FRANCIS

AnPer — Anonymus Peruginus, in: *L'Anonyme de Pérouse, Traduction et Introduction*, par Pierre-B. Beguin, Paris, 1979.

Bonaventura LM — Bonaventure, *Major Life of St. Francis*, in: *St. Francis of Assisi. Writings and Early Biographies. English Omnibus of the Sources for the Life of St. Francis*, Chicago, 1973, 627–787.

1 Cel — Thomas of Celano, *First Life of St. Francis, English Omnibus*, 225–355. New translation in: R. Armstrong, W. Hellmann, W. Short, *Francis of Assisi: Early Documents. Vol. I: The Saint*, New York 1999, 180–297.

2 Cel — Thomas of Celano, *Second Life of St. Francis, English Omnibus*, 357–543.

3 Comp — *Legend of the Three Companions*, ibid., 885–956.

Jordan — *Chronicle of Brother Jordan of Giano*, in: *Early Franciscan Classics*, Paterson, NJ., 1962, 235–272.

LegPer — *Legend of Perugia, English Omnibus*, 975–1091.

SpecPerf — *Mirror of Perfection*, ibid., 1117–1265.

JOURNALS, WORKS IN SERIES

FL — *Franciscaans Leven*, DenBosch-Utrecht, 1917ff.

FrancDigest — *Franciscan Digest, A Service for Franciscan Spirituality*, Manila, 1991ff.

FranzSt — *Franziskanische Studien*, Münster-Werl, 1914–1993.

Laur — *Laurentianum*, Roma, 1960ff.

PL — *Patrologiae cursus completus*, Series Latina, accurante J.P.Migne, Parisiis, 1844–1905.

WissWeis — *Wissenschaft und Weisheit*, Mönchengladbach-Düsseldorf, 1934ff.

Preface

This study on Francis of Assisi's Salutation of the Virtues has grown far beyond the expectations which I had when I started this study in 1996. I had just finished the English translation of my book on *Francis and Islam*, and was looking for a suitable topic in the field of Franciscan studies which I could develop in greater depth. Because of my age—I was born in 1929—and my being a laryngectomee since September 1995, I felt that a major study was no longer possible, especially also since I had still other commitments which I did not want to give up. These considerations limited my choice. To write a commentary on one of Francis' major writings, for example, was therefore out of the question. If I would decide to study one of Francis' writings, it would have to be one of the smaller, lesser known ones. Further, its study should be of more than just historical interest. It should, at the same time, also contribute to the praxis of Franciscan readers today in that it would help them to translate the views and ideals of Francis and his first brothers into action in the context of the present world.

At that moment, an observation, made by David Flood, came again to my mind. In the conclusion of his *Francis of Assisi and the Franciscan Movement*, he characterizes the Salutation as "a synthesis of movement action." As such, it describes the basic forces or foundational virtues through which the movement, in opposition to Assisi's system, was to realize its historical mission in the world by confounding the evil in whatever form it presented itself and so redeeming the world that had fallen away from God's original plan with humankind. Moreover, Francis wrote the Salutation at a time when the brotherhood went through a crisis of identity due to the increased influx of learned brothers who wanted to move in a different direction than the one envisaged by Francis.

Recalling this observation, my choice was soon made. For, when read from this perspective, the Salutation would provide me with an entry into the basics of an authentic Franciscan praxis. It would, moreover, indicate how Francis analyzed the dangers that had led to the critical situation of the brotherhood, and how he hoped to overcome this crisis by reminding the brothers of the six virtues that were in his eyes the foundation of the life and mission of the brotherhood. Finally, although in light of the previous reasons for my choice this was now of lesser importance, the Salutation was one of the smaller writings of Francis which had not received much attention in the English-speaking world.

During my research on the Salutation, I never came to regret the choice I had made. It proved a very exciting and rewarding experience to read the Salutation as a reminder which Francis thought necessary within the historical context of the crisis in the brotherhood. Further, comparing the Salutation with relevant passages from Francis' other writings, I was able to unveil gradually, verse by verse, the amazing riches as well as the remarkable depth of views and ideas which in this small writing lay hidden behind its condensed poetic form. In this way, I obtained in the course of time a clearer insight into the social ethics of Francis, as I called it, as well as into the deeper underlying motive, theological in its formulation, but socio-political in its intent, which moved Francis and his brothers in their actions: the restoration of paradise, the making of a world that was more in conformity to God's original plan.

For the reader, this verse by verse commentary in which each virtue is studied separately has the disadvantage that at times it may become somewhat repetitive, especially since, as Francis observes, none of these basic forces or virtues can exist without the other. Each one presupposes the other and hence cannot be treated without referring to the others. I have tried, however, to reduce these repetitions to a minimum. On the other hand, the separate treatment of each virtue has the advantage that our individual commentary on each of the six foundational virtues becomes like a small monograph that can also be read independently of the others.

This study would never have been completed were it not for the continuous encouragement I received from Fidelis, my most beloved wife and constant helper, and from Wim (Anselm) Moons, OFM, my friend and brother, who always with great interest after the progress I was making and helped me to focus again on my study when I got distracted by becoming too involved in other activities. My sincere thanks go also to Dr. Jaime Vidal, Director of Franciscan Press, and his editorial board who accepted my study for publication, and, very especially, to Dr. Terrence Riddell who generously offered to revise and edit my text.

Synopsis

The Salutation of the Virtues has not received much attention in the English speaking world. This is not surprising as the title is not very appealing to people of our time. An author like Raoul Manselli does not help much to change this situation when he describes *The Salutationof the Virtues* as a "devotional outpouring," nor does Regis Armstrong, who characterizes *The Salutation of the Virtues* as the writing that "is perhaps most clearly influenced by chivalry or the troubadour tradition."[1] Alasdair McIntyre, who in his *After Virtue: A Study in Moral Theory* pleads for a renewed interest in the virtues, and more concretely for the establishment of communities where people strive together to find the way towards a virtuous life in the midst of the world and its structures, was not able to awaken an interest in Francis' *The Salutation of the Virtues*.[2]

However, on closer examination the *Salutation* appears to be an important document to obtain a deeper insight in the spirituality of Francis and the early Franciscans. For it was composed by Francis at a time when the brotherhood went through a crisis of identity. At this crucial moment Francis used also his poetic skills to remind the brothers of the virtues, the values, that are foundational to the Franciscan brotherhood and its evangelical mission of peace in the world.

The Salutation of the Virtues can therefore be characterized as a

[1] R. Manselli, *St. Francis of Assisi*, Chicago, 1988, 309; R. Armstrong, *St. Francis of Assisi: Writings for a Gospel Life*, New York, 1994, 191.

[2] Alasdair MacIntyre, *After Virtue: A Study in Moral Theory*, London, 1985.

poetic reminder or even a poetic testament which Francis composes so that the brothers may take to heart and never forget the virtues, God's holy forces, that are to shape the brotherhood in its continuous struggle to build an alternative society against the forces of evil that are threatening the brotherhood and its original ideals.

Reading *The Salutationof the Virtues* in this context, i.e. the historical context of Francis and his early brothers, it is clear that *The Salutation of the Virtues* is not in the first place an ascetico-spiritual document supporting the individual brother in his striving for personal holiness.[3] Rather, it must be understood as a socio-political document encouraging the brothers to stand firm in their struggle for social transformation, i.e. their struggle for a world which is governed, not by sin and evil, but by the virtues, led by Queen Wisdom. For as these virtues proceed from the most holy God, they will confound the forces of evil and thus be instrumental in establishing God's kingdom, God's lordship on earth: paradise restored.

As such, *The Salutation of the Virtues* can be described as a Franciscan social or political ethics, which challenges Francis' followers at the beginning of the third millennium in their commitment to the realization of God's reign on the basis of the virtues that constitute the very heart of the Franciscan way of life according to the form of the gospel which the Lord, and no one else, revealed to Francis.

In my commentary, I will in a first chapter deal with a number of introductory questions such as authenticity, literary genre, origin, audience and structure. In the next chapters, I will give an extensive exegesis of each of the four parts of *The Salutation of the Virtues*.

In the first part, Francis' poetic testament opens with a greeting of Queen Wisdom and her Lady Virtues who, in a kind of royal procession, are solemnly introduced before the brothers. This greeting is

[3] See D. Flood, *Francis of Assisi and the Franciscan Movement*, Manila, 1989, 168–173. "We may not reduce Francis' doctrine of the virtues to a personal ascetical attitude. We must allow the entire project of life of Francis and his first brothers as it found expression in the Rule, to resonate as background. In the first brotherhood poverty and humility also have a social significance. As a community the brothers wish to unmask, to expose the ideals of their society as a false way of salvation. Their concrete life as brothers, that is their social choices regarding labor, salary, position and housing (RegNB 7), was meant to demythologize the new merchant society that was developing in Assisi." A. Jansen, "Lofzang op de Deugden II," *FL* 75 (1992) 173.

accompanied by the wish that the Lord, from whom they proceed, may save them from the difficult situation in which the brotherhood finds itself (1–4). Introducing here these six virtues that form the very basis of the brotherhood as an alternative society, Francis clearly reminds his brothers of the shape and character of the alternative society, paradise, that he and his brothers are committed to realizing in the name of God and after the example of Jesus.

The second part is a short intermezzo, in which Francis informs his brothers about the way they will be able to acquire and to preserve the virtues (5–8). Francis stresses that to die first is an essential condition for acquiring and possessing a virtue. As to the relation between the virtues among themselves, Francis follows the traditional doctrine.

In the third part, Francis assures his brothers that, if they allow the virtues, God's holy forces, to work in and through their works *(operatio)*, they will confound Satan and with him the evil that in its many forms threatens the brotherhood and the world in which they live (9–14). In naming these many forms of evil, Francis indicates that he and his brothers have made a thorough analysis of the evil forces that dominated the society of their days and tried to determine its future direction. To withstand these forces and to confound them in the strength of God's holy virtues is the mission the Lord gave to Francis, namely, to live according to the model of the gospel, exemplified in the life and death of the poor and humble Jesus.

Finally, in the last part, Francis describes the obedient brother who, through his obedience to the Spirit and to his brother, is ready to give his life, as Jesus did, by being subject and submissive to every human creature and even to beasts and wild animals (15–18). These final verses were added because of problems within the brotherhood with regard to being subject to all and probably also because of questions in connection with going among the Saracens. In these verses, Francis once again opens up the perspective of paradise where all people of the world, Christians and Muslims, and all beasts and wild animals can live together in peace, just as God had willed it from the very beginning of creation. In this way Francis hopes, at the end of his life, to motivate his brothers so that, in spite of all difficulties and hardships, they will continue to commit themselves to this ideal, this utopia, in the footsteps of Jesus.

CHAPTER ONE

Introductory Questions

After the commentary which Sigismund Verhey wrote in 1960 on *The Salutation of the Virtues* (SalVirt) in the broader context of his study on the theological anthropology of Francis,[1] the German and Dutch speaking worlds remained silent about this writing of Francis for almost 25 years. In 1984, Leonhard Lehmann was the first to devote again a study to *The Salutation of the Virtues* in his doctoral dissertation on universalism as a fundamental characteristic of the prayers of Francis.[2] In 1989, Ron Reijsbergen took *The Salutation of the Virtues* as the subject for his master's thesis in which he paid special attention to a structural analysis of *The Salutation of the Virtues*.[3] A year later, in 1990, Theo Zweerman showed a similar interest in the structure of *The Salutation of the Virtues* in an article based on a lecture given during a seminar on Mysticism in the Franciscan Order.[4] Together with E. v.d.

[1] S. Verhey, *Der Mensch unter der Herrschaft Gottes. Versuch einer Theologie des Menschen nach dem hl. Franziskus von Assisi*, ch. 6: Das Lob der Tugenden, Düsseldorf, 1960, 107–133.

[2] L. Lehmann, *Tiefe und Weite. Der universale Grundzug in den Gebeten des Franziskus von Assisi*, ch. 9: Der Gruß an die Tugenden, Werl 1984, 221–246.

[3] R. Reijsbergen, *Omkeer van een verdwaalde mens. Poging tot een maatschappijhistorische interpretatie van de Lofzang op de deugden van Franciscus van Assisi*, Den Haag 1989. It is remarkable that the structural analysis which forms the central part of his thesis and receives more attention than the socio-historical interpretation, is not mentioned in the title.

[4] Th. Zweerman, Mystik bei Franziskus von Assisi. Unter besonderer Berücksichtigung der "Salutatio Virtutum", in: *Mystik in den franziskanischen Orden*, ed. J-B Freyer, Kevelaer 1993, 20–46.

Goorbergh, Zweerman published a revised and enlarged edition of this article in 1998.[5] In line with Lehmann but independently from him, André Jansen studied *The Salutation of the Virtues* in a commentary on the prayers of Francis, published in 1992.[6] Finally, in 1999, Hans Sevenhoven wrote a short introduction to *The Salutation of the Virtues*, emphasizing Francis' interest in using unconventional methods to get his message across to his brothers and to the people.[7] Outside the Dutch and German speaking worlds, there appeared on the European continent in recent years only one article in Spanish by Martin Steiner.[8]

In the English-speaking world, it was David Flood who drew attention to *The Salutation of the Virtues* in his *Francis of Assisi and the Franciscan Movement* (1989) wherein he resumed the main ideas of an article written a year earlier.[9] There he wrote that *The Salutation of the Virtues* "easily comes across as a conceit of Francis" own spirituality, a sweet and exalted hymn to the virtuous life. In truth, it offers a synthesis of Franciscan action. It celebrates the movement's commitments." As such "it deserves careful study," within the historical context of the Franciscan movement which "clashes with other social forces" of those days. Unfortunately, Flood limits himself to only a few interesting remarks. Following Flood's dialectic approach, I study *The Salutation of the Virtues* as one of the many texts where Francis describes the ongoing struggle of the brotherhood in its confrontation with the world they have left but which, in many open as well as hidden ways, tries to get hold of the brothers again; the struggle, that is, between the Spirit of the Lord and the spirit of the flesh.[10] Thus in *The Salutation of the Virtues* Francis invites his brothers to remain committed to the praxis of the virtues as they have come to understand them within the brotherhood

[5] E. v.d. Goorbergh and Th. Zweerman, *Was Getekend: Franciscus van Assisi* , Assen 1998, 93–118.

[6] A. Jansen, "Lofzang op de deugden," *FL* 75 (1992) 61–74; 167–182.

[7] H. Sevenhoven, "Het theater van de deugden," *FL* 82 (1999) 99–105.

[8] M. Steiner, El "Saludo a las virtutes" de S. Francisco de Asis, *Selecciones de Franciscanismo* 16 (1987) no. 46, 129–140.

[9] D. Flood, "The Confusion of Evil: Franciscan Nonviolence," *Haversack* 11,3 (February 1988) 3–5. See also his *Francis of Assisi and the Franciscan Movement*, Quezon City, 1989, 168–173.

[10] This theme occurs in more than 15 places of the writings of Francis, as Optatus van Asseldonk observes. Verso un cuore puro con la pura, semplice e vera pace dello spirito (RegNB 17,15), *Laurentianum* 33 (1992) 481–531, here 486, note 17.

and so to become channels of the Spirit's transformative power in overcoming the opposing forces of evil in the world.

It is clear that my dialectic approach differs considerably from the approach followed in the recent studies mentioned above. However, before starting my commentary on the text, I will deal first with a number of introductory questions.

AUTHENTICITY

The authenticity of *The Salutation of the Virtues* is solidly established by Thomas of Celano, who in his Second life of Saint Francis quotes the opening verse of *The Salutation of the Virtues* at the end of a reflection on what true simplicity really is (2 Cel 189). Moreover, the oldest manuscripts, including Codex 338 of Assisi, insert *The Salutation of the Virtues* among the writings of Francis, even though they do not explicitly mention Francis as the author.[11]

Besides these external criteria, there are also internal criteria, based on the text itself, which bear witness to its authenticity. Important here are several parallel texts in which similar ideas are expressed and similar terms are used.[12] The most relevant are found in *Regula non bullata* 17:14–16; 16, 1 and 6, and in the Second Letter to the Faithful, verses 45–48 and 63–69.[13] These texts show very clearly the dialectic, the strug-

[11] Lehmann 222, where further literature can be found.

[12] "Much more characteristic, however, is the use of terms like *corpus*, *caro* and *spiritus*, as also *mundus*... In sofar is precisely the Salutation of the Virtues typical for the way of thinking, or rather the biblical way of thinking of St Francis." K. Esser, *Die Opuscula des hl. Franziskus von Assisi*, Grottaferrata, 1989, 422. Cf. Lehmann 222–223.

[13] "In general, the 'lines of force' of the Salutation develop out of the early years and are named fully for the first time in Early Rule XVII 14–16" (Flood 3–4). The main texts mentioned here read as follows: RegNB 17:14–16: "But the Spirit of the Lord wishes the flesh to be mortified... And it strives for humility and patience, and the pure and simple and true peace of the spiritual person. And above all things it always longs for the divine fear and the divine wisdom and the divine love of the Father, and of the Son, and of the Holy Spirit"; RegNB 16:1 and 6: "The Lord says: Behold, I am sending you as lambs in the midst of wolves... Be subject to every human creature for God's sake"; 2 LetFaith 45–48: "We must not be wise and prudent according to the flesh; rather, we must be simple, humble and pure. And let us hold ourselves in contempt... We must never desire to be over others; rather we must be servants and subject to every human creature for God's sake.

gle between the spirit of the flesh and the Spirit of the Lord, in which the brothers are caught. And since they can be considered as parallel texts of *The Salutation of the Virtues*, it is clear that the dialectic approach is indeed best suited for reaching a proper interpretation of Salutation of the Virtues.

LITERARY GENRE

Song of Praise, under the influence of the troubadours

The Salutation of the Virtues belongs to the literary genre of the *Lauda* (song of praise), as it shows a clear hymnic character. Like other such texts, it fits the image of Francis as troubadour. In this context many authors speak of an influence of the minnesong, the courtly love lyric. The fact that the virtues are personified and addressed as *domina*, as lady, seems especially to point in that direction. Summing up their view, Armstrong writes: "Of all the writings of Francis, this is the one that is perhaps the most clearly influenced by chivalry or the troubadour tradition."[14] None of the authors, however, is able to quote a similar text from the courtly lyric. Beside the personification of the virtues and their greeting as *domina*, they refer only to the idea of service to the Lady as one of the essential characteristics of courtly love,[15] an idea which could

---

And upon all men and women, if they have done these things and have persevered to the end, the Spirit of the Lord will rest"; ibid. 63–69: "All those who are not living in penance... [but] practice vice and sin and walk after wicked concupiscence and evil desires; who do not observe what they have promised and bodily serve the world by the desires of the flesh, the cares and anxieties of this world, and the cares of this life, deceived as they are by the devil.., they are blind because they do not see the true delight, our Lord Jesus Christ. They do not have spiritual wisdom because they do not have within them the Son of God who is the true wisdom of the Father... See, you blind ones, you who are deceived by our enemies, the flesh, the world, and the devil."

[14] R. Armstrong, *St. Francis of Assisi: Writings for a Gospel Life*, New York, 1994, 191. See also Lehmann 221–222; Reijsbergen 44. In the most recent translation of Francis' writings, we read: "Francis greets each virtue in a fashion typical of a medieval troubadour." R. Armstrong, W. Hellmann, W. Short (eds), *Francis of Assisi: Early Documents. Vol I: The Saint*, New York, 1999, 164.

[15] "Courtly love is realized in the submission of the man who considers himself as servant of his lady and tries to fulfil all her wishes" (Joachim Bumke, *Höfische*

very well fit Francis. The difficulty is that in greeting the virtues as his Queen and his Ladies, Francis is first and foremost concerned not about his service to them but about the Lord saving them (1–3) so that they may be able to confound the evil, the vices and sins, that were affecting the brotherhood. For these reasons, some authors are more cautious in their conclusions. Thus Lehmann concludes that one should not overestimate the influence of the courtly love lyric, which should rather be seen as an undertone of *The Salutation of the Virtues*.[16]

Reijsbergen pursues the matter somewhat further. He mentions two

---

Kultur, Literatur und Gesellschaft im hohen Mittelalter, München 1986, II, 504). Jansen remarks: "Francis links the personification of the virtues with courtly love. 'Lady' was the solemn title for a noble woman. In the original courtly love the knight dedicated himself to a symbol and personification of an ideal. Such an ideal had a strong transforming power. In this way courtly love could easily be used as a model for a pedagogy of the virtues" (70). H. Nolthenius refers specifically to Lancelot as a figure with whom Francis might have associated himself, especially in his emphasis on humble service. She writes: "Francis' most remarkable association is Lancelot (L'Ancelot: the little servant) in the shape that Chrétien de Troyes gave to this knight of Arthur in his *Chevalier de la Charrete*, the knight of the little cart... This Charrete is the cart of shame, a riding pillory. "At that time," Chrétien says, "the Charrete was so gruesome that it was said: when you see and meet the Little Cart, make a sign of the cross and think of God that no evil may come upon you." Whoever had to take place in the cart, could be insulted and booed with impunity and had lost his standing forever. Yet, Lancelot does just that when, at a certain moment, the Charrete is the only means of transport that can take him to his Beloved, Guenièvre, the wife of King Arthur, who had been abducted and had to be liberated... Loving service through humiliation appears to be the key idea of Chrétien's epic... That the young Francis read the story of Lancelot must be doubted: it was typical court literature. But... the content of Chrétien's romances of chivalry was definitely known to the people and must have been discussed frequently. One can hardly escape the conclusion that the Cart of Shane, as symbol of the element of humiliation in the courtly love, must have been known to our *miles Christi* when, out of love of God, he allowed himself to be booed and wanted to be the least of the least... It is perhaps for this reason in particular that one should not dismiss the knightly aspirations of the young Francis as an unimportant, passing dream of a boy: he kept ideas from that period in his life which would have a great influence on his spirituality" (*Een man uit het dal van Spoleto. Franciscus tussen zijn tijdgenoten*, Amsterdam, 1988, 210–211). A more detailed elaboration can be found in J. v. Lotringen and I. Nije Bijvank, "Liefde en vernedering. De ridderlijke idealen van Franciscus en Lancelot," *FL* 72 (1989) 112–126. See also below in our general observations on verses 1–4.

[16] Lehmann 221–22.

possible points of contact. First there is the stress which troubadours place on the total surrender to love. Francis could have given this a religious interpretation. Next, Reijsbergen refers to the theme of the *obediensa* between beloved. There exists thus a relationship between love and the surrender of one's own will in *obediensa* to the other. According to Reijsbergen, a somewhat similar idea can be found in Salutation of the Virtues 14–18 where Francis formulates the love of God in its consequences of obedience and the surrender of one's own will. Both possible points of contact are in my opinion too general to be convincing and seem rather farfetched. How much did Francis really know about these themes from the courtly love lyric? And if he knew them, how deeply did they influence him, especially at the end of his life after he had tried for so many years to follow closely in the footsteps of the poor and humble Jesus? Reijsbergen ends by saying that, if we compare the form of *The Salutation of the Virtues* with examples from the courtly love lyric, we can notice a certain similarity. However, he considers this similarity not very striking and thinks that it can be fully explained by the fact that *The Salutation of the Virtues* came into being at the same time and in the same place as many songs of the troubadours. Further, Francis may have used the art of the troubadours to impose some order on his feelings of enthusiasm and to express his ideas in such a way that they could be passed on.[17]

A further similarity may be found in the description of the ideal society by the troubadours. Joachim Bumke, an authority in this matter, writes: "In opposition to the negative characteristics of the medieval reality, the court poets developed the image of a society which was free from all that made life burdensome and oppressive in those days and from which all economic and social forms of coercion, and all political conflicts were banned, while only the desire for moral and social perfection motivated people into action. This extreme unrealistic image of society was apparently conceived as a contrast to the existing reality and has to be interpreted in this line."[18] If as we later will see, Francis intends *The Salutation of the Virtues* as a reminder to the brothers of the original

[17] Reijsbergen 44–49.

[18] Bumke I,12. This text is also quoted by O Schmuck-Th Jansen, "Nachhall zu einem Geburtszentenar," *CollFranc* 56 (1986) 246. In the second volume, Bumke writes: "Courtly love was a social utopia. Love stood for a new, better society; a society which did not exist and which could not exist in reality: it existed only as a

ideals, namely, that they have left the world and have committed themselves, in the strength of the Spirit of the Lord, to build a new, alternative world, a restored paradise, which is radically opposed to the existing world, then there exists here a close affinity with the troubadours' image of a new society. However, except for the virtue of love, the other virtues which Francis mentions do not figure very prominently in the courtly lyric.[19] Therefore, it remains rather doubtful that Francis has been influenced by the poems of the troubadours. A more likely source for Francis' vision of a new world, the restored paradise, is rather to be found in the Scriptures and in the tradition of the church. All in all, on the basis of the present evidence, it seems fair to conclude that, if there exists any relationship at all, it remains limited to a rather indirect relationship. As such it will not any further be considered in our interpretation of The Salutationof the Virtues.

---

poetic project in the mind of the poets. What distinguished the society of love from the reality, was the poetic assumption that all evil and all ill-mannered behaviour would be excluded where love would reign. In the French *Roman de la Rose* the reign of love was an enclosed garden. On its walls all that was not allowed to enter, was pictured: hatred *(haine)*, felony *(felonie)*, villainy *(vilanie)*, greed *(covoitise)*, avarice *(avarice)*, envy *(envie)*, sadness *(tristece)*, old age *(vieillece)*, hypocrisy *(papelardie)* and poverty *(povreté)*. Thus the whole reality of everyday life was excluded. Only those were admitted who were ready and able to dedicate their life to courtliness *(cortoisie)*, pleasure *(deduiz)*, cheerfulness *(leece)*, beauty *(biautez)*, riches *(richece)*, largesse *(largece)*, frankness *(franchise)*, leisure *(oiseuse)* and youth *(jonece)*. Such an ideal picture reflected the wishful thinking of a small, noble elite..." (II, 528–529). It is interesting to note that the *Roman de la Rose* excludes poverty from the enclosed garden while the poverty which Francis and his brothers strive after is holy and opens for them the gate to paradise which was lost through the sin of appropriation. See below II C d.

19 A good survey of the virtues of a knight in the courtly lyric can be found in Bumke II, 416–430. He quotes various lists which, even though some expressions are the same, indicate a quite different perspective from Francis': generosity, chastity, meekness, manly goodness, wisdom, bravery (416). Often steadfastness and measure, temperance, are mentioned; they are considered as "sisters, children of one and the same virtue" (418). See also F. Cardini, The Warrior and the Knight, in *The Medieval World*, ed. J. Le Goff, London, 1990: "The *Song of Roland* offers a first important model of the codification of the *ritterliches Tugendsystem* — the chivalric system of virtues. It turns around the two poles of *prouesse* (valor) and *sagesse* (wisdom), or the particular variety of wisdom sharpened by experience usually expressed in terms of prudence. The terms are complementary; when they are

Didactic poem or penitential song

Whereas in Codex 338 of Assisi space is left open for musical notes in the text of the Canticle of the Sun, this is not the case with the text of The Salutationof the Virtues. For this reason H Nolthenius concludes that The Salutationof the Virtues was not meant as a song to be sung, but rather as a didactic poem to be recited.[20] Several authors agree with Nolthenius' characterization, but add some further specifications of their own. Thus, according to Jansen, *The Salutation of the Virtues* had its place as a didactic poem within the preaching of penance which the brothers had to announce through their exhortations and praises (RegNB 21:1). *The Salutation of the Virtues* therefore can also be described as a penitential song.[21] In a similar vein, Reijsbergen defines *The Salutation of the Virtues* more specifically as a call to conversion.[22] E. v.d. Goorbergh and Th. Zweerman add that, because *The Salutation of the Virtues* are an echo of the experiences which Francis had during his

---

both present and in harmony, the result is *mesure*, controlled equilibrium. The valiant knight who is not wise is a madman; the wise man who cannot show proof of valor is vile" (81). That this perspective is quite different from Francis' is clear from the following observation: "...the Christian God of Roland, even if he is often lovingly referred to as the "Son of Mary," is in reality the terrible God of Israel, the *Dominus Deus Sabaoth*, Lord of battle and of vengeance" ibid. And a few pages later Cardini writes: "Romanesque portals and capitals abound in allegorical figurations of the combat between the virtues and the vices, represented as opposing warriors or as knights and monsters. This was an inviting interpretation of the tourney, as it opened the way to infinite possibilities for allegorization... Huon de Méry's poem, *Le Tournoiement d'Antéchrist*, offers one example of this: Christ's shield bears a vermillion cross...; he jousts against Satan, whose insignia is a strip of Persephone's tunic (in another version the Devil is "the knight of the dragon" and has a dragon as his blazon). The archangels and the cardinal and the theological virtues fight at Christ's side, along with the specifically knightly virtues of *Prouesse*, *Largesse*, *Courtoisie*, and *Débonnaireté*" (101).

[20] Nolthenius 275.

[21] Jansen 62–63.

[22] Reijsbergen 40. However, Reijsbergen is not convinced by Nolthenius' argument about the absence of space for musical notes. The copyist may not have known about the existence of a melody, or he may have thought that the melody could no longer be traced.

life, it might also be called a "didactic poem on life."[23] I can agree with all these descriptions. They remain, however, very general and do not clearly envisage the concrete, more specific content of *The Salutation of the Virtues* which does not mention the words penance or conversion as such but rather emphasizes the struggle between good and evil or, more precisely, the confounding of the evil by the virtues that come from God. It is this struggle the brothers ought to be involved in. It is this struggle also which eventually should figure in a more precise characterization of this didactic poem.

Play

As Jansen had earlier, Sevenhoven places *The Salutation of the Virtues* within the context of Francis' preaching. However, stressing Francis' familiarity with the world and the language of the courtly lyric and the chansons de geste of Arthur and Lancelot, of Charlemagne and Roland. He characterizes The Salutationof the Virtues as a play. Hence the title of his article: Theatre of the virtues. When the play opens, he presents, just like the troubadours, his ladies to the public. Also, when introducing the vices, he uses another instrument from the world of the theatre, namely, the mask. The virtues rip off the masks of the vices. They unmask their temptation as fraud and deceit. In this way, following one of the didactic methods of his days, Francis wishes by means of his play to help people in the training of their memories, so that they will keep the lady virtues always before their eyes and hopefully will allow them to become their source of inspiration in the struggle against the forces of evil.[24] Sevenhoven touches here on an important aspect of every didactic poem, song or play—an aspect that certainly cannot be ruled out

[23] "With Nolthenius we prefer to call the Salutation a 'didactic poem' rather than a prayer in the strict sense. Because Francis' life experience resonates in the Salutation, one could call it also a 'didactic poem on life' *(levensleerdicht).*" v.d. Goorbergh-Zweerman 94. Unfortunately, they do not further specify here which life experiences in particular play a role in the composition of Salutation of the Virtues. Later they refer to SalVirt as "a possible reflection of Francis" conversion *(Neerslag van Franciscus' bekering?).*" They also mention that "Francis acquired the virtues through a long struggle against the 'armed strong one' (cf. Adm 27:5; RegNB 22:21–24). Hence it is not improbable that he composed this didactic poem on life on the basis of this experience" (105–106).

[24] Sevenhoven, passim.

here, given Francis' concern to keep his brothers and others on the right path through his admonitions and exhortations. However, as is clear from what I mentioned earlier about Francis and his being influenced by courtly lyric, I am not convinced that the courtly lyric has to be seen as a direct source of inspiration for Francis. Moreover, as I hope to show later, "to unmask" is not the most obvious translation of the Latin verb *confundere.*

Song of victory

In the third part of *The Salutation of the Virtues*, using the present indicative tense, Francis affirms that the virtues confound the sins and vices. Lehmann interprets this as implying that Francis was conscious of the victory of the virtues and sings about it in a joyous, festive tone. Later, in his conclusion, he writes that the victory of the virtues over sins and vices constitutes the theme of *The Salutation of the Virtues*.[25] A similar view can be found in Flood's more recent publication. Following his dialectical approach, he writes that "in his Salutation of the Virtues, Francis did not rejoice at his virtuous behavior; he celebrated the political success of the movement."[26] In my view, however, rather than celebrating the victory of the virtues, Francis here reminds his brothers that, at this particular moment in the history of the brotherhood, when the virtues are in danger and hence need to be protected and saved by the Lord, they must not give up. On the contrary, convinced of the power of the God-given virtues, they must continue their struggle, trusting that victory will surely be theirs. In this context I would rather agree with Flood who, later in the same publication, characterizes *The Salutation of the Virtues* as a celebration of the strengths of the movement.[27] If the brothers would use these strengths, they would indeed break the opposition of the dominant forces of their society, of their culture and inaugurate a new age.

[25] Sevenhoven 227 and 245.

[26] D. Flood, *Work for Everyone. Francis of Assisi and the Ethic of Service*, Quezon City 1997, 22.

[27] Ibid. 56.

Scheme for a sermon

In this view, *The Salutation of the Virtues* has its origin in the itinerant preaching of the brothers. In chapter 9 of the *Regula bullata*, Francis admonishes his brothers that, in their preaching, they must speak to the people "of vices and virtues, punishment and glory in a discourse that is brief, because it was in few words that the Lord preached while on earth" (3). Francis gave his brothers this admonition to go out and preach. True to his style of first doing personally all that he desired from his brothers, he also left them an example. He gave them the scheme for a sermon. He did something similar in Admonition 27, which in speech and content is quite similar to *The Salutation of the Virtues*.[28] I find it very difficult, however, to see in *The Salutation of the Virtues* a scheme for a sermon. It is so different in style and composition from the much simpler scheme for a sermon Francis gives to all his brothers in RegNB 21. Rather than as the scheme for a sermon, I would therefore prefer to read *The Salutation of the Virtues* as a reminder, a program of life calling the brothers to action, for, as Francis says, all his brothers should preach by their deeds (RegNB 17:3).

Prayer

Both Lehmann and Jansen deal with *The Salutation of the Virtues* in their commentary on the prayers of Assisi. They do so for various reasons. According to Lehmann, *The Salutation of the Virtues* cannot be understood if we separate them from Francis' living relationship with God, his Lord. It is because they are the Lord's, that Francis calls them "ladies." In other words, behind the personified virtues stands the Lord. This vital link with the Lord is further confirmed by the place the Lord occupies at the beginning and at the end of *The Salutation of the Virtues*. For these reasons Lehmann considers it justified to call *The Salutation of the Virtues* a prayer, for it has its beginning and its end in the Lord. In this prayer Francis directs himself to the Lord, asking him to save and protect the virtues.[29] Jansen stresses that Francis greets and addresses

[28] Lehmann 221; Esser 428–429; J. Campbell, Les écrits de saint Franÿois d'Assise devant la critique, *FranzStud* 36 (1954) 223. Reijsbergen speaks of "a short, all-encompassing sermon about the virtuous life" (39).

[29] Lehmann 228–229.

the virtues. Thus the first part has a similar structure as the Salutation of the Blessed Virgin Mary. Also the content must be seen in line with the Salutation of Mary. The virtues are for Francis home and tabernacle of the Lord. Here lies the main reason why they are greeted and sung of. In them Francis implicitly praises the Lord who pitched his tent, his tabernacle on earth.[30] In as far as they read *The Salutation of the Virtues* first and foremost as a prayer, Lehmann and Jansen pay little or no attention to its historical context in their interpretation.

Poetic reminder or poetic testament

Near the end of his commentary, after he has studied various aspects of *The Salutation of the Virtues*, Lehmann writes that "*The Salutation of the Virtues* can be considered as a short summary of the original aims of the lesser brothers; as their program of life in the form of a poem; as a mirror of their ideals; a song of their life; a song in which they turned to God and reminded each other of their ideals."[31] It is difficult to understand why Lehmann keeps this description of the literary genre of *The Salutation of the Virtues* until the end and instead places so much emphasis on *The Salutation of the Virtues* as a scheme for a sermon. Moreover, if from the very beginning he had interpreted it as a reminder, his commentary as a whole would certainly have taken a different direction.

A similar remark about *The Salutation of the Virtues* as a reminder can also be found in Reijsbergen. When speaking about the date, he observes that "*The Salutation of the Virtues* seems like a compact expression of Franciscan evangelical life. As such *The Salutation of the Virtues* should be seen as a reflection *a posteriori*, in retrospect, on a life experience which had matured in the course of many years rather than as an a priori formulated and therefore theoretical program."[32] Unfortunately, Reijsbergen hardly considers the life experience of Francis and his brothers in its historical context, that is, the context of the everyday struggle between the brotherhood whose life is to be governed by the Spirit of the Lord, and the world which is ruled by the spirit of the flesh.[33]

[30] Jansen 62.

[31] Lehmann 244.

[32] Reijsbergen 43.

[33] Reijsbergen devotes the entire sixth chapter, pp. 129–163, to "An outline of a histor-

It is clear that, with some reservations, I can recognize myself and my views in the characterization which Lehmann and Reijsbergen give of *The Salutation of the Virtues* as a reminder, a remembrance, and a reflection a posteriori on the life experience of Francis and his brothers. In their characterization they come close to Flood's description of *The Salutation of the Virtues* as "a synthesis of Franciscan action," in which the brothers "celebrate the movement's commitments" in order to remember these commitments and keep them alive within the movement. However, since Flood sees and interprets the movement's commitments dialectically in opposition to the commitments of the world, a commentary along his lines will fundamentally differ from other ones. For it will not remain on the individual plain, limiting itself to a more spiritualizing approach, as is customary in our days;[34] rather, it will be concerned to emphasize the social and political implications of the

---

ical context." However, in its introduction he observes that "because of the limited possibilities, [he] did not examine the specific, local circumstances of Umbria." Rather, he restricts himself to a number of more general remarks relating to "certain aspects of medieval culture like expressions of emotions and patterns of thought." Thus he tries to give "a picture of the medieval society which has produced this text [i.e. SalVirt]" (129).

[34] Mary Grey writes about this: "[Het is] wel duidelijk dat het ethos van het individualisme het vooralsnog grotendeels heeft gewonnen. De meeste mensen in West-Europa en Noord-Amerika schijnen er nu alleen maar aan te kunnen denken hoe zij en hun directe familiekring, voor welke zij zich verantwoordelijk voelen, er materieel op vooruit kunnen gaan... Boeken over spiritualiteit concentreren zich voor het grootste gedeelte op onze gevoelens en op de vraag hoe we ermee in contact kunnen komen, en counseling is een zich explosief ontwikkelende industrie geworden. De groei van deze tendens heeft vele oorzaken: in een cultuur waarin privatisering zich dagelijks uitbreidt ten koste van het openbare leven is het geen wonder dat de persoonlijke navolging van Jezus of het overnemen van die gedeelten van zijn boodschap die toevalligerwijs het persoonlijke ordenen zonder de publieke moraal uit te dagen of te inspireren tot sociale gerechtigheid, de overwinning behalen. Ook is het mogelijk terug te vallen op een lijn van christelijke traditie om dit te ondersteunen... [zoals] het Moravisch piëtisme en het quietisme, welke beide hun brandpunt hadden in een verborgen gebedsleven en in een cultivering van het innerlijke leven. Deze individualistische navolging van Jezus laat zich ook verbinden met wat in bepaalde delen beschouwd wordt als de mislukking van de bevrijdingstheologie, bijvoorbeeld in het post-Sandinistische Nicaragua. Wanneer het zoeken naar de God van gerechtigheid door omvorming van de politieke en sociale structuren op niets lijkt uitgelopen te zijn, komen evangelistische groepen die de ontgoochelden ertoe overhalen de 'innerlijke' boodschap van Jezus te volgen

Franciscan commitment, the Franciscan action for the transformation of their society.

As a reminder, *The Salutation of the Virtues* is open-ended. Whenever new problems emerge, as e.g. regarding obedience, the text can be extended. In fact, this seems to have happened in verses 15–18, which do not follow the same pattern as the previous verses and also have a different subject than verse 14.[35] This implies that Francis feels free to move beyond the original structure of *The Salutation of the Virtues* as a song of praise or a didactic poem. Apparently it is not the song or the poem, but the reminder of their commitments to his brothers which is of vital importance to Francis. The song or the poem is for Francis only an instrument which he can use whenever he sees fit. *The Salutation of the Virtues* does not stand alone as a reminder but forms part of Francis' mission in the years after he had resigned, namely to exhort and admonish his brothers by his words and especially by his example.[36] And as *The Salutation of the Virtues* is written toward the end of Francis' life, we may describe this poetic reminder also as a poetic testament.

SITZ IM LEBEN

Itinerant preaching

Lehmann and others who see *The Salutation of the Virtues* as a scheme for a sermon think that its origin lies in itinerant preaching. As Lehmann writes, it is there that *The Salutation of the Virtues* is at home. For Francis did not want to send the brothers on their preaching mission without giving them an example or at least a scheme for a sermon. Did he not always first do himself what he asked of others?[37] However, as I observed earlier, *The Salutation of the Virtues* does not very much look like a scheme for a sermon. Further, itinerant preaching is far too wide a

op als paddestoelen." "Jezus, guru van het individualisme of het hart van de gemeenschap? Christelijk leerlingschap en profetische kerk," *Concilium* 1997/1, 118–119.

[35] See below under C 3; see also note 38.

[36] LegPer 85 and 87; SpecPerf 16 and 81c.

[37] Lehmann 221. See what has been said above, I, 3.

context to be helpful in the interpretation of Salutation of the Virtues. Also, I think that the Sitz im Leben is to be found, first of all, within the brotherhood itself, unless there are obvious indications to the contrary. Within the brotherhood, then, Francis observed that the situation was not in accordance with the way he had come to see and appreciate things in the light of the Gospel. He was therefore deeply concerned to do whatever was within his ability to advise and motivate the brothers to change this situation. It is within the context of this concern that we have to look for the origin of *The Salutation of the Virtues*, rather than in itinerant preaching, though the latter may well have profited by making good use of the insights formulated in *The Salutation of the Virtues*.

The everyday life of the first brothers

Struck by the admonition of *The Salutation of the Virtues* to be "subject and submissive... even to all beasts and wild animals" (17), Casutt suggests that "we place ourselves as realistically as possible in the situation of the lesser brothers. In the first years, they had no house, not even a place to lodge. Whatever the situation of the weather, they lived in the open air. Often they slept under a bush or in the woods or under a ledge. They prayed for hours and even whole nights kneeling or sitting in the grass. They were then continuously exposed to wild animals. One need not think straightaway of wolves, although in that time they roamed through the forests of Umbria. But there were plenty small wild animals that attacked the brothers. Forest ants, beetles, worms and other small insects crept into their habits, tormented their bodies when they rested for a few hours on the forest soil." According to Lehmann, Casutt has thus very aptly described the Sitz im Leben of Francis' peculiar understanding of obedience.[38] I think, however, that the explanation is rather farfetched. I rather prefer to read this passage in the context of the Earlier Rule 16, about the brothers who by divine inspiration want to go among the Saracens and other nonbelievers. Referring to his own personal experience, Francis opens this chapter with the words of the Lord: "Behold, I am sending you as sheep in the midst of wolves" (RegNB 16,1). He had gone among the Saracens as a "sheep," without

[38] L. Casutt, *Das Erbe eines großen Herzens*, Graz, 1949, 178. Quoted by Lehmann 240–241.

any weapons, without any power and might, in a nonviolent, peaceful way to discover that the "wolves" were no wolves and that sheep and wolves could live together. It is this experience which has deeply influenced Francis' description of obedience, of being subject and submissive even to all beasts and wild animals, as found in The Salutationof the Virtues 16.[39] It does not explain, however, why Francis should come up with such a description in the last part of *The Salutation of the Virtues*. What situation within the brotherhood required it?

The Crisis of Obedience during the last years of Francis' Life

Since in the last verses of *The Salutation of the Virtues* the virtue of obedience receives such strong emphasis—in fact, more place is given to obedience than to all of the other virtues, including poverty![40] — Hardick and Grau think that *The Salutation of the Virtues* finds its origin in the crisis of obedience which overshadowed the last years of Francis' life.[41] The place that is devoted to the virtue of obedience is very remarkable indeed. It even looks as if Francis' preoccupation with obedience is such that it makes the well balanced text of *The Salutation of the Virtues* break through its structure. For one gets the impression that, from verse 15 onward, we have to deal with an addition to the original text.[42]

This addition had become necessary because, in Francis' experience, the brothers, or at least some of them, were no longer observing the obedience of the Spirit and the obedience of one's brother in mutual service to one another, as he had envisaged it in the Earlier Rule 5:14–15.

[39] For an interpretation of this text, see J. Hoeberichts, *Francis and Islam*, Quincy, Il. 1997, 61–66. Lehmann also refers to RegNB 16, and especially to verse 6: "One way [of living spiritually among the Saracens] is not to engage in arguments or disputes, but to be subject to every human creature for God's sake." It is here that he finds the explanation for Francis' insistence in SalVirt 16, that the obedient person must be "subject and submissive to all persons in the world." He further quotes RegNB 16:2 about the simplicity of the doves but, strangely enough, he does not consider RegNB 16:1 (239).

[40] See Esser 429.

[41] L.Hardick and E. Grau, *Die Schriften des heiligen Franziskus von Assisi*, Werl, 1980, 131.

[42] See Reijsbergen 61.

Rather, they had started obeying other authorities which would protect them from the risks involved in obeying the Spirit, being subject to one another and even to every human creature. Hence Francis decided to remind them by adding a further explanation to the text of the Salutationof the Virtues on obedience.[43] This reminder became even more urgent after the publication of the Later Rule in 1223. For not only did the recommendations about being subject to every human creature disappear from its much reduced chapter on the brothers who want to go among the Saracens (ch. 12), they are also no longer found in the Later Rule as a whole.[44] However important the issue of obedience may have been for Francis, it explains the Sitz im Leben only as far as the last additional part of *The Salutation of the Virtues* is concerned. What about the rest of the text?

Francis' Depression

In verse 13 we read that "holy Charity destroys (confounds) every temptation of the devil and of the flesh and every carnal fear." Jansen asks whether this verse could possibly refer to some temptation in Francis' own life. It is known that Francis went through a period of severe depression between 1220–1223. Nolthenius interprets this depression as a stage in Francis' mystical way to union with God. If this is true, Francis gives us here, in his own typical reserved manner, a glimpse of his mystical journey. At the same time, it would give us some indication regarding the Sitz im Leben of this verse.[45] Although I think that this verse, just like the other verses of Salutation of the Virtues, is to be interpreted in the context of the brotherhood rather than in the context of Francis' personal inner life, I do not exclude the possibility of a more personal interpretation. But again, this does not explain the Sitz im Leben of the rest of the text. For this we have to look for some broader

[43] In my description of the crisis of obedience I base myself on the text of the SalVirt where the obedience to the Spirit and to one's brother are explicitly mentioned. I differ here from Hardick–Grau (36), according to whom the crisis of obedience refers more specifically to the brothers "who go wandering about with no regard for the discipline of the Rule" (LetOrder 45).

[44] For the meaning of "being subject" as an essential element in the spirituality of Francis, see Hoeberichts 60–70. The reference to RegB 12 can be found on page 69.

[45] Jansen 179–180, where he refers to Nolthenius 213–220.

context in which all the virtues mentioned in *The Salutation of the Virtues* are being threatened.

The Conflict with the Learned Brothers

Writing about true simplicity in his second life of Francis, Celano mentions that Francis does not approve "all simplicity, but only that simplicity which is content with its God and considers everything else as of little value. This is that simplicity which glories in the fear of the Lord and knows not how to do or to speak evil. This is that simplicity that examines itself continually and is careful not to condemn any one... This is that simplicity that does not set the highest value on hellenic honours (cf. 2 Maccabees 4:15) but chooses rather to act than become learned and to teach. This is that simplicity that, in all that concerns the divine laws, leaves wordy circumlocutions, ornaments and embellishments, vain displays and curiosities, to those who are marked for a fall... The most holy father demanded this virtue in both the learned and the lay brothers, for he did not consider it contrary to wisdom, but true wisdom's sister, though he thought it easier to be obtained and more ready to be used by those who are poor as regards learning. Therefore in *The Salutation of the Virtues* he composed, he says: "Hail, Queen Wisdom, may the Lord save save you with your sister, pure, holy Simplicity" (189).

Reading this text, there slowly emerges before our eyes a brother who is not content with God and God's will, but attaches great value to other earthly things. He does not examine himself critically, but is ready to condemn others. He wishes to be learned and to hold a teaching position rather than to realize the Franciscan way of life by his deeds. He enjoys indulging in words, the more the better, in order to show his learning, his brand of wisdom that cannot be reconciled with simplicity. Thus he has strayed far from the original ideal. And he is not alone. Towards the end of Francis' life, there were many such brothers. This is evident from the story of True Joy, where the brother at the door answers Francis' request for admission: "Go away, you are a simple and illiterate man; we are so many and of such quality that we have no need of you" (11).

The presence and activity of these many learned brothers within the brotherhood most likely provide the Sitz im Leben of *The Salutation of the Virtues*. Their understanding of learning and wisdom and their way of life formed a real threat to the true wisdom of the Spirit and the other virtues which were to guide the brothers in following Jesus. Since their influence was growing, Francis wished to counteract the impact the learned brothers had on the brotherhood with their false wisdom and their evil way of life, and so try with God's help to save the virtues from the threat they were under. This is what prompted Francis to compose *The Salutation of the Virtues*,[46] in which he reminds the brothers of the true Queen Wisdom and her lady companions in the hope that the brothers will allow themselves to be inspired and moved by them in fulfilling their calling to establish an alternative to the world they have left (RegNB 5:10). Hence according to Francis, the practice of the virtues is not in the first place meant to promote the virtuous life or the moral excellence of the individual brother, but to help the brothers with all God's strength and virtues to disentangle themselves and their movement from the hold that the spirit of the world has on their society and to devote themselves fully to the realization of their vision of a new world.[47]

It is this Sitz im Leben which explains very well why Francis starts *The Salutation of the Virtues* by introducing Queen Wisdom, followed by the other virtues. Moreover, this is in line with the fact that, in the second Letter to the Faithful, Francis interprets the conflict between the Spirit of the Lord and the spirit of the flesh as a conflict between those

[46] Not only the SalVirt, but several of Francis' other writings find their origin in problems the movement was facing. Typical in this context is the frequent use of terms like "admonition," "exhortation," etc. So also the title Commonitorium which, in many manuscripts, is given to the Second Version of the Letter to the Faithful and which therefore the new English translation prefers: Later Admonition and Exhortation to the Brothers and Sisters of Penance (Armstrong, Hellmann, Short 45). If these problems would not have existed, we might wonder whether Francis would have written these letters and even his Testament. It is with these writings as L. Keck states with regard to the writings of the New Testament: "Although many factors were at work in the creation of these twenty-seven pamphlets... it is unlikely that we would have these texts at all had the authors, users, and canonizers regarded the Christianity they knew and faced as flawless. In other words, the New Testament as canon, like its constituent pieces before they were canonized, not only expresses the faith and ethos of early Christianity but also addresses them in order to correct them. To overlook this is to fail to understand the New Testament historically." "Rethinking New Testament Ethics," *Journal of Biblical Literature*, 115 (1996) 5.

[47] Flood, *Francis of Assisi*, 170–172.

who possess the true spiritual wisdom and those who do not but rather are "deceived by our enemies, the flesh, the world, and the devil." They "practice vice and sin and walk after wicked concupiscence and evil desires; [they] do not observe what they have promised and bodily serve the world by the desires of the flesh, the cares and anxieties of this world and the cares of this life" (64–69).[48]

Once Francis had composed *The Salutation of the Virtues*, the problems with the learned brothers were not over. For they were also the brothers mainly responsible for the crisis of obedience within the brotherhood which I described above and which, I think, moved Francis to the addition of verses 15–18 to the text of Salutation of the Virtues. The addition therefore has its Sitz im Leben in Francis' conflict with the learned brothers.

DATE

The date of *The Salutation of the Virtues* is intimately linked with its Sitz im Leben. Hence Hardick-Grau place *The Salutation of the Virtues* in the last years of Francis' life, when Francis tried to find a solution for the crisis of obedience that had arisen among the brothers on account of the abuses that certain brothers made of the freedom inherent to the wandering life of the beginning.[49] Lehmann is not convinced by this argument. According to him, the somewhat utopian vision of obedience which Francis proposes in *The Salutation of the Virtues* cannot be the result of abuses. However, since he sees the experience of Francis' presence among the Muslims reflected in certain formulations of *The Salutation of the Virtues*, especially in regard to being subject to all people in the world, Lehmann too agrees on a late date, which is certainly to be fixed after Francis' return from Egypt in the beginning of 1220.[50]

Jansen offers various reasons for a late date. First he refers to the similarities between *The Salutation of the Virtues* and the second Letter to the Faithful. From this we may assume that perhaps *The Salutation of the Virtues* was composed during the same period as the second Letter to

[48] We differ here from Jansen (61) who, after quoting 2 Cel 189, observes that we cannot draw much out of this story with regard to the Sitz im Leben of the SalVirt.

[49] Hardick-Grau 131.

[50] Lehmann 223 and 239.

the Faithful which, according to most authors, was written some time after 1221.[51] Next, Jansen draws attention to the admonition in the Later Rule 9,3–4. It is as if one hears in this text a summary of *The Salutation of the Virtues*. This could imply that both documents are from the same time, i.e. around 1223. I have to confess, however, that I cannot hear a summary of *The Salutation of the Virtues* in Francis' admonition to his brothers that "in their preaching, their words must be well chosen and chaste... speaking to them of vices and sins." Finally, Jansen suggests that the words "every temptation of the devil and of the flesh and every carnal fear" (13) may refer to a state of depression which Francis suffered between 1220 and 1223. Perhaps *The Salutation of the Virtues* was written shortly afterwards.[52]

After referring to Lehmann and his objections to Hardick-Grau, Reijsbergen observes that it is not possible to fix a certain date for the composition of the Salutationof the Virtues. However, because of the deep insights of *The Salutation of the Virtues* which reflect Francis' experience of many years, he too opts for a late date.[53]

Although I have indicated that I do not agree with all the arguments given so far, I am also in favour of a late date. As regards the main body of the text, the many similarities to the Second Letter to the Faithful are also for me a clear indication that *The Salutation of the Virtues* must have been composed at about the same time as the Letter, i.e., some time after 1221. As regards the last part, my analysis of the verses 15–18 gives me reason to believe that they were probably written even after the official papal approval of the Later Rule by Honorius III with his decree *Solet Annuere* of November 29, 1223.

STRUCTURE

Whereas Verhey does not pay any attention to the structure of the Salutationof the Virtues, more recent authors like Lehmann, Reijsbergen, Zweerman and v.d. Goorbergh-Zweerman do so rather

[51] Jansen 61–62. According to G.P. Freeman, the Second Version of the Letter to the Faithful may even have been written during the last years of Francis' life between 1224–1226. *Gelukkig wie in Jezus' voetspoor gaat*, Utrecht, 1981, 73 ff.

[52] Jansen 63; 179–180.

[53] Reijsbergen 43–44.

extensively. I will briefly summarize their findings and eventually add my own observations.

Lehmann

According to form and content, the Salutationof the Virtues can be divided in three parts which, on account of their almost rhythmic composition, can be characterized as strophes. Strophe A consists of verses 1–4, each of which is composed in a four-line rhythm. Its theme is indicated in the first word, *Ave*. It is a salutation of the virtues. Strophe B comprises the verses 5–8. In comparison with the previous verses, they sound more like prose, whereby the salutation changes into statements. Their theme is the human person and the virtues. The main verb is *habet* while its counterpart is *offendit*. Verse 8 is joined to verse 7 through *et*. At the same time it also forms the link with strophe C through the verb *confundit*, which introduces the theme of what follows. Strophe C covers the entire second half of the song: verses 9–18. Whereas strophe B speaks about the virtues in general, strophe C presents the virtues one by one. Thereby the same order is followed as in strophe A. The theme of strophe C can be formulated as the working of the virtues. The central verb of each verse is *confundit*. It is the opposite of *salvet*, which is the main verb in strophe A. The virtues must be protected, saved; it is then that, through their working, they will be able to confound, to destroy vices and sins. The tripartition of the text as a whole can be extended to the individual strophes where most verses have three parts. Further, the triad's form corresponds to its content: three pairs of virtues are presented.

Once attention has been drawn to this triple structure, the question may be asked whether Francis' reverence for the Blessed Trinity lies hidden behind this structure. Lehmann is not convinced. The identification of Queen Wisdom with Christ may be somewhat justified on account of a text in the second Letter of the Faithful where Francis writes about "the Son of God who is the true wisdom of the Father" (67). But when Lady Poverty is said to refer to the Father and Lady Charity to the Holy Spirit, it becomes clear how artificial and forced such interpretation really is. Lehmann is therefore personally not interested in pursuing this trinitarian interpretation. In the end he is willing to admit that "Francis' preference for the number 3 may have something to do with his reverence for the Blessed Trinity. The undeniable triple structure of *The Salutation of the Virtues* could be seen then as a reflection of the Holy Trinity, while the emphasis on the inseparable union of all virtues could point to the unity in the Trinity, which Francis mentions more often."[54]

Reijsbergen

Reijsbergen distinguishes between a surface structure or pattern and a depth structure which lies underneath the surface structure and concerns the deeper meaning and intention of the text.

In the section about the surface structure, Reijsbergen deals with the division of *The Salutation of the Virtues* into three parts and some general characteristics of its structure and style. He does so in much the same way and with the same result as Lehmann to whom he refers. His observation regarding verses 15–18 is interesting.

Previously, he had already drawn attention to the fact that these verses form a kind of addition because they have a different structure. Now he points out that these verses have a different subject as well, namely the human person (strophe B) who possesses the virtues (strophe A). To prove this he refers to the possessive pronouns *suum* and *sui*. It is not clear to me precisely what Reijsbergen means. However, he is correct in saying that a different subject has entered the scene. For *obedience, obedientia*, does not have a body or a brother, nor can it be the subject of the predicate *subditus et suppositus*. Because of the fact that these verses have a different subject, the virtuous person, Reijsbergen concludes that verses 15–18 form an independent unit which relates back to the entire Salutationof the Virtues and constitutes its climax (63). I cannot agree with this conclusion. The subject of verses 15–18 is not the virtuous person, but the obedient person. Hence, these verses do not relate back to the entire Salutation of the Virtues, but form an addition to verse 14 which had become urgent because of problems that had arisen within the brotherhood with regard to obedience. He ends his analysis by saying: "Heart and centre of *The Salutation of the Virtues* is the human person, for whom it is possible to receive the virtues which proceed from God and to let them flow out again in his/her life through the destruction (confounding) of the vices and sins."[55]

[54] Lehmann 225–228.

[55] Reijsbergen 57–66.

Whereas Reijsbergen devotes about ten pages to the surface structure, his study of the depth structure occupies more than sixty pages: 67–127. It is not my intention to give a summary of Reijsbergen's analysis. I limit myself to some of his more important conclusions. In the first section of his analysis Reijsbergen deals with the situation at the beginning and at the end of the text. He concludes with the observation that *The Salutation of the Virtues* "opens with a reverential greeting of the divine in the form of the forces which proceed from God. In the end it depicts the human person in whose life these forces are active. The vices and sins of the human person are taken away by the virtues... Thus the situation at the end of the Salutationof the Virtues touches the situation at its beginning for the sinner returns to the original harmonious order of creation. *The Salutation of the Virtues* describes the return of the human person to his/her creator."[56] Reijsbergen builds here on his view that the last part of *The Salutation of the Virtues* forms an independent unit which speaks about the virtuous person. Above I expressed already my disagreement with this view. Apart from this, *The Salutation of the Virtues* nowhere mentions the idea of a return. Moreover, the description given by Reijsbergen is far too general. This does not accord well with the fact that Francis in his writings is not so much interested in formulating a general theory about one or another aspect of a person's spiritual life, in this case about the requirements for a sinner's return to God, but rather in addressing concrete problems that have arisen especially within the brotherhood. However, it is not at all clear from Reijsbergen's conclusion which these concrete problems in reality are and who the brother or brothers are that are involved.

In the second section of his analysis, Reijsbergen speaks about the various persons mentioned in *The Salutation of the Virtues*. They can be placed in different groups. "The divine group is composed out of the Lord, the Spirit and six virtues. Since Francis believes in God as Trinity, the assumption arises that Christ is perhaps represented by the six virtues so that the divine group comprises the Blessed Trinity... Thus we have found a first trace for a trinitarian interpretation of *The Salutation of the Virtues*."[57] This interpretation sounds rather farfetched. Moreover, later on, in the fourth section about the obedient person, the virtues do not point just to Christ, but to the three divine persons.

[56] Reijsbergen 72.

[57] Reijsbergen 74–76.

Asking there which particular virtue can be characterized as a specific activity of one of the three divine persons, Reijsbergen starts with ascribing to Christ the virtues of wisdom (RegNB 17:16; 2 LetFaith 67) and obedience (RegNB 5:15; LetOrder 46). Next he refers charity to the Spirit (RegNB 5:14; 17:16) together with simplicity (RegNB 17:15). According to the latter text, humility could also be referred to the Spirit, but in fact it is ascribed to the Father, as is poverty. "Poverty points to the Father. It is the poverty which Christ and his mother preferred above all else in this world" (2 LetFaith 5; RegNB 9:5). In the Rule of 1223 the brothers are admonished "not to feel ashamed since the Lord made himself poor for us in this world (6:3) ... Humility, too, can be called a transcription of the Father. For Francis calls God humility in the Praises of God (4) and mentions the humility of God in the Letter to the Order (27–28)."[58]

The arguments do not sound very convincing. I fail to see why on account of the fact that Jesus and his mother prefer poverty above all else in this world, poverty should point to the Father, and not to Jesus himself. Further, the Praises of God speak not only about God as humility but also about God as love, charity, and wisdom. Why then choose humility as referring to the Father, while wisdom refers to Christ and charity to the Spirit? Moreover, the first Admonition speaks explicitly about the Son of God who "daily humbles himself as when he came from the royal throne into the womb of the Virgin; daily he comes to us in a humble form" (16–17). The way Reijsbergen ascribes a particular virtue to one of the three divine persons looks therefore rather arbitrary. It appears not so much to be based on Francis' interpretation of the virtues but on the need to find a division into three which corresponds to the three persons of the Blessed Trinity. As I have serious doubts about the existence of a trinitarian depth structure in *The Salutation of the Virtues*, I am also doubtful about the other conclusions which Reijsbergen reaches with regard to the depth structure on the basis of his trinitarian interpretation.

Zweerman

Zweerman has become convinced that some poems and prayers of

[58] Reijsbergen 96–97.

Francis have to be read as mystical texts, even though they have been neglected as such in recent studies. He refers here especially to *The Salutation of the Virtues*, Admonition 27 and the Praises of God: three texts which in his view are all connected with the LaVerna event. In *The Salutation of the Virtues*, in which Francis describes the life of the human person as a struggle, Zweerman discovers at least two Christograms. They indicate that in his struggle the human person is intimately connected with Christ. However, the way in which Zweerman proceeds is so artificial that I cannot accept his views. To give just one example, Zweerman sees a double diagonal line between verse 5 and the verses 15–16:

> v.5 *nullus homo... in toto mundo (A1) habere moriatur (B1)*
> v.15–16 *habet mortificatum (B2) omnibus hominibus... in mundo (A2)*

The only reason for seeing connecting diagonal lines between these two verses which are so very different as far as their content is concerned is the presence of some similar words. No attention is even paid to the place and the meaning the words have in the respective verses. I fail then also to understand how Zweerman can see any connection between the two verses, let alone discover here a Christogram. The same holds good for the Christogram he finds between v. 1 and v. 10 where the adjectives *sancta* and *pura* change place:

> v.1 *sancta pura simplicitate*
> v.10 *pura sancta simplicitas*

Zweerman also plays on the presence of the vowel A and the vowel O. *The Salutation of the Virtues* starts with A (*Ave*) and closes with O (*Domino*). The first virtue is *sapientia*, the last *obedientia*. The predominant verbs are *salvare*, *habere*, *offendere* and *confundere*; where once again the vowels A and O occur. This would refer to *Alpha* and *Omega*, the Greek letters often connected with the Christogram. Here too, the interpretation looks very artificial and far-fetched. Yet Zweerman uses these Christograms as a basis for his characterization of Francis' mysticism as a dramatic mysticism.[59]

[59] Zweerman 20; 27; 38–41. Zweerman gives some other examples of Christograms and number symbolisms which he and others discovered in some texts of Francis. Thus he found a Christogram in what he calls the Book of Admonitions, while

v.d Goorbergh-Zweerman

Most ideas expressed in Zweerman's article can also be found in the book he published together with Edith v.d. Goorbergh OSC. However, in their book they propose a different surface structure for the Salutationof the Virtues. According to them the first part comprises vv. 1–5. They argue as follows: "The salutation: *Ave* (v.1) is followed by the addresses: *you* (vv.1–4) together with the possessive pronouns: *your* (vv.1–3) and the personal pronoun *of you* (v.5). On the basis of these addresses we determine our division."[60] They seem to forget what they themselves write, namely that in verse 5 "the human person is placed before our eyes in a drastic fashion, for whoever wishes to possess the virtues mentioned in the previous verses, must first die." It is clear then that with verse 5 there starts something entirely new: after the introduction of the virtues it is now the human person who receives all our attention. Moreover, verse 5 is also in ideas and terminology closely connected with verses 6–7. They all three speak about the having or not having of one of the foundational virtues: *unam habere; unam habet; unam offendit, nullam habet.*

Further, as regards the depth structure, v.d. Goorbergh-Zweerman, too, follow a trinitarian interpretation of the three pair of virtues, as Reijsbergen did before them. They do not add anything new to his earlier considerations, except that they see in the way in which the three pair are grouped a trinitarian christogram: wisdom and obedience refer to

---

Rotzetter discovered one in the Canticle of Brother Sun. Rotzetter's interpretation was supported by Lehmann, who observed that the prevalence of the vowel O in the first line and of the vowel A in the last line could possibly refer to *Alpha* and *Omega.* As to the symbolism of numbers, Zweerman thinks that the 33 lines of the Canticle of Brother Sun and of the Praises of God are a reference to the years of Jesus' life. He also points to the numbers 6, 4 and 24. The Salutation of the Blessed Virgin Mary contains 6 invocations starting with *Ave*. In the SalVirt there are 6 virtues. Admonition 27 has 6 verses in which, if the regularity would not have been interrupted, there would have been 6 x 4 = 24 virtues and vices. The RegNB has 24 chapters, while in the central part of the Praises of God there are 24 short invocations starring with *Tu es*. As to the symbolic meaning of these numbers, number 6 points to God's creative activity; number 4 to the totality of the cosmic reality and number 24 to the activity of the Holy Spirit and the glory of God (31–33).

[60] v.d. Goorbergh-Zweerman 99, note 18.

the Son, while simplicity and love refer to the Holy Spirit. The two lines of these virtues cross in the middle where poverty and humility reflect the Father. Thus, so they conclude, the virtues in their mutual relationships give us an inkling of the relationship between Father, Son and Holy Spirit as well as of the active presence of the tri-une God in the hearts of the faithful. As I observed already with regard to the trinitarian interpretation of Reijsbergen, I am not convinced by their interpretation, which seems to me rather artificial. Moreover, v.d. Goorbergh and Zweerman themselves are not always certain of their own interpretation when trying to relate the virtues to one of the Persons of the Trinity.[61] All these conjectures make the interpretation as a whole very doubtful.

TARGET GROUP

To whom was *The Salutation of the Virtues* addressed? Lehmann observes that from the text itself it is not clear whether *The Salutation of the Virtues* is meant for a big or a small audience. At the end of his observations, however, he is inclined towards the conclusion that originally *The Salutation of the Virtues* was intended for the brothers only. The main reason is that *The Salutation of the Virtues* may be seen as a kind of summary of the original ideals of the lesser brothers. Moreover, it describes the obedience in such breadth and with such radicality that it can hardly be considered as valid for everybody.[62]

This conclusion is supported by Jansen. He does find, however, an indication in the text itself which, quite remarkably in his view, uses the expression "his brother." Further, speaking about "obedience of the Spirit and obedience of one's brother," the text appears, according to Jansen, to be influenced by the ideas which are proposed to the brothers in the Earlier Rule 5:14–15: "through the charity of the Spirit, they should voluntarily serve and obey one another."[63] Elaborating this suggestion somewhat further in the light of what we wrote above about the

[61] "Our supposition that Francis, when speaking about the virtue *Queen Wisdom*, meant especially the presence of God's Son in our life, receives a certain affirmation by the mentioned parallels." "One may venture to suppose that, also in his Salutation, Francis thought especially of the working of the Holy Spirit when mentioning the virtue of *pure simplicity*" (v.d. Goorbergh-Zweerman 114).

[62] Lehmann 244.

[63] Jansen 174, especially note 21.

crisis of obedience, we may add that it looks as if Francis in the final verses of *The Salutation of the Virtues* wishes to address a situation among the brothers which threatens the ideal of the Earlier Rule 5. Some brothers namely no longer obey the Spirit and each other, neglecting the mutual service, the mutual subjection and submissiveness to each other through washing one another's feet (RegNB 6:4). Obeying the spirit of the flesh, they have established other priorities which are more in conformity with their learning and the status they claim on account of it.

Reijsbergen, on the other hand, is of the opinion that the text does not contain any indications as to the person or persons to whom it is addressed. "The song is in its surface structure to be seen as a prayer or meditation. Further, it does not contain any words which would clarify that Francis intended *The Salutation of the Virtues* especially for the brothers, or the Poor Clares or the penitents. The text appears to have been written in view of the human person in general, the hearer or the reader."[64] I doubt, however, whether this is true because it looks far too abstract for a man like Francis who is above all interested in the concrete situation of the brotherhood and its commitment to live up to its calling in the world. For me it is therefore the brotherhood which is addressed. Thereby it is not the individual brother and his conversion which are first and foremost in Francis' mind, but rather the brotherhood and its original ideal, its original calling to offer an alternative to the existing society—a calling which they received from the Lord when on the Lord's divine inspiration they left the world.

CONCLUSION

The Salutation of the Virtues is a song or a didactic poem in which Francis reminds his brothers of the virtues that are characteristic of the way of life they have chosen in accordance with the gospel as an alternative to the ways of the world they have left on divine inspiration. This reminder has become urgent, especially in the last years of Francis' life, because the presence and activity of the learned brothers threaten to undermine the original option of the brothers and to allow the sins and vices of the world to enter the brotherhood itself. In fact, Francis sees it already happening around him. Out of a false sense of wisdom, the

[64] Reijsbergen 63.

learned brothers start appropriating to themselves the ministry of the brothers and the office of preaching (RegNB 17:4). They start asking privileges of the Roman curia to avoid the eventual hardships and persecution the obedience to their option in the Spirit may entail (Test 25–26).[65] And they pride themselves on their achievements to such an extent that they feel they can easily do without Francis and his ideals (TrueJoy 11). It is with this very painful problem in mind that Francis composes *The Salutation of the Virtues*, in an effort to make the brothers who have wandered away return to the original ideal. Thus *The Salutation of the Virtues* stands in the middle of the struggle within the brotherhood between the spirit of the flesh and the Spirit of the Lord. It is from within this very same struggle, this dialectic process, that I wish to read and understand *The Salutation of the Virtues*.

[65] A translation of the papal letters containing privileges granted to the lesser brothers during Francis' life can be found in Armstrong, Hellmann, Short 558–564.

CHAPTER TWO

Salutation of the Virtues and Prayer for their Salvation

vv. 1–4

In the light of the conclusions reached in the previous chapter, I will follow the dialectical method in my interpretation of *The Salutation of the Virtues*. That is, I will read and interpret *The Salutation of the Virtues* as a writing of Francis which has its Sitz im Leben in the struggle which, especially in the last years of his life, Francis was involved in with those learned brothers who went their own way and drifted ever further from the original ideals of the brotherhood. In this connection we think that Francis did not in the first place intend the description of the struggle between good and evil in *The Salutation of the Virtues* as a rather general advice of how an individual brother can lead a virtuous life but very concretely as a reminder to his brothers of what they originally promised the Lord when they left the world and its dominant value system and in their newly formed brotherhood set out on the road towards a new society, governed by quite different values.

In my commentary, after giving the text of a particular section, I will first make some general observations regarding that section as a whole before I will give a more detailed exegesis of each verse. When dealing with each virtue in particular, it will appear how intimately connected they are among each other. Or, as Francis says, "Whoever possesses one, possesses all" (6). Hence, it is not possible to speak about one of the virtues without also mentioning the others. I will however, as much as possible, try to avoid repetition.

TEXT

1.	Ave, regina sapientia	Hail, Queen Wisdom,

Dominus te salvet	may the Lord save you
cum tua sorore	with your sister,
sancta pura simplicitate.	holy pure Simplicity.
2. Domina sancta paupertas,	Lady, holy Poverty,
Dominus te salvet	the Lord save you
cum tua sorore	with your sister,
sancta humilitate.	holy Humility.
3. Domina sancta caritas,	Lady, holy Charity,
Dominus te salvet	the Lord save you
cum tua sorore	with your sister,
sancta obedientia.	holy Obedientia.
4. Sanctissimae virtutes,	Most holy Virtues,
omnes vos salvet Dominus,	the Lord save you all,
a quo venitis	from whom you come
et proceditis.	and proceed.

GENERAL OBSERVATIONS

Queen, Lady, Sister

The text personifies the virtues and addresses them as ladies or even as queen. Many see in this address the influence of the minnesong or a remnant of his earlier dreams about becoming a knight.[1] It is very possible that Francis was influenced by current forms of poetry and song.[2] There is, however, no indication that *The Salutation of the Virtues* either in its form or its content depends directly on the minnesong. If we want

[1] Hardick-Grau: "In the address 'Lady' Francis retains the knightly, chivalrous feelings of his youth. He does not dedicate himself to worldly women, but to the virtues in true courtly love" (130). Lehmann: "In a spirit of chivalrous courtliness and courtly chivalry Francis greets the virtues as ladies and presents them in pairs as sisters" (245). Reijsbergen quotes Lehmann and concludes: "The biographers tell us that Francis often sang about God's goodness in French songs. In this context it does not look strange if Francis were in fact inspired by the popular art of the troubadours of his time" (44–45). Jansen: "Francis links the personification of the virtues with courtly love. 'Lady' was the solemn title for a noble woman" (70).

[2] See the discussion in the Introduction.

to look for ideas that have more directly contributed to *The Salutation of the Virtues*, we must look elsewhere in the theological and liturgical tradition of the church and, of course, especially in Francis' own experience with his brothers.

The personification of the virtues was a well-known tradition in the Middle Ages, a tradition which had been greatly influenced by the *Psychomachia* of Aurelius Prudentius Clemens (384–405). In this work he deals with the struggle between virtues and vices within the human soul. It is this struggle which inspired many medieval artists in their sculptures and paintings. And so, even today, we can still see the lady virtues, often in full panoply, fighting evil, in miniatures, capitals and church portals.[3] It is therefore not surprising that Francis personifies the virtues as he too must have seen these images and reflected upon them. He need not have read the *Psychomachia* for that! Nor one of the medieval treatises on virtues and vices.[4] Moreover, the struggle between virtues and vices must have been the subject of a good number of sermons which Francis heard from his youth onward. Later, he even urges his brothers to preach about "vices and virtues, for the instruction and edification of the people" (RegB 9:3).

That the virtues are called Ladies, *Dominae*, has everything to do with the fact that, as Francis states, the virtues come and proceed from the Lord, *Dominus* (4), and thank their continued existence to him (1). This essential, theological link is clearly underlined in the text itself where in verses 2 and 3 *Domina* and *Dominus* figure next to each other.[5] The virtues are thus inseparable from the Lord. It is in fact through them that, as will become evident further on in *The Salutation of the Virtues*, the Lord exercises his gracious Lordship over men and women, sharing with them the power of his lifegiving Spirit (RegNB 17:15; SalBVM 6) and undoing the evil influence of Satan, the world and the flesh that dominate the society of those days.[6] Rather than seeing the influence of the minnesong behind the title of Ladies—an influence

[3] Nolthenius 273–274; Hardick-Grau 130; F Cardini, I musulmani nel giudizio dei crociati all'inizio del Duecento, *Archivio Storico Italiano* 146 (1988) 371–388; here 377; see also Introduction, note 17;

[4] For a survey of these treatises, see *Vertus et Vices (Traités sur les)*, in: *Dictionnaire de Spiritualité* XVI, Paris 1994, 497–502.

[5] Lehmann 228–229.

[6] See Verhey 108–109, quoted by Lehmann 228–229.

which may or may not be there—I prefer to emphasize the deep theological insight which Francis expresses by using this particular title. If there is any influence of the minnesong at all, it has been radically transformed by Francis in *The Salutation of the Virtues*.

Francis describes the virtues as sisters and makes them almost, as in a procession, stride along in pairs before our eyes. Looking for an image which may have influenced Francis in this description, we may, with Nolthenius, refer to psalm 44 (45) where the queen as a bride is led to the king while "virgins follow in her train... and enter the king's palace with joy and exultation" (15–16). This psalm verse is repeatedly quoted in the Common of the Virgins. As such it was certainly known to Francis. Though it does not have a textual similarity to *The Salutation of the Virtues*, nevertheless its picture of a royal wedding procession may well have been in the back of Francis' mind when he introduced the virtues in this particular way in his *The Salutation of the Virtues*.[7] At least, this explanation based on the prayer tradition of the church appears to be more likely than a possible reference to ladies-in-waiting in some *chanson de geste*.

The Lord Save You

The Lord holds the central place in the first strophe. For he is not only the one from whom all virtues come and proceed; he is also the one who can save the virtues. It is precisely in this latter capacity as possible saviour that Francis addresses the Lord in all the four verses of the first strophe, asking him to save queen Wisdom and the other virtues. Most translations render the Latin verb *salvare* as "to protect, to keep."[8] On

[7] Nolthenius 273–274. Reijsbergen sees no textual similarity between psalm 44 (45) and the Salutation of the Virtues. He finds it difficult to give a proper evaluation of Nolthenius' suggestion, but thinks it worthwhile to keep it in mind (45). v.d. Goorbergh-Zweerman, however. suggest the opposite, namely that "with the repeated wish: *May the Lord preserve you*, the virtues are sent off" (99). This seems rather strange to me. How could Francis send them off after he has barely introduced them and before he even has explained how people can acquire these holy vortues and what they will effect once people possess them.

[8] Lehmann: "Der Herr schütze dich" ("May the Lord protect you"). Hardick-Grau: "Der Herr erhalte dich" (May the Lord keep you). Jansen and Reijsbergen: "De Heer moge u behouden" (May the Lord keep you). Armstrong-Brady and

account of the Sitz im Leben of *The Salutation of the Virtues*, however, I prefer the translation "to save." For Francis considers the situation within the brotherhood to be such that the virtues characteristic of his gospel way of life are in danger[9] of being defeated and thrown out, just as he, Francis, is thrown out when he knocks at the door of the Portiuncula and asks to be allowed in.[10] Hence he prays to the Lord to save the virtues from this threatening defeat so that they will be able to continue to play their role in the struggle between the Spirit of the Lord, who is active in and through them, and the spirit of the flesh. To translate the verb *salvare* as " to protect, to keep" does not seem to do justice to this Sitz im Leben and to the struggle to keep the Spirit of the Lord alive within the brotherhood and not let it be destroyed by some misguided brothers.

Holy, Most Holy

The virtues are called holy, or even most holy, because they come and proceed from the holy God. The holiness of God is one of the most cherished attributes of God, and this especially in the invocations "holy Father" or "most holy Father" which together occur 21 times, 13 times in the Office of the Passion. In most of these places in the OffPas Francis inserts the invocations "holy Father" or "most holy Father" to replace the word God or Lord.[11] This shows the profound impression they have made on Francis, especially within the context of Jesus' passion. Trying to relive this passion and to enter deeper into the meaning of this mystery, it was not enough for Francis to mention God or the Lord. Rather, he found it necessary to introduce God as the holy or most holy Father, a name which Jesus himself used in his prayer at the eve of his passion in the farewell discourse of John's gospel (17:11).

Armstrong, Hellmann, Short: "May the Lord protect you." Flood: "The Lord save you."

[9] The idea of the virtues being in danger can also be found in Zweerman-v.d.Goorbergh: "because they are exposed to dangers, God's guarding care is invoked with the wish: *May the Lord preserve you*" (100). They do not, however, specify here the nature of these dangers nor where they come from.

[10] See the story about the True Joy 9–14.

[11] See Walter Viviani, *L'ermeneutica di Francesco d'Assisi, Indagine alla luce di Gv 13-17 nei suoi scritti*, Roma 1983, 257

He did so especially in the first six psalms of his OffPas where, praying with the suffering Jesus, he placed the invocation of the holy or most holy Father nine times in Jesus' mouth. Surrounded by enemies in his passion, Jesus had no one to turn to but his holy, his most holy Father. And although the situation was very critical and looked almost hopeless, Jesus kept praying for help (1:4–5) trusting that his holy, most holy Father would not leave his Son in the hands of the wicked who had risen against him (2:9). And he was not to be disappointed. The holy Father held his right hand (6:12) and snatched his life from the strongest of his enemies (3:5). He, the most holy Father, saved him (14:1–2); and so Jesus rose from death and his most holy Father received him with glory (6:11–12). He was his strength and, in his strength, shattered the enemy (14:3–4). Suffering and death did not have the last word. The holiness of God, the Father, ultimately overcame the suffering and death which sinful men had inflicted upon Jesus. It is therefore especially in Jesus' struggle against suffering and death that God's holiness manifests itself most clearly as that particular characteristic of God which cannot co-exist with sin and evil and hence has to oppose them and eventually conquer them. Thus humankind and the world are, in principle, snatched away from the power of sin and evil; they are made holy again and returned to the domain of the holy Father. For whatever is holy, does not (any longer) belong to the world of sin and evil, but is at home with the holy God, the source of all holiness.[12]

It is this same faith and trust in the holy Father who overcame sin and death which are at the heart of the passages in the Second Letter to the Faithful 56–60 and in the Earlier Rule 22:41–55, where Francis quotes extensively from Jesus' prayer in the farewell discourse. In the Second Letter to the Faithful Francis exclaims: "Oh how holy and how loving, pleasing, humble, peaceful, sweet, lovable and desirable above all things to have such a brother who laid down his life for his sheep and prayed to the Father *for us*." Thus Francis presents Jesus as a brother who, like a good shepherd, gives his life for him and his brothers and at the end of his life recommends them to the care and protection of his holy Father. For they, whom the Father gave to Jesus and to whom Jesus gave the words he had received from his Father, have to stay on in a hostile world. It is for them that Jesus prays that the holy Father will protect, bless and

[12] See G.P. Freeman, Kinderen van de hemelse vader, *FL* 81 (1998) 251–258, here 256.

sanctify them, so that they may be freed from all that causes dissension and threatens the unity among them, and be holy in being one as Jesus is one with his holy Father.The hostile world of sin and division has to make place for the world of unity and holiness that comes from God.

In the Earlier Rule 22, Francis wishes that he and his brothers may "hold onto the words, the life and the teaching and the holy Gospel of [Jesus] who humbled himself to ask his Father for us and to make his name known to us" (41). Also at the centre of the long quotation from the farewell discourse, which then follows, Francis introduces Jesus praying to his holy Father that he may protect Jesus' followers from the evil one and sanctify them in the truth so that they may not be divided but completely one. Their unity will be a sign to the world of the Father's holiness, of his sanctifying power which is stronger than the evil one.

In *The Salutation of the Virtues*, too, Francis refers to the struggle between holiness and sin. It is here the holy, most holy virtues of the most holy God and Father, which take up the struggle against the unholy forces of Satan which dominate the world. And Francis is confident that the virtues will overcome Satan and all his works. More than that, he is sure about it. For in the text he does not use the optative, expressing a wish, but the indicative, stating a fact *(confundit)*. When and where the brothers possess the holy virtues that proceed from God, the holy Father, they cannot but confound the evil and restore the world to God's original design, the paradise of the beginning. For through the holy virtues God, the holy Father, their protector, their guardian and defender, their strength (PraisesGod 2 and 5), is with the brothers and works his redeeming, liberating and sanctifying power through them for the life of the world.

The number of virtues, their selection and relationship

Francis greets six virtues: wisdom, simplicity, poverty, humility, charity and obedience. With the exception of charity, they do not belong to the traditional sets of virtues, namely the three theological virtues of faith, hope and charity and the four cardinal virtues of justice, prudence, temperance and fortitude. This indicates that Francis did not want to write some rather theoretical treatise about virtues and vices, several of which existed in his days. For in that case he would definitely have taken these traditional divisions into account. Rather,

Francis had his own agenda which was essentially determined by the concrete situation of the brotherhood which he felt it his duty to guide by his word and example.

This is further confirmed by the fact that the monastic triad of poverty, chastity and obedience is not followed by Francis. Apparently a treatise based on these pillars of the religious life did not fit Francis' intentions, which centred first and foremost around the actual way of life of his brothers and the problems he encountered there.[13] Finally, in his selection of virtues Francis does not continue the trinitarian line of the Earlier Rule 17:16, where he writes that the Spirit of the Lord "always longs for the divine fear and the divine wisdom and the divine love of the Father, and of the Son, and of the Holy Spirit." For the divine fear of the Father is not at all mentioned in *The Salutation of the Virtues*. A trinitarian interpretation of the three pair of virtues, as proposed by Reijsbergen and by Zweerman-v.d Goorbergh, seems therefore less likely.

It is evident then that the six virtues are not selected by Francis for any theoretical or structural reason, but because he felt the brothers needed to be reminded of the essential importance of these virtues for their way of life. In other words, they are the foundational virtues of the brotherhood and of its mission in the world.[14] Their foundational character is confirmed by the fact that they are among the virtues that are

[13] Hardick-Grau: "Francis always thinks concretely, never abstractly" (130).

[14] On another occasion, when writing Admonition 27, Francis proposes another set of virtues in which some of the virtues of Salutation of the Virtues, namely love, wisdom, humility, poverty are accompanied by a number of other virtues: patience, rest, meditation, fear of the Lord, mercy and discernment. Jansen suggests that, in placing special emphasis on quiet and meditation, Francis may have been influenced by a stay with the hermits of Camaldoli to which he had been invited by cardinal Hugolino in 1220 after he had returned from his tiring journey to the Middle East. A. Jansen, Words of Salvation of Saint Francis. A Commentary on Admonition 27, *FrancDig* IV, 2 (December 1994) 1–24, here 3. It remains surprising, however, that two important virtues, namely simplicity and obedience, are completely absent from Admonition 27, while other virtues like rest, meditation and discretion are mentioned only here. Does this imply that in this admonition Francis uses, or borrows from, or is inspired by, an existing monastic text or existing monastic sayings in which he finds many things which he considers important also for his own brothers at that particular moment and which he therefore proposes to them in this admonition, but that when it comes to the foundational virtues of the brotherhood and its mission, Francis rather includes

most frequently mentioned in the writings of Francis.[15] Being foundational, these virtues possess, next to their unity of origin in the Lord, a clear unity of purpose. For as *virtutes*, that is as forces, powers of the Lord, they are meant to empower the brothers so that by their virtuous way of life they will be able to overcome sin and evil in the world and to build a new, different world that is more in accordance with God's plans. There exists thus a most intimate relationship between the virtues: they are sisters of each other, having a common origin in the Lord and a common goal which does not first and foremost lie on the personal, ascetical plain: their personal holiness, but rather on the level of the transformation of society in the power of the Lord: a new, alternative world, a sisterhood and brotherhood that embraces all people without exception.

Besides this common relationship between the six virtues, there also exists, according to van Asseldonk, a special relationship between the virtues within each pair. This relationship is supposed to be of a causal nature and is expressed by the proposition *cum*, which in the medieval Latin of Francis' writings does not only mean together with but also through, by means of.[16] According to van Asseldonk, therefore, Francis does not only ask that Queen Wisdom be saved together with her sister Simplicity—both come from the Lord and derive their continued exis-

---

simplicity and obedience, while omitting quiet, meditation and discretion. Or, in other words, does this imply that when it comes to the specific character of Franciscan spirituality, Salutation of the Virtues is to be preferred as a source because it reflects more directly the experiences and the struggles of Francis and his brothers than *Admonition* 27 with its more monastic background? I am inclined to give an affirmative answer to the questions.

15 Outside Salutation of the Virtues, wisdom in the sense of the true wisdom of God and of the virtue of (spiritual) wisdom is mentioned 10 times; simplicity is mentioned only once in Fragm. 1:52, as a variant of the Earlier Rule 17:15, but the adjective *simplex* and the adverb *simpliciter* occur more frequently, the latter even 4 times in the Testament. Poverty is mentioned 13 times, of which 3 times together with humility. Humility itself occurs 15 times, once as a divine name (PrGod 4). Charity is mentioned 19 times, while obedience is found 42 times. Yet, as remarked above, obedience is one of the virtues which is missing in Admonition 27. See v.d. Goorbergh-Zweerman 112, note 62. However, in their counting they include also the Salutation of the Virtues as well as the Fragments.

16 O. v Asseldonk, Verso un cuore puro con la pura, semplice e vera pace dello Spirito (RegNB 17,15), *Laurentianum* 33 (1992) 506–507; Jansen 63; Steiner 131. Hardick-Grau come to the same conclusion without referring to the special mean-

tence from him—but he also points to the special role of simplicity through which Queen Wisdom is to be saved. The same holds good for poverty and humility, as well as charity and obedience. It seems to me, however, that this might lead to a certain artificiality and move us away from the real message contained in verses 5–7, that the relationship between the virtues is completely mutual. As much as wisdom is saved through simplicity, so also simplicity is saved through wisdom[17] as well as through the other virtues. This is but natural, as the virtues are all sisters of each other. Further, the virtues could also have been paired differently. Love and wisdom could have been combined as they are in Admonitions 27:1, or poverty and obedience, as is implied in Admonitions 2, where the original sin of disobedience is the sin of appropriation. Yet, these different combinations would in no way lead to a different exegesis, because we cannot explain tone virtue without the others. This implies that, since the actual pairing shows a particular preference of Francis at the time he composed *The Salutation of the Virtues*, we will certainly have to take this preference into account in our exegesis, as it will help us to understand better how Francis, in his own mind, saw the specific meaning of each virtue within the context of the situation of the brotherhood. Yet, on the other hand, we should avoid wanting to read too much in it.[18]

DETAILED EXEGESIS

Ave—Hail

In his other writings Francis uses this greeting only in the context of the place and role of Mary in the mystery of the incarnation. Thus he uses it seven times in the Salutation of the Blessed Virgin Mary. It echoes there, of course, the greeting in Luke's gospel passage of the

---

ing of *cum*: "Thus 'pure Simplicity' creates the favourable climate for 'Queeen Wisdom'; Simplicity becomes the sister of Wisdom who cannot exist without her" (300).

17 "In every greeting, two virtues complement one another: one presupposes the other." Lehmann 230.

18 We may refer here to the Trinitarian depth structures that Reijsbergen en Zweerman discover in the three pair of virtues. See I E 2–3, also for the doubts we expressed there about the validity of such interpretation..

annunciation of the angel Gabriel to Mary, which Francis quotes once directly in the Exhortation to the Praise of God (4). Using this greeting here, Francis is likely to have in mind the same context of the incarnation, of God's Spirit overshadowing Mary and making her the mother of Jesus. In fact, it is through the virtues, which proceed from God, that God's power, the power of God's Spirit, is present among the brothers.[19] Or as Francis writes in the Salutation of the Blessed Virgin: "Hail... all you holy virtues which through the grace and the illumination of the Holy Spirit are poured into the hearts of the faithful so that from unfaithful people you may make people faithful to God" (6). It is precisely those faithful, possessing God's virtues through the power of God's Spirit, who become mothers of Jesus when they give birth to him through their holy works, their works of virtue performed in the power of the Spirit of the Lord (2 LetFaith 53). It is these works that are absent wherever the spirit of the flesh dominates the world (RegNB 17:11) and the people have become unfaithful, with the result that in such a world Jesus cannot be born. It is Francis' great concern that, although he sees the spirit of the flesh making inroads among the brothers, this unfaithfulness not take hold of the brotherhood as well. To this end, the brothers should not let themselves be blinded by a false sense of wisdom, but open their minds and hearts to the true wisdom and her sister virtues that come from God.

Queen Wisdom

It is not charity or poverty which Francis greets first, but Queen Wisdom. In calling wisdom "queen," Francis may have been influenced by liturgical readings from the Wisdom literature, especially on feast-days of Mary and in the Office of Mary. Thus we read on the feast of the Birth of Mary (8 September): "The Lord possessed me, Wisdom, at the beginning of his ways, before he made anything, from the beginning. From eternity I was ordained, from the days of old, before the earth was made. The deep was not and I was already conceived.., before the hills I came to birth... When the Lord prepared the heavens, I was there.., when he laid down the foundations of the earth, I was with him and ordered everything.., ever at play in his presence, at play everywhere

[19] Jansen 67.

in his world, delighting to be with the sons of men. And now, my children, listen to me. Blessed those who keep my ways. Listen to my discipline and be wise. Blessed those who listen to me, who watch day after day at my gates and keep guard at my doorposts. Those who find me, find life and will obtain salvation from the Lord" (Proverbs 8:22–35).

And in the readings of the Office of Mary, we hear: 'From eternity, in the beginning, I was created, and for eternity I shall remain. I ministered before him in the holy tabernacle, and thus was I established on Zion. In the holy city I found rest, and in Jerusalem I wield my authority. I have taken root in a privileged people, in the Lord's property, in his inheritance" (Ecclesiasticus 24:14–16).[20] As the liturgy applies these texts to Mary, who is Lady and Queen, (SalMary 1), it is but a little step to apply the title queen to wisdom as well, especially also because she is close to the Lord and involved with him in the work of creation and salvation. Moreover she lives in the holy city, Jerusalem, in a palace where people watch at the gates.[21] It is Queen Wisdom's ways the brothers should follow and so find life for themselves and for others, especially for those who are the victims of a society which does not allow itself to be governed by Queen Wisdom.

What are, concretely speaking, the ways of Queen Wisdom? What are we to think about? In verse 6 Francis states that "whoever possesses one of the virtues and does not offend the others, possesses all." This implies that whoever possesses wisdom, possesses also simplicity, pover-

[20] S. van Dijk, *The ordinal of the papal court from Innocent III to Boniface VIII and related documents*, completed by J. Hazelden Walker, Fribourg 1975, 470. Further, during the month of August, the office readings were taken from the Book of Proverbs. The first responsory was: "From the beginning the Lord created me, before the earth was made," followed by the verse: "When the Lord prepared the heavens, I was there." Another responsory is taken from the Book of Wisdom: "Grant me wisdom, assistant at your throne" (9:4), together with its verse: "Send her from the holy heavens and from your throne of glory to be with me and toil with me, that I may know what is pleasing in your eyes" (9:10). ibid. 341–342. These last texts are also quoted by Jansen 68.

[21] Jansen does not refer to the liturgical use of the readings from the Wisdom literature and their application to Mary in order to explain the title "queen." His explanation is more general, more abstract and, in my opinion, less convincing: "The illumination by the Holy Spirit is the beginning of God's operation. From this perspective wisdom is the first of all virtues and may well be given the title of queen" (68).

ty, humility, charity and obedience of the Spirit and of one's brother which manifests itself in an attitude of being subject and submissive to all persons in the world. Several brothers could not see how these virtues, and particularly simplicity, could be combined with wisdom. In fact, they thought that simplicity went contrary to, and was incompatible with, wisdom (2 Cel 189). Thus Francis finds the understanding of the true meaning of wisdom lacking within the brotherhood. His brothers, at least some of them, do not have the true "spiritual wisdom," that is the true wisdom of the Spirit, as he has seen it revealed in Jesus Christ, "the Son of God who is the true wisdom of the Father" (2 LetFaith 67; cf. 1 Cor 1:24 and 30).

This observation of Francis about Jesus as the true wisdom of the Father, together with the virtues he mentions as being one with wisdom, leads us almost necessarily to the beautiful passage in the First Letter to the Corinthians 1:18–31 where Paul speaks about the wisdom of God as opposed to the wisdom of the world. And this all the more so because *The Salutation of the Virtues* develops the same theme.[22] However, according to the register of scripture references of Eßer's critical edition, Francis' writings do not contain any explicit or implicit reference to this passage of Paul's letter. This looks highly improbable to me. In this matter I prefer, therefore, to follow Boccali.[23] Besides the just mentioned reference to 1 Cor 1:24 and 30 in the Second Letter to the Faithful 67, he finds another reference to the same passage in the Second Letter to the Faithful 45: "We must not be wise according to the flesh," which refers to 1 Cor 1:26.

To this may be added *The Salutation of the Virtues* 10: "Simplicity confounds all the wisdom of this world *(sapientiam huius mundi)*." Eßer,[24] very strangely, sees in this verse a reference to 1 Cor 2:6, which speaks about "the wisdom of this age" *(sapientia huius saeculi)*, instead of the more obvious 1 Cor 1:20: "Hasn't God made foolish the wisdom of this world." Boccali is more correct by referring here to 1 Cor 3:19 where Paul speaks indeed about the wisdom of the world. I prefer however to refer to 1 Cor 1:20 and, implicitly, to the larger passage of verses 18–31, of which it is a part. The main reason for this preference is that, in the repeated use of the verb *confundit* (confounds, puts to shame) after every

[22] We agree here with Jansen 66.

[23] I.M. Boccali, *Opuscula S. Francisci et Scripta S. Clarae Assisiensium*, Assisi 1978, 464.

[24] Esser is followed by Lehmann 234.

virtue in the second part of *The Salutation of the Virtues*, I hear a clear echo of another verse of this passage, namely verse 27, where Paul describes the confounding power of God's wisdom as he had experienced it in his own life as a follower of Jesus. It turned the standards of the world, its wisdom, which he had followed in his actions before his conversion, completely upside down: "God has chosen what is foolish in the eyes of the world to shame *(confundat)* the wise and what is weak in the eyes of the world to shame *(confundat)* what is strong." Of course, I cannot establish with certainty what Francis had in mind. However, given the similarity of the problem both Paul and Francis face, namely the conflict between God's wisdom and the wisdom of the world, between the wisdom of the Spirit and the wisdom of the flesh, I cannot but conclude that *The Salutation of the Virtues* resonates with ideas and words of Paul's beautiful explanation to the Christian community in Corinth of the ways in which God's wisdom confounds the wise and mighty of this world.[25] And I am rather amazed that Esser and Boccali do not refer to this at all.

In 1 Cor 1:18–31, Paul writes: "The word of the cross is foolishness for those who will perish; however, for those who will be saved, that is for us, it is the power of God. For it is written: 'I shall destroy the wisdom of the wise and bring to nothing the learning of the learned *(prudentiam prudentium)*.' Where are the wise? Where are the scribes? Where are the thinkers of our age? Hasn't God made foolish the wisdom of this world?.. We preach Christ crucified: a scandal to the Jews and foolishness to the Gentiles; but to those who are called, whether Jews or Greeks, he is God's power and God's wisdom. For God's foolishness is wiser than human wisdom and God's weakness is stronger than human strength. Look at your own calling, brothers and sisters. There were not many wise according to the flesh, nor many powerful, nor many belonging to noble families. But what is foolish in the eyes of the world God has chosen to shame the wise and what is weak in the eyes of the world God has chosen to shame what is strong. All that is not noble in the eyes of the world and contemptible God has chosen, and what is nothing, to destroy what is, so that no one should glory in his sight. Thanks to him, however, you are in Christ Jesus who by God has been made for us wisdom, and justice, and sanctification, and redemption, in

[25] For a further discussion of the meaning of the verb *confundere*, see below my commentary on verse 8 in III B e.

order that, as has been written: If anyone glories, let him glory in the Lord."

In this passage Paul not only presents his message of the cross as a critique of the human wisdom of the Corinthians and the standards by which it operates, he also develops what one could call a new epistemology of the cross. For what is at stake is the [Corinthians'] perspective on God and their life together as a community. They are asked to think in a different way, to see through a new lens which corrects their myopia. Particularly, they are asked to redefine wisdom and power in the light of Jesus' crucifixion and death. For at this climax of Jesus' life divine wisdom and power are revealed in self-giving love which looks like foolishness and weakness in the eyes of the world. As such they contradict the criteria and expectations of the Corinthians and show clearly that their value system has become obsolete. Further, Paul's message of the cross presents not merely a new logic or a new cognitive enterprise, but includes living as well as thinking. An epistemology consistent with the scandal of the cross makes people fools for Christ's sake and a spectacle to the world Yet, it is they who remove the masks behind which society hides itself and who see reality as it actually is in God's eyes.[26]

[26] These ideas have been taken, almost literally, from Charles B. Cousar, Paul and the Death of Jesus, *Interpretation* 52 (1998) 44–46. Transposed to the present world, they are very much part of Asian liberation theology. Thus e.g. Choan Seng-Song, a Presbyterian Taiwanese, speaks about the "politics of the cross" which is the natural consequence of God's politics of taking the side of the poor against the rich, against "the barbarism of power." For "what transpired in the final struggle of Jesus with power politics was the power and wisdom of the cross." This politics of the cross, however, does not mean weakness and ineffectiveness. Indeed, "the powerless cross proves so powerful that throughout the centuries it has empowered countless persons to struggle for justice and freedom... The politics of the cross has taken form in resistance, in revolt, in revolution. But above all it has inspired a great many persons to believe in self-sacrifice as the most powerful weapon against self-serving political power. It has encouraged them to use nonviolence, not just for tactical reason but out of love, to carry the cause of the people to the court of rulers." *Third-Eye Theology*, Maryknoll, 1990, 222. 231; *Tell Us Our Names*, Maryknoll, 1984, 176–180. Quoted from Peter C. Phan, Kingdom of God: A Theological Symbol for Asians, *Gregorianum* 79 (1998) 295–322, here 306–309. Similar ideas are emphasized also in various documents of the Federation of Asian Bishops' Conferences (FABC) where the bishops urgently plead for an Asian spirituality of *kenosis* which will inspire the church in Asia to become the servant of the Asian peoples. See my *Francis and Islam*, 175–186.

Read against the background of Paul's message to the Corinthians, the holy wisdom Francis speaks about is the wisdom of the weak, crucified Jesus who became contemptible, like nothing, in the eyes of the world. Or—to use more Franciscan terms that have the same meaning—holy wisdom is the wisdom of the poor, humble and obedient Jesus. Jesus revealed this wisdom, God's wisdom, during his life here on earth by becoming "a poor man and a transient who lived on alms" (RegNB 9:2) and by allowing himself in the end to be made "a worm and no man, the scorn of men and the outcast of the people" (2 LetFaith 46; cf. Ps 21:7); and he continues to reveal this divine wisdom in the Eucharist where "daily he humbles himself as when he came from the royal throne into the womb of the Virgin" (Adm 1:16). It is the ways of this holy wisdom which Francis wishes his brothers to follow "simply and without gloss," i.e., without any learned rationalization (Test 39), in loving service, being "subject and submissive to all people in the world" (SalVirt 16), and so to confound Satan and all his subtlety (SalVirt 9).

Many learned brothers, however, cannot see it this way. Blinded as they are by the enemy (2 LetFaith 69), they lack the eyes of the Spirit (Adm 1:20) and become an easy prey for the enemy's subtlety. Rather than being poor, living without calling anything their own, they want to appropriate to themselves the office of preaching (RegNB 17:4) because this gives them a certain status in church and society. Rather than to offer their body, created in the image of Christ's body, in service and obedience to their Creator, they want to glory in their knowledge, whereas there is nothing in which they can glory as their own, except in their infirmities (Adm 5). Rather than to live according to Spirit of the Lord speaking to us in the Scriptures, they wish to know the words alone, so that they may be esteemed wiser than others (Adm 7:2).[27] These learned brothers find support among the church officials who are most eager to use their talents as preachers to realize the policies of the

[27] According to Armstrong, "the concern for wisdom or knowledge... is a prominent theme in the Admonitions... *Sapiens* and *sapientiores* appear one time each in the admonitions. *Sapienter* can be found twice, as can *sapientia*. While *scientia* is present four times, and various forms of the verb *scire* are present seven times. All of this confirms the belief that the pursuit of knowledge and the risks it presents is one of the strong themes of the admonitions." Prophetic Implications of the "Admonitions," *Laurentianum*, 26 (1986) 454–455, note 194.

church.[28] The learned brothers can therefore always approach the curia for letters that will strengthen their position before bishops, priests and people.

Francis strongly objects to this way of behaviour, even during the last days of his life. He is not at all impressed by the reasoning of these brothers that, according to the leaders of the church, they can render a great service to the church and the people through their preaching. Hence, in his Testament he writes: "And I firmly command all of the brothers through obedience, that wherever they are, they should not be so bold as to seek any letter from the Roman curia... neither under the guise of preaching or even for the persecution of their bodies; but wherever they have not been received, let them flee into another country to do penance with the blessing of God" (25–26). This severe admonition is clear evidence that Francis feels very strongly about the way the learned brothers rationalize their behaviour with the support of the curia. He radically rejects their way of understanding the situation because it is not at all in conformity with God's wisdom as revealed in the poor and humble Jesus. It is his life with all its radical demands which the brothers should follow in all simplicity, without any rationalization.

Thus Francis discovers by his own experience the truth of Jesus' saying in the gospel of Matthew that God's wisdom is kept hidden from the wise and the learned, and revealed only to children (Mat 11:25), i.e. to the simple. The fact that the true wisdom is hidden from the wise and learned is not, however, meant by Francis as a condemnation of learning as such. Francis has a great respect for theologians and preachers provided they use their learning to "minister spirit and life" (Test 13), and not to seek their own advantage. Nor does Francis with his view on true wisdom wish to take a stand in the debate between the affective theology of the monasteries, based on contemplation, and the scholastic, more dialectic theology of the universities, based on reason.[29] It may even be asked whether Francis was at all aware of this debate. On the other hand,

[28] Cf. 2 Cel 148 where we find a good example of how Pope and curia want to make use of the brothers in the interest of their policies by playing on the need of the church for "bishops and prelates from among the brothers who excel all others by their learning and example."

[29] Reijsbergen draws attention to this debate when sketching the historical context on pages 131–133. We are not convinced, however, that it plays a role in the Salutation of the Virtues.

it is quite clear that his theological insights are the fruit of his contemplation, i.e. his looking at created reality with great admiration, experiencing it as God's good gift of love which, sadly enough, is often not treated with the respect due to it, and interpreting it in the light of the gospel with a strong commitment to praxis, i.e. to establishing or rather to bringing back God's kingdom of justice and peace as revealed in the life and the liberating, redemptive praxis of the poor and humble Jesus (RegNB 9:8; 23:3; Test 14; 22–24).

Being contemplative and experiential, Francis' approach to wisdom and theological learning is thus also highly pragmatic. Concretely this means that, in accordance with God's creative and redemptive plans, he is very much concerned about realizing the brotherhood with its own particular value system as an alternative society in the hierarchical and patriarchal world of his days. However, reflecting on its situation, he sees how learned brothers succeed in obtaining a recognized, respectful place in church and society. Because of this place, this position they start identifying themselves again with the dominant valuesystem of those days where everything centres around power, possessions and prestige. They are forgetting that they have left that world and its value system, and chosen a way of life which makes them look foolish in the eyes of the people, but of which they themselves ought to know that it is the only right one (cf. RegNB 9:7), because it is confirmed by the life of Jesus himself.

It was this forgetfulness of the true, spiritual wisdom about the strength of the weak and the importance of those who are nothing which undermined the very foundation of the life of the brotherhood and of its mission in church and society.[30] That is why Francis saw the problems within the brotherhood basically as the result of a conflict between the different understandings of wisdom and the different ways of seeing and knowing that have developed among the brothers due to different value and language systems stemming from the different posi-

[30] See e.g. LegPer 114, where, at the Chapter of Mats, the "wise and learned brothers" with the help of Cardinal Hugolino tried to secure a safe and respectful place for the brotherhood in the church by "appealing to the rules of Benedict, Augustine and Bernard which teach all kinds of things in order to lead an orderly life (*quae docent sic et sic ordinate vivere*)." Francis ends his reply by warning them that "God will use [their] knowledge and wisdom to confound them." For the whole story, see our commentary on the virtue of simplicity.

tions the brothers occupy. For this reason he wanted the learned brothers from their position of learning to make their own epistemology of the cross. He wanted them to see and to know the true wisdom of God revealed in the poor, crucified Jesus, and simply live by it. Then, and then only, would they be able again, in the strength of holy wisdom, to confound the wisdom of the world that is creeping back into the brotherhood, and return to the ideals of the Gospel which they promised to observe. This interpretation of the situation by Francis explains, as we have already indicated above, why Francis opens his reminder to the brothers—which *The Salutation of the Virtues* is meant to be—with wisdom and calls her "queen." For the very life of the brotherhood rises or falls with the absence or presence of true wisdom.[31] Wherever she is absent, the brothers are not able to trace the footsteps of their poor and humble Lord and follow them. Rather, they remain stuck in the world of possessions, power and prestige, and the violence and injustice which inevitably go with them.

On the other hand, wherever Queen Wisdom reigns, the brothers are able to see the way the Lord reveals to them as to how they are to live according to the form of the holy Gospel. And in wisdom's strength, wisdom's virtue which comes from God, they will be able to walk that way and to realize a true brotherhood in mutual service as an alternative to the violent and oppressive society of those days. It will be again as "when the Lord laid down the foundations of the earth, and I [Wisdom] was with him and ordering everything... Blessed those who keep my ways and listen to my discipline. Those who find me, find life and will obtain salvation from the Lord" (Proverbs 8:29–35). It is this vision of the place and role of Queen Wisdom within the context of the actual situation of the brotherhood as Francis sees it which also explains why Queen Wisdom is accompanied by her sister, Simplicity. For the learned broth-

[31] v.d. Goorbergh-Zweerman suggest that Francis probably starts his Salutation of the Virtues with Queen Wisdom because "at the begining of his life as a convert Francis chose the spirituality of the desert monks as his example." They come to this rather far-fetched suggestion via the following reasoning: "It is interesting that, according to 1 Celano 21, Francis initially wore a hermit's habit, that is the dress of the desert monks, and that he put this off only after he had heard Jesus' missionary discourse. If we take as our starting point that Francis was indeed captivated by the spirituality of the desert monks, it is important to know in this context that these monks called the imitation of Christ *wisdom (sapientia)*. For their life was one long search for the simple God-directed existence" (105).

ers will only be able to know and understand the true wisdom if, with all their learning, they will open themselves in all simplicity for God's revelation in the poor and humble Jesus, and are ready in all simplicity to accept and realize the radical demands which Jesus' revelation entails, without rationalizing or trying to find excuses whenever the going becomes difficult.

with your sister, holy pure Simplicity (v.1)

It is clear then that Queen Wisdom cannot exist without her sister Simplicity.[32] Simplicity is indeed the indispensable condition of possibility for the existence of true wisdom.[33] But what does Francis exactly have in mind when he speaks about "simple" and "simplicity"? As simplicity is the only virtue which in addition to "holy" carries a second adjective, namely "pure," we will pay special attention in our exegesis to those passages in his writings where the adjectives "simple" and "pure" occur together. Of particular importance here is a text of the Testament where the adjective "simple" is used twice, once together with "pure" and next with the expression "without gloss" (39).

The oldest text where "simple" and "pure" are found together is the Earlier Rule 17:15, which forms part of the original end of the the Earlier Rule. In this passage Francis and his brothers remind one another con-

[32] It is somewhat surprising therefore that the virtue of simplicity does not at all occur among the virtues mentioned in Admonition 27, whereas it occupies such a prominent place in the Salutation of the Virtues as well as in Francis' other writings, especially the Testament. Does this mean that in this admonition Francis uses an existing monastic text or existing sayings which he finds important enough to convey to his brothers but without first adapting them fully to his own insight and experience? See also II B, note 14, III B b, note 3 and IV B a, note 3.

[33] Francis stands here in an old tradition. Several Eastern Fathers stress that simplicity is a necessary requirement for faith, true wisdom and one's relation with God. Philoxenos exhorts to receive the Scriptures "with a simple faith that does not reason." Isaac of Ninive writes: "Let us walk in simplicity, and not in knowledge, before God." And according to Ps. Macarius, we must "search God with simplicity." Simplicity is also seen as a return to the original state of innocence where all artificiality is excluded and a person is immune to evil. Finally, Martyrius Sahdona praises a person happy whose "eye has been purified from the trouble of the clouds of this world and has been made simple and straight to see the Lord in the cloud of light." Simplicité, in *Dictionnaire de Spiritualité*, vol. 14, Paris 1990, 904, 906.

cerning the ideals of the brotherhood and how they can only realize them by becoming involved in the ongoing struggle between the spirit of the flesh and the Spirit of the Lord. It is this Spirit of the Lord which "strives for humility and patience, and the pure simplicity and true peace of the Spirit."[34] In this striving the Spirit of the Lord is radically opposed to the spirit of the flesh whose priorities are altogether different. The spirit of the flesh "strives greatly towards having words, but little towards deeds *(operatio)*. And it does not seek the religion and holiness of the spirit within *(in interiori spiritu)*, but it wishes and desires to have a religion and holiness outwardly apparent to people" (11–12). What does this description of the opposition between the spirit of the flesh and the Spirit of the Lord mean in the mind of Francis when read within the concrete historical context of Assisi?

Assisi offers peace to its citizens. For, with great pomp, the warring parties have signed a peace treaty in the name of God and to the glory of their Lord Jesus Christ in an assembly of the people on November 9, 1210. The external appearance of religion and holiness is on their side: with the blessing of God they have a beautiful document, which regulates everything in the smallest detail. But for whom? When looked at from the point of view of the people who, individually or collectively, benefit from this treaty, it is evident that this document protects and safeguards the interests of the emerging classes in the urban society: traders, bankers, lawyers, notaries who in their dealings rely very much on words. However, these practitioners of "the culture of the word"—and this is what bothers Francis—are little interested in deeds, in *operatio:* i.e. the liberating, transforming activity in the power of the Spirit through which men and women bring Jesus to birth again in this world, give him a new concrete, historical existence in their surroundings (2

[34] The manuscripts present us with different readings. Esser prefers here the reading: "the pure and simple and true peace," which is found in Clarenus whose quotations, according to Boehmer, form the oldest tangible witness of the RegNB, and in An, the manuscript preserved in the Library of the Antonianum in Rome which, according to Flood, in several places certainly contains the oldest reading. The great majority of manuscripts, however, reads "et puram simplicitatem." For this reason Lehmann does not understand why Esser relegates this reading among the variants (226, note 16). Van Asseldonk mentions as a possible further argument in favour of this reading the fact that the fragment of the Worcester codex which contains a later version of the RegNB, chooses also the reading "et pura simplicitas"—a choice made probably by Francis himself or during his lifetime (502).

LetFaith 48–53; cf. Test 39).[35] Because of this absence of deeds, the ruling classes of Assisi do not bring peace to the many poor and marginalized in Assisi and surroundings, notwithstanding the peace treaty they have signed. On the contrary, the poor and marginalized are excluded; they do not count. Peace is only for those who have possessions and are willing to collaborate in increasing Assisi's wealth. They alone have a right to speak and can take part in the decision- making process. That the poor, the sick, the lepers and all those others are the victims of this system, this ideology, so be it. For does Assisi's prosperity not prove that God is with them, indeed, and so demonstrate the truth of its ideology? Of course, because God blesses them, Assisi's rich are willing, out of charity, to give from their wealth to the poor. They do know their obligations as religious people!

Francis and his brothers reject this situation, which is the result of the hold that the spirit of the flesh has on the people of this world. If ever the brothers are to change this sinful system, they will have to free themselves, to keep themselves "pure" from "the wisdom of the world and the prudence of the flesh" (10). Instead of devoting all their energy to the increase of possessions and power, as the citizens of Assisi do, they have in the strength of the Spirit of the Lord to strive to be "simple." For true peace cannot be ensured by possessions and power which

[35] Commenting on this passage from the Second Letter to the Faithful, Zweerman writes: "Precisely in this text about God's dwelling among the faithful, the aspect of action is undeniable. The specific passivity of receiving results in *carrying Jesus* and *giving birth to him through holy works*. In Francis' writings, the expressions *operatio* and *facere* are therefore not to be seen as a sign of the tendency according to which holiness is to be achieved by immersing oneself in action *(Wirkheiligkeit)*. Rather they express his typical desire that the outside of life should correspond to the inside." a.c. 44. I find this comment rather meagre, and even a little misleading. Of course, Francis wants that the outside corresponds to the inside. But he also wants very much that this correspondence manifests itself concretely and historically in and through a person's works *(operatio)*. And it is precisely this concrete, historical dimension which Francis has in mind, because it is only through those works, inspired by the Spirit of the Lord, that Jesus can be born again in the life of the individual person and of the society. Francis' emphasis on the *operatio* is all the more remarkable because the *Glossa ordinaria*, the accepted short explanation of the Scriptures at that time, commenting on the underlying text of the gospel (Mt 12:50), writes: "Brothers and sisters by believing; mothers by preaching." *PL* 114, 129. See G.P. Freeman, Kinderen van de hemelse vader, *FL* 81 (1998) 251–258, here 254.

divide people and favour the rich and the powerful at the expense of the poor and the weak. On the contrary, true peace for all people can only be obtained when people in all simplicity, without striving after positions of power and status, without taking pride in themselves and in their good works and deeds as if they were theirs rather than God's (6), are ready to open themselves up to the inspiration by the Spirit of the Lord and in the strength of that same Spirit to humbly serve (5 and 15) the poor and marginalized, even if that means that because of their choice for and their identification with the poor and marginalized they will be mortified and despised, reviled and rejected (14) as in fact they are by the people of Assisi. It is the true wisdom of God as revealed in Jesus (16) but which is foolishness in the eyes of the world, versus the false wisdom of the world.

To make this choice for the poor and marginalized in a world which believes in possessions and power is difficult. In fact, it is only in the Spirit of the Lord that people can overcome the opposition of Assisi and commit themselves to living in solidarity with the poor and marginalized. However, even in the brotherhood where all are supposed to find their inspiration and their strength in the Spirit of the Lord and to know where true wisdom is to be found, some of the brothers have fallen for the prevailing ideology of the rich and mighty and want to be part of their world. According to Admonition 7, which carries the title: "Good works *(operatio)* must follow knowledge," they are especially to be found among the learned brothers who use their knowledge of Scripture to obtain positions of respect and authority in society from where they can preach the word of God to others without having themselves to become involved in action. Interested only in a merely external, worldly-minded knowledge which does not touch and transform them personally or move them into action, they are killed by the letter instead of being brought to life by the Spirit of Sacred Scripture.

In this situation it is not surprising at all that because of their external, worldly-minded knowledge these brothers are even able to find all kinds of words and subtle arguments that will excuse them from living the gospel in all simplicity, without any show of learning or any desire for status and power. Thus, unfortunately, these brothers fail to realize their calling; that is, they fail to follow the example of the poor and humble Jesus, who is the true wisdom of the Father (RegNB 17:16), and to extend to the people his greeting of peace in words, but above all in deeds, not of power and might, but of simple, humble service that does not exclude anyone but brings all people together in true peace. It is with regard to these brothers who were "pursuing offices of authority" that Francis "was filled with sorrow" because they "had left their former works and had forgotten their earlier simplicity after they had found new things" (1 Cel 104; cf. LegPer 70–71). And as he himself "hoped always to make a new beginning [and therefore] wished to go back again to serving lepers" (1 Cel 103), so he prayed "that God's mercy might free these sons and asked most earnestly that they might be kept in the grace that had been given to them" (1 Cel 104). In spite of Francis' prayers and example, this group of brothers continued to grow and its influence became stronger after he died. In fact it was this group which later on would become engaged in preaching the crusades and collecting money to buy arms and to send troops to the Holy Land to wage a war, not to bring peace.[36]

The words "simple," "pure," and "humble" occur in a similar context of being "wise and prudent according to the flesh" and of "deeds" *(operatio)* in the Second Letter to the Faithful 45–53—written before 1223 (Armstrong) or even in the last years of his life: 1224–1226 (Freeman)—to which passage we referred already when trying to determine what Francis meant with the *operatio* that is missing there where the spirit of the flesh reigns. The passage runs as follows: "We must not be wise and prudent according to the flesh; rather, we must be simple, humble and pure... We must never desire to be over others; rather we must be servants and subject to every human creature for God's sake. And upon all men and women, if they have done these things and have persevered to the end, the Spirit of the Lord will rest... They will be children of the heavenly Father whose works they do. And they are spouses, brothers and mothers of our Lord Jesus Christ... [We are] mothers when... we give birth to him through our holy deeds *(operatio)* which should shine before others as an example." It is evident then that "simple" and "pure" have to be understood against the background of the brotherhood which is threatened by the growing number of brothers who "are wise and prudent according to the flesh." As such they desire to be over others, whereas they are called to keep themselves pure from such desires and

[36] See Christoph T. Maier, *Preaching the Crusades. Mendicant Friars and the Cross in the thirteenth Century*, Cambridge 1994.

simply to be subject to every human creature for God's sake.[37] This is the holy deed *(operatio)* which is demanded from the brothers and through which they give birth to Jesus and render him concretely and historically present in their world.

In this way, being "simple, humble and pure," the brothers will build a new, alternative society, a brotherhood, which is diametrically opposed to the society of those days whose hierarchical structures are based on possessions, power and might and where because of the absence of the deeds *(operatio)* worked in the Spirit of the Lord Jesus cannot be born again nor receive a new historical existence. Hence, when Francis and his brothers insist on being simple, humble and pure, they do not do so for reason of personal ascetical motives in order to promote personal holiness or virtuousness; rather, they are moved by a clear insight into the sinfulness of the dominant culture in which Jesus is very much absent, and by their commitment to transform this situation through the praxis of a different set of values than the ones accepted by the surrounding world.

In the opening address of his Letter to the Order—written around 1220 (Esser) or around 1225 (Schmucki, Armstrong, Freeman)—Francis uses the adjective "simple" in combination with yet another adjective, namely "obedient." After addressing himself in a general way "to all the reverend and much beloved brothers," he mentions some brothers more specifically according to the office they hold in the brotherhood: "to Brother Elias, the minister general of the Order *(religioni)* of the Lesser Brothers, his lord,... to all ministers and custodians." To the last officials, he adds then somewhat strangely: "and priests of this same brotherhood who are humble in Christ." This addition can be explained in that in the central part of the letter Francis addresses the priests more in particular, which finds its climax in v. 28: "Look, brothers, at the humility of God... Humble yourselves as well." After this special mention, Francis then continues: "and to all the simple and obedient brothers, from those who have joined first to those who have done so recently." He does not address here the brothers non-priests as a special group, as Schmucki

[37] See e.g. 1 Cel 103–104: Whereas Francis "wished to go back again to serving lepers, to be held in contempt, as he once had been,.. he saw many pursuing offices of authority... He was filled with sorrow that some had left their former works and had forgotten their earlier simplicity after they had found new things."

supposes,[38] but all his brothers, from first to last. All of them, whether they are priests or not, have to be simple and obedient.

The adjectives "simple" and "obedient" are joined here so as to mutually explain and reinforce each other. But why does Francis add the adjective "obedient," instead of the more familiar "pure" or "humble"? From a dialectical point of view, the answer is not difficult to find. Francis must have been unfavorably impressed at that moment by what he had come to see as the disobedience of the learned brothers. Under the influence of the wisdom of the world, they did not look at their learning as a ministry to share the Spirit and life of the Scriptures with their brothers (Test 13). On the contrary, they were using their learning to get the other brothers to accept their interpretation of the way in which the brotherhood should develop and obtain a respectable place within the pastoral policy of the church as well as among the people (LetOrd 15; Test 25–26). It is in fact because of this situation that Francis mentions especially the priests and reminds them of the humility of Jesus. This shows Francis' great concern about this development which, in his eyes, is a deviation from the original ideals to which he and the first brothers had committed themselves in obedience to the divine inspiration (RegNB 2:1.9). By adding the adjective "obedient," he wants to call the brothers back to the beginnings. Just like in those early days, all the brothers, the brother priests included, should simply, without asking any questions or making any reservations, open themselves to the promptings of the Spirit of the Lord. In obedience to that same Spirit they should not desire for any respectable position in church or society (2 Cel 148); rather, they should dedicate themselves fully to their calling as lesser brothers by following Jesus who in his humility is for us the "wisdom of the Father."

"Simple" or "simply," with or without other qualifications, occurs most frequently in the Testament: five times in all. Depending on the context, it has different shades of meaning, though in all cases the under-

[38] O. Schmucki, La lettera a tutto l'Ordine di San Francesco, *L'Italia Francescana* 55 (1980) 245–286; English translation: "St. Francis's Letter to the Entire Order," *Greyfriars Review* 3,1 (April 1989) 1–33, here 2–3: "He [Francis] addresses the two categories of friars who make up the entire order, namely, 'the priests of the fraternity' and 'all the simple brothers'... [A] certain tension between the apparent superiority of the 'brother priests' and a feeling of frustration on the part of the 'simple brothers' was probably making its appearance."

tone of its opposite "learned" can be heard. The first time, "simply" occurs in v. 4, where Francis writes: "And the Lord gave me such faith in churches that I would simply pray and speak in this way: We adore you, Lord Jesus Christ..." "Simply" here means that the prayer mentioned in this text is not long and complicated; it does not need any special learning nor does it require any special books, like psalters or breviaries, nor has it to be said in a special place, like a choir. On the contrary, it is short, can easily be learned by heart and can be said without any difficulty by every brother wherever he finds himself.

Next, "simply" is found in the passage of the Testament where Francis describes how the very first rule came into being. He recalls: "And after the Lord gave me brothers, no one showed me what I should do, but the Most High himself revealed to me that I should live according to the form of the Holy Gospel. And I had this written down in a few words and simply and the Lord Pope confirmed it for me" (14–15). What the Lord revealed to Francis was not a long treatise, but just a few texts which formed the very core of the gospel. Francis had them written down simply, just as they had been given to him by the Lord. He did not add anything to them by borrowing from other existing rules or from the words of popes, bishops or theologians in order to further explain the meaning of those few texts. For how could these, especially the latter, be of any help to enlighten him? They did not, and even could not tell him about the real meaning of the gospel, because they were so much caught up in the spirit of the world (cf. AnPer 17d; 3 Comp 35). Rather than go to them for advice, he had allowed the words of the gospel directly to act upon his mind and heart and there to sink in deeply. In their simple directness, these gospel words were sufficient for him: they clearly showed him Jesus' way and, at the same time, inspired and moved him to follow Jesus on that way. Francis did not need anything more nor anything else. The words and the example of Jesus were enough.

When Francis writes this at the end of his life, is it possible that his remembrance and the way he formulates it, have been influenced by all the problems that had arisen around the rule? In a story in the Legend of Perugia, we read how at a chapter, called the Chapter of Mats, where five thousand brothers were present, "several wise and learned men approached the lord cardinal [Hugolino]. They asked him to persuade blessed Francis to follow the advice of the wise brothers and to let himself be guided by them. And they appealed to the rule of St. Benedict, St. Augustine, and St. Bernard who taught all sorts of things to lead an orderly life *(ordinate vivere)*. Blessed Francis listened to the admonition of the cardinal, took him by the hand and led him before the brothers assembled in chapter. He then spoke to the brothers as follows: "My brothers, my brothers, God called me to walk in the way of simplicity and showed me the way of simplicity. I do not want you to mention to me any rule neither of St. Augustine, nor of St. Bernard, nor of St. Benedict. The Lord has told me that he wanted me to be a new fool in the world; and the Lord does not want to guide us by any other way than by that knowledge; but God will confound you through your knowledge and wisdom... The cardinal was dumbfounded and said nothing in reply; and all the brothers were gripped by fear" (114).

The third place in the Testament where Francis uses "simple" is v. 29: "And although I may be simple and infirm, I wish nonetheless always to have a cleric who will say the office with me as it is contained in the Rule." Ten verses before, in v. 19, Francis has described how in the beginning they were *idiotae*, i.e. "illiterate" or "uneducated."[39] Does he here refer to this? This would then mean that although Francis is not a learned, but rather a simple, uneducated person, and sick too, yet he wants to say the office as well as his mental and physical condition allows him.

The most important passage in the Testament where "simply" occurs twice with two different qualifications, is found in verse 39, just before the blessing at the end of the Testament: "But as the Lord has given me to speak and to write the Rule and these words simply and purely, so shall you understand them simply and without gloss, and observe them with holy deeds *(operatio)* until the end." Already, in v. 15, Francis had spoken about "simply" writing down the words that the Lord had revealed to him. In the present text, Francis also refers to the Lord who has given him to speak and to write but he further reinforces "simply" by adding "and purely." In the light of what we have found so far, it is evident that Francis wants to make it clear that, as God has given him to speak and to write, he cannot possibly alter anything. He would not even dare to think about it. For how could he, Francis, pretend to know better than the Lord! Fully confident that the Lord from whom

[39] Armstrong-Brady translate: "simple." The Dutch translation has "ongeletterd," the German "ungebildet" and the French "sans éducation."

all good comes, wishes nothing but good for him and his brothers, he wholeheartedly, without any reservation, accepts what the Lord inspires in him. That is what he will speak about, what he will write down "simply and purely." And he is not going to let himself be influenced by the learned brothers. Referring to some learned commentaries, they may want to write something different that is more suitable to their desire for a respectable place in church and society. But Francis will not allow any brother, how learned he may be, to come between him and his Lord. Rather, he will keep himself "pure" and free from their advice, even if this means that he is no longer welcome with them who have become "so many and of such high quality" *(tot et tales)* that they do no longer need such "a simple and illiterate man" (*simplex et idiota;* TrueJoy 11).

After Francis has spoken about how, under the inspiration of the Lord, he wrote the Rule and the Testament "simply and purely," he admonishes his brothers for the last time that, in the same way, they must "understand the Rule and the Testament simply and without gloss, and observe them with holy deeds *(operatio)* until the end." The addition "without gloss" makes it quite clear that Francis has in mind here especially the learned brothers. For they are the ones who because of their learning are most capable of appealing to all kinds of theological authorities to make glosses to the Rule and the Testament and claiming that "they are to be understood in this way" (38). Francis sees in their activity a great threat to the brotherhood, and therefore "through obedience strictly commands all his brothers, cleric or lay, not to place glosses on the Rule and [the Testament]."

According to Freeman and Sevenhoven in their commentary on the Testament, "the Latin word *glossa* was a technical term for the learned annotations which, at the univerities, were made on the Scriptures or other theological or legal texts. And the expression *sine glossa* (without gloss), which resounds like a slogan throughout the thirteenth century, symbolizes the resistance against a subtle explanation of the bible which causes the bible's strength to be lost in fine-drawn, sophisticated argumentations which extinguish the spirit; the resistance against an interpretation of rules which is so learned, that nothing is left of the rules or that they even turn into their opposites. More positively formulated, the expression "*sine glossa*" symbolizes a new way of dealing with the Scriptures, which are no longer reserved for the learned, but accessible to everyone, including to a merchant's son from Lyons or Assisi who had no scholastic education, but was smart enough to see what life according to the gospel is all about and to take care that this spirit does not get lost."[40]

By using the expression *sine glossa*, Francis wishes his brothers not to make any subtle commentaries on his Rule and Testament. For with the brothers the danger exists, in fact he has seen it happening already, that such commentaries lead the brothers away from the original ideal of the brotherhood: to live according to the form of the gospel. What he, Francis, has formulated simply and purely, by divine inspiration, the brothers should accept as such: as simple words coming from the Lord, as simple words of true wisdom. In faith and confidence they should surrender themselves to these words and the call, the challenge they contain. They should not make any reservations out of fear for the consequences of this challenge. They may indeed have to face hard times, and even persecution. But even then, they should not try to water down the call that God in his wisdom gives them, nor, inserting themselves as preachers and priests in the pastoral policies of the church, should they seek refuge in a respectable position in church and society (Test 25–26). Rather, they should understand the Rule and the Testament "simply and without gloss and observe them through holy deeds *(operatio)* until the end."

Here again we meet the word *operatio*, which we met earlier already in the Earlier Rule 17 and the Second Letter to the Faithful. It is the keyword in the very last reminder that Francis gives his brothers in his Testament, just before he is to bless those who persevere in this holy *operatio* against the unholy forces of evil at work in the world and also in the brotherhood. Not allowing anyone or anything to come between them and God, "who is the fullness of good, every good, the true and supreme good, who alone is good, merciful and gentle, delectable and sweet,.. who alone is kind, innocent and pure" (RegNB 23, 9–10), the brothers are to commit themselves simply and without delay to faithfully living the word of God by holy deeds, not counting the cost.

[40] G.P. Freeman—H. Sevenhoven, The Legacy of a Poor Man V, *FrancDigest* 6,1 (April 1996) 12–13. For the exegesis of v. 39, see also Hardick-Grau 297–301; van Asseldonk 505–509. Further also L. Izzo, Semplicità, in *Dizionario Francescano*, Padova 1983, 1687–1702, here 1698–1699. Surprisingly, "simple, simplicity" does not occur in the index of A. Rotzetter, *Franz von Assisi. Ein Anfang und was davon bleibt*, Zürich 1981.

Through those holy deeds, that may seem utterly foolish to the world, but are wise in the eyes of God, they will give birth to Jesus in the power, the virtue of the Spirit of the Lord. And because of this faithfulness until the end "they will be filled in heaven with the blessing of the most high Father and on earth with the blessing of his beloved Son with the most Holy Spirit" (Test 40).

After our examination of the texts where Francis uses "simple" or "simply" with or without further qualifications, we get a good picture of all that Francis has in mind when in *The Salutation of the Virtues* he presents "holy pure Simplicity" in his small procession of virtues. It is definitely not the simplicity of Brother John the Simple which Celano highly recommends in his Second Life by telling us that Francis rejoiced in it and proposed it to the other brothers for imitation. "When St. Francis would stand in any place to meditate, whatever gestures or movements he would make, John the simple would himself repeat and copy. For if Francis spat, he spat; if Francis coughed, he coughed. He joined his sighs to Francis' sighs; and he accompanied Francis' weeping with his own. When the saint raised his hands to heaven, John raised his too, diligently watching him as his model and copying everything he did. The saint noticed this, and asked him why he did these things. He answered: "I have promised to do everything you do; it would be dangerous for me to omit anything." The saint rejoiced because of the brother's simplicity, but gently forbade him to act like that in the future. Not long afterwards this simple brother went to the Lord in that purity of life. The saint often proposed his life for imitation, and with great joy he called him, not Brother John, but Saint John" (2 Cel 190; LegPer 19). Celano's description presents us here with a caricature of the virtue of simplicity which is miles apart from the simplicity as it emerges from Francis' writings.

Simplicity, according to Francis, is the opposite of merely copying a model without much further thought as to the reasons behind a particular action. As is evident from our exegesis of Francis' writings, it is rather to be seen as the fruit of a mature decision made after a close look at and an analysis of the situation, in Francis' case the situation prevailing in the world of Assisi and, later, in the brotherhood itself. In this context, then, we discovered that, negatively, pure simplicity means not to be wise according to the flesh or the world, i.e. the world of Assisi; not to accept its ideology; not to show of one's learning to look wiser than others; not to use one's learning in subtle commentaries or sophisticated arguments to find excuses or to make reservations with regard to the observance of the gospel; not to strive after a respectable place in the system; not to let anyone or anything come between oneself and God. Positively, pure simplicity means to stand with an open mind before God and to be receptive to the words that he speaks; to surrender in faith to the word of God, the supreme good who only wishes what is good for us; to let the word of God directly act upon our mind and heart; to be obedient to the promptings of the Spirit of the Lord; to follow the example of Jesus who is the true wisdom of the Father; to commit oneself wholeheartedly to live the gospel in holy deeds and so to offer an alternative to a sinful world by bringing Jesus to birth again, giving him a new historical existence in a world where otherwise he would be absent.[41]

Many of these characteristics of Franciscan simplicity can be found in a description given by Celano and to which I referred earlier in the general introduction: "Not all simplicity was approved by [Francis] but only that simplicity which, being content with its God, considers everything else as of little value. This is that simplicity that glories in the fear of God, that knows not how to do or to speak evil... This is that simplicity that chooses rather to act than to learn or to teach. This is that simplicity that, in all the divine laws, leaves wordy circumlocutions, ornaments and embellishments, vain displays and curiosities, to those who are marked for a fall, and seeks not the bark but the pith, not the shell but the kernel, not the many things, but the much, the greatest and the lasting good" (2 Cel 189).

Lady, holy Poverty

Redaction criticism of the Earlier Rule shows that only at a later stage in its development did the rule of Francis and his brothers state that "all the brothers should strive to follow the humility and poverty of our Lord Jesus Christ" and that they appealed explicitly to the example

[41] "Thus one can say that the holy, pure simplicity is that gift of God which enables the human person, freed from all 'worldly' and 'carnal' hindrances, to integrate God's word and God's gifts and to let them become operative for his or her own salvation, for the good of others and, above all, for the glory of God." Verhey 112–113. Although fundamentally correct, Verhey's conclusion could have been more concrete and challenging, if he would have contextualised his exegesis more clearly.

of Jesus "who was a poor man and a stranger and lived on alms, He and the Blessed Virgin, and the disciples" (RegNB 9:1 and 5; RegB 6:2–3). Apparently it had only then, at that particular moment, become necessary to make this statement about their ideal, based on the person and life of Jesus.[42] Until then they had not felt the need to appeal to the example of Jesus' poverty. The foundational texts of the first chapter had been enough. There Jesus had told them to sell everything they had and give it to the poor and to follow him (2). These words in which they found expressed what they had been looking for after their profound feeling of dissatisfaction with the system of Assisi (AnPer 11; 3 Comp 29) had been enough for them. Poverty was not an issue at the beginning.[43]

In fact, the word "poverty" in reference to the life of the brothers does not occur in the RegNB. It occurs for the first time in the Later Rule 5:3–4: "As payment for their work they may receive whatever is necessary for their own bodily needs and those of their brothers, but not money in any form; and they should do this humbly as is fitting for servants of God and followers of most holy poverty." Immediately after this passage, Francis continues in the Later Rule 6: "The brothers shall not appropriate anything to themselves, neither a house nor a place nor anything at all. Instead, as pilgrims and strangers in this world who serve the Lord in poverty and humility, let them go begging for alms with full trust. Nor should they feel ashamed since the Lord made himself

[42] All other references to Jesus' poverty, too, occur in the later writings: the Later Rule 6,3: "Nor should they feel ashamed since the Lord made himself poor for us in this world"; 2 LetFaith 5: "Though he was rich beyond all other things, in this world he willed to choose poverty, together with the most Blessed Virgin, his mother"; LetLeo 3: "In whatever way it seems best to you to please the Lord God and to follow his footprints and his poverty"; LastWill Clare 1: "I, brother Francis, the little one, wish to follow the life and poverty of our most high Lord Jesus Christ and of his most holy mother and to persevere in this until the end."

[43] See, for example, L. Lehmann, who writes: "At the turning point in his life, Francis did not in the first place discover poverty as it is presupposed later on whem they like to speak about Francis' marriage with Lady Poverty. In reality, Francis discovered first of all the poor. He declared his solidarity with them; he lived not only as they did, but with them, among them. After he had left the world, he found a new place, a new location at the fringes of society. He lived among the lepers, among all those excluded and abandoned." Franziskus und die utopische Bewegung heute, *FranzStud* 61 (1985) 86–106, here 89. Francis' "discovery of the poor" and his solidarity with them will be developed later on in this chapter.

poor for us in this world. This is that summit of the most high poverty which has established you, my most beloved brothers, as heirs and kings of the kingdom of heaven, and has made you poor in things but exalted you in virtue. Let this be your portion which leads you into the land of the living. Hold on to this, my most beloved brothers, with all your strength and do not wish to possess anything else forever under heaven for the sake of our Lord Jesus Christ."

This lyrical outburst about the summit of the highest poverty and its insistence on holding on to poverty as the brothers' only legitimate possession at the exclusion of everything else for the sake of their Lord Jesus Christ is unique in the writings of Francis. Holy poverty is the climax of following Jesus; holy poverty makes the brothers heirs and kings of the kingdom of heaven; holy poverty is to be the portion, the share of food that will be sufficient for the brothers' pilgrimage to the land of the living. Everything else, Queen Wisdom included, has to give way here to holy poverty. She is the only virtue that really matters. If the brothers cherish her as their only possession for the sake of Jesus, they will be rich in virtue, for in possessing poverty they possess all the other virtues.

What is the reason for this outburst? In my view the reason has to be found in the situation of the brotherhood. Apparently the situation with regard to the practice of poverty has become such that Francis feels his original ideal might be in danger. Hence he resorts to this high praise of poverty as the core value of Jesus' life in the hope thus to motivate the brothers not to fall to the ever present temptation of covetousness and avarice, of wanting to appropriate things and to hold on to them, and instead to return to the original ideal. Also, in the years afterwards, Francis keeps reminding his brothers of their devotion and loyalty to holy poverty, even though no longer in the exuberant way of the Later Rule. Thus, in the Testament of Siena, Francis urges his brothers "always to love and to be faithful to our Lady Holy Poverty" (4). In a similar vein, he writes in his Last Will written for Clare: "I, brother Francis, the little one, wish to follow the life and poverty of our most high Lord Jesus Christ and of his most holy mother and to persevere in this until the end" (1).

Against the background of these reminders, it is surprising that a similar emphasis on poverty is absent from other writings of the same time. Thus, in *The Salutation of the Virtues*, poverty is one of the six in the procession of virtues led by Queen Wisdom, and not, so it seems, the most important one. For, as already mentioned, in the last verses of *The Salutation of the Virtues* obedience receives more place than all the other virtues, including poverty, together.[44] Something similar can be seen in Francis' final Testament. Certainly, Francis recalls there how the brothers "who came to receive this life gave to the poor everything which they were capable of possessing"; they were "to give themselves to honest work" and if they were not paid for their work, they were "to have recourse to the table of the Lord, seeking alms from door to door" (Test 16.20.22). And after this recall, Francis issues a special warning as regards one aspect of their life of poverty, namely, the brothers should "beware that they by no means receive churches or poor dwellings or anything else which is built for them, unless it befits the holy poverty which we have promised in the rule" (Test 24). Both the recall of the poor and humble beginnings and the warning as regards the acceptable type of buildings are important enough to Francis to be explicitly mentioned in his Testament. Yet, within the context of the Testament as a whole and considering the severity of the language used and of the measures to be taken, it seems that other issues, especially those of asking privileges from the Roman curia (25), of praying the office according to the rule and of of not being Catholics (30–33), figured more prominently in Francis' mind when he dictated the Testament than the issue of poverty. The latter is still present, but does not receive the same strong emphasis as in some of his other writings.[45]

This short survey of Francis' writings shows very clearly that a development has taken place. Whereas poverty and the example of the poor Jesus do not figure in his writings initially, later they receive a more important place. Poverty after the example of the poor Jesus becomes in the *Regula bullata* even the gospel virtue which constitutes the very heart of the life and work of Jesus. Poverty has indeed become an issue, though not the only one nor the all-overriding one! But exactly what is the issue? What is this poverty all about? What was the original

[44] See above I C 3

[45] See K. Esser, *Das Testament des heiligen Franziskus von Assisi*, Münster 1949, 129–130. Also in the Second 2 Letter to the Faithful and in the Letter to the Order, Francis does not raise the issue of poverty. For a critical approach to Esser's views, see G. Miccoli, Francis of Assisi's Christian Proposal, *Greyfriars Review* 3,2 (August 1989) 136–138.

experience that made Francis and his brothers leave Assisi and sell all their possessions? How did they organise their lives thereafter? What did they want to achieve by following this way of life? What threats later endangered the original ideal of poverty?

In his youth Francis' mind is fully occupied by the world of Assisi and its interests. At that time Assisi is involved in the struggle of freeing itself from the feudal system and obtaining a place among the cities, the "communes" of Central Italy.[46] Whether Francis took part in the destruction of the Rocca above Assisi, the symbol of the foreign, imperial power, during spring of 1198, we do not know. He was involved, however, in the war with Perugia, Assisi's archrival, for in November 1202 he was taken prisoner by the Perugian troops. After his release from captivity, Francis returns to Assisi where he continues to devote his energy to the realization of the economic goals which the people of Assisi have set for themselves: to increase as much as possible the goods of the city. Thus the young Francis is described as one who "thought only of making money and of taking care of the cloth shop" of his father (AnPer 4a; 3 Comp 3). And he might well have continued along these lines, were it not that, as he writes in his Testament, the Lord himself led him among the lepers (2).

It is there that Francis' eyes are opened and he becomes conscious of the sinfulness of the system of Assisi which shows itself in all its ugliness and repulsiveness in that it expels the lepers and declares them dead in a liturgical ceremony. Of course, the expulsion is justified as a public health measure. But this convenient excuse cannot hide the fact that within the system of Assisi there is simply no place for the lepers as they are a liability rather than an asset to the interests of the commune. And the same holds good for all those others: the poor, the sick and the beggars by the wayside (RegNB 9:2). For they cannot contribute to the economic growth of Assisi, to the increase of Assisi's wealth based on an ever greater appropriation of the goods of creation even though God did not destine for a few privileged people only, but for all (Adm 2; RegNB 17:17). Appropriation, then, is the name of the sin of Assisi in which Francis collaborated. It is this sin that divides people and victimises the lepers and the poor, a victimization which is felt even more strongly because of the many natural disasters which caused a shortage of food,

[46] In this and what follows I am greatly indebted to David Flood, *Francis of Assisi and the Franciscan Movement*, Quezon City 1989.

especially for the poor and powerless.[47] Yet they too were entitled to a place at the table of the Lord. After this discovery, it is for Francis "no longer the leper who stinks, but the money and the vainglory."[48]

Confronted by this situation, Francis thus passes through what could be called a negative experience of contrast. He knows intuitively that the situation of the lepers is fundamentally wrong. They should not be treated the way they are. At the same time, knowing this, Francis knows the way lepers should be approached: as human beings, created by God in God's own image and hence our brothers and sisters.[49] As a

[47] See Nolthenius 233–234. She writes: "Francis lived in what Jacques Le Goff has called 'the universe of hunger.' Storms, earthquakes, floods, too much rain, too little rain, locust, wars: agriculture could not cope with all this when the world was empty. Now that the population was increasing, its impotence was catastrophic. Society was in a phase of transition between a feudal system that was losing its patriarchal character, and an aggressive early capitalism whose strivings led to a crooked economic situation; thus the poor fell everywhere between wall and ship. Hundreds of them. And besides hunger, sickness. Thanks to undernourishment, filthiness, and ignorance, epidemics had free play, every summer anew; and whoever survived could freeze to death when there was a severe winter. There were always corpses lying along the main routes of Europe, stripped of their last possessions by fellow paupers, and not even pitied by those passing by... Towns like Assisi must have been swarming with beggars, timid, skinny, moaning beggars—as today with cats."

[48] Freeman-Sevenhoven, The Legacy of a Poor Man, *FrancDigest* 3, 1, (14. See also Flood 30–31.

[49] See also Lehmann: "The contrasts which Francis experienced in Assisi, made him especially receptive for the call from the Gospel. They gave him the negative picture against whose background the positive picture of an alternative form of society could really stand out and take concrete shape in a brotherhood based on the Gospel." Franziskus und die utopische Bewegung heute, 90. In his article: The Jesuit Martyrs in El Salvador: Liberation Christology and Spirituality, *New Theology Review*, 11, no. 2 (May 1998) 32–42, Roger Haight has the following to say on the negative experience of contrast: "The experience of poverty, oppression, and general social suffering that lies at the basis of liberation theology is a negative experience of contrast (E. Schillebeeckx, *God the Future of Man*, New York 1968, 136, 153–154, 164; Patricia McAuliffe, *Fundamental Ethics: A Liberationist Approach*, Washington 1993, 1–38). A negative experience of contrast is provoked by a situation which one spontaneously knows is wrong. In such an experience, of injustice, for example, one knows intuitively that such a situation should not be; it is evil, it is negative. One can have this experience without being able to explain why it is wrong or how to fix it. One simply knows instinctively and connaturally that it cannot or should not go on. Such experiences are common, and all of us

result a radical turnabout in the understanding and appreciation of values takes place in Francis' life: all that was at first bitter for him, like the meeting with a leper, has now become sweet. And all that previously was sweet now has the bitter taste of sin. Due to this experience of contrast and its subsequent conversion, Francis cannot but leave the world of Assisi and its value system which held him captive (Test 1–3). Francis has made his choice: he chooses openly for the victims of the socio-economic system which dominates Assisi. "Strengthened by God's grace, he became such a friend to the lepers that, as he himself declared in his Testament, he lived among them and served them with loving eagerness" (3 Comp 11). However, the people of Assisi do not agree, as Francis was soon to find out the hard way. His father curses him when they meet, while many others mock and abuse him and call him all sorts of names; almost all consider him a fool (AnPer 9b–c; 3 Comp 23). But Francis does not give up. And it is precisely in this continuous conflict with the social forces controlling Assisi that Francis becomes ever more clear about his choice and ever more strongly confirmed in it.

All that happened during Francis' personal history of conversion repeats itself when the Lord gives Francis brothers. It is the Most High himself and no one else—neither the pope, nor the bishop of Assisi (AnPer 34b and 17d; 3 Comp 49 and 35)—who reveals to him that he should live according to the form of the holy Gospel (Test 14). The brothers find this form of the Gospel expressed in four texts which summarize, as it were, the Gospel. They function for the brothers as a kind of rule of life with the help of which they can explain to themselves and eventually also to others (Test 15) where it is they, as a brotherhood, stand in church and society. These four texts form the content of the first chapter of the Rule of 1221. The first two texts occur also in an old story in which a priest finds these texts for Francis and his first two brothers, Bernard and Peter, because "they themselves did not know very well how to read the Gospel book" (AnPer 11a).

---

have had them. They can arise out of interpersonal relationships or general social situations... Two qualities are attached to the negativity of this experience. The first is that in knowing that something is negative one implicitly knows what is positive, the way things should be. This is necessarily the case because without this one could not perceive the negative as negative. This is the contrast in the negative experience. As Aristotle said, we know justice in our experience of injustice. The second is the urge to resist the negativity, to negate the negation, to right the wrong. This could and often does translate into action" (33–34).

These texts make it very clear that, from that moment on, Francis and his first brothers reject the possession of goods which forms the basis for the socio-economic order of Assisi and which they, as citizens of Assisi, have helped to promote. They do not show any hesitancy whatsoever about their intentions. As soon as they have heard these gospel texts from the priest and have recognized them as their rule of life, brother Bernard, who is rich, leaves to sell his possessions. Next, they call the poor of the city together and distribute among them the money from the sale of their possessions (AnPer 11b; 3 Comp 29). This story gives a good picture of what the brothers had in mind, even though they were not able as yet to formulate it clearly and in as many words. They wanted to build a new society, not on the basis of the appropriation and possession of goods, through which the rich of Assisi take advantage of and exploit the poor, but on the basis of the Gospel, which invites the brothers and all people of good will to share the goods of God's creation with each other, and especially with the poor (RegNB 1:2).

The consequence of this clear choice against Assisi which is dominated by the wisdom of this world and the spirit of the flesh (RegNB 17:10–11) is that the brothers place themselves outside the existing society. As Flood observes, they do not just change place within the system, giving up "a sunny and well-appointed apartment in Assisi's household for a dingy corner in the servants' quarters," where they live poorly and humbly, sharing the condition of Assisi's lower classes. No, they left that world; "they stayed outside the material and spiritual services which the commune bestowed on its citizens and subjects. Outside Assisi and within its territorial circumscription, they worked out the distinctive patterns of their daily life."[50]

This is not an easy task. For by leaving the world of Assisi, its economy, its value ystem, its cultural and religious traditions, Francis and the brothers are literally and figuratively nowhere. This implies that, in their attempt to give a more concrete shape to their ideal of a new, different society, they have to rely entirely on themselves. Here too neither pope nor bishop can help the brothers. Even the existing religious communities cannot be of service because, living soberly within the system of property, they have accumulated possessions and have themselves

[50] Flood 15.

become part of the established order.[51] The Jesus as he is given concrete shape in the life of these communities therefore cannot be the Jesus of the brotherhood. Traces of this Jesus and his footsteps are nowhere to be found yet.[52] Rather, they themselves have to place Jesus' footsteps on this earth and give Jesus a new historical existence in their world (cf. 2 LetFaith 53). This implies that, over and over again, the brothers will have to discover for themselves what Jesus demands from them in their new situation. Hence, in their continuous confrontation with the world of their time, they will always anew have to make their own choices on the basis of their original intuition of a new society where, according to God's plan of creation and salvation manifested in Jesus' life and death, there is place for everyone and all, and no one is excluded from sitting at the table of the Lord (Test 22; RegNB 9:8).

Concretely, this means that, after their rejection of the sinful economic system of Assisi, the brothers have to start looking for a new, a different economic basis for their life. Or to say it very simply, it is of course very praiseworthy for the brothers to leave Assisi, but they will all the same have to eat, because without eating even the most beautiful ideal is doomed to failure. They will quickly have to take a clear decision in this regard. For if they do not determine soon very concretely where they precisely stand, they will be absorbed again by the system of Assisi and follow once more the ways in which Assisi's citizens deal with these matters. But then it is also finished with the goal they have set themselves: to follow in the footsteps of Jesus (RegNB 1:3). For Assisi whose

[51] Cf. Miccoli's observations on Francis' attitude towards the existing monastic orders: "Francis singled out and rejected the occasions and means which historically had transformed the monastic orders. They had, in fact, become great complexes endowed with goods and income, and thus powerful institutions standing at the apex of the social hierarchy. For Francis,... the choice of poverty is a choice radically opposed to the movements at work in history... [It results from his] full awareness of the values at work in his society and of the features which the various forms of religious life had assumed. In this way he affirmed and defended the special nature of his own vocation and witness" (152–153).

[52] D. Flood, Die wirtschaftliche Grundlage der franziskanischen Bewegung in ihrer Entstehungszeit, *WissWeis* 44 (1981) 186–187. Miccoli says the same in different words: "Francis in effect lived a religious experience which, as far as its original core is concerned, had no link or reference to the ecclesiastical tradition of his time. Even his contemporaries and those after recognized this more or less obscurely... when they described him as the 'new man' *(novus homo)*" (131).

affairs are not guided by the Spirit of the Lord, but by the spirit of the flesh, cannot see and recognize the truth of who Jesus is and where it is he leads us (Adm 1:15; 2 LetFaith 65–66).

Francis and his brothers elaborate the economic implications of their choice to leave Assisi in the present chapter seven of the Rule of 1221. There they answer the questions which have arisen within the brotherhood as regards work, the remuneration for their work, and their livelihood. The fact alone that the brothers ask these questions and answer them, shows already that the brothers think quite differently about these matters than their surroundings. If this were not the case, it would not have been necessary for them to write anything at all in this regard.

The first decision the brothers make, is that they will support themselves through their work, their production of goods and services. And there is more than enough work available in Assisi. The growing economy has always room for good workers who can be employed as day-labourers in the fields and in the workshops. Moreover there is plenty of work in the houses for the poor and the lepers, for the newly found wealth and affluence have also their victims: the sick and weak who are pushed to the side. For these reasons, the brothers do not find it difficult to get a place in the production process, whereby they show a definite preference for working in the houses for the poor and the lepers.

The rejection of the economic system of Assisi does not mean therefore that the brothers place themselves outside the economic reality. On the contrary, through their work, through their production of goods and services, they do take part in the economy. However, they do so not on Assisi's terms, but on their own. They do not allow Assisi to define their work, for this would imply their re-integration within its economic system.[53] Thus wherever the brothers are employed, their work has for them a totally different function than within the system of Assisi. The brothers do not work to become rich or to gather possessions, for they do not wish to return to the system of Assisi even though the people of Assisi are keen to integrate them and offer them posts as administrators, managers or supervisors (RegNB 7:1). The brothers refuse these posts because they do not work to develop and strengthen the sinful economic system of Assisi. They do not want to bear any responsibility for Assisi's

[53] Flood 20.

economic institutions, nor do they have any intention of helping Assisi along in reaching the goals which it has set for itself.[54]

They work, then, in order to make the life of their brotherhood possible while, at the same time, giving preference to works of service that will contribute to the development of an alternative form of society. For this reason they do not want to receive more than they need, and certainly not money. That is, they do not want to accumulate possessions, nor do they want to be part of the system and play the money game of the rich and powerful, who kept the big money, *denaro grosso*, in which all the major transactions were done, for themselves and paid the labourers in little money, *denaro piccolo*, with which they could buy the daily necessities of life but never become a threat to the well-guarded interests of the ecclesiastical and communal establishment. Rather, labourers and all those others at the fringes of the Assisian system were forced to remain forever small, powerless, and socially insignificant: victims of a two-tiered monetary system pressed upon them by the ruling classes.[55] Placing themselves outside this system and its built-in injustices, the brothers discover that they can get along well without money! A world without money is possible. Even in such a world the brothers are not without the means of life.

However, especially with their refusal to receive money, the brothers go directly against the economic rules of Assisi. The people of Assisi are not prepared to accept the brothers' refusal and try continually to entice them into the world of money. To protect themselves against these various attempts, the brothers consider it necessary to devote a

[54] Ibid. 22.

[55] For this and what follows, see Flood 26–27; see also the article in which Flood for the first time worked out these ideas more in detail: Franciscans and Money, *Haversack* 4,2 (December 1980) 12–21 Further also his: *Work for Everyone. Francis of Assisi and the Ethic of Service*, Quezon City 1997, 36–39. About the matter in question, he writes there: "Assisians used Luccan and Pavian coin, the former a weak currency, the latter a solid one. The different coins circulated in different spheres, given their different functions. When the bishop of Assisi, Guido, and the prior of San Rufino, Rainaldo, agreed to arbitration in 1216, they agree as well to pay a fine if they did not abide by its terms. They specified good money as the medium of satisfaction. The case was serious. A lot of Assisians, and the brothers' colleagues at work first of all, never got to see the good money. They had to survive on Luccan coin" (36). The problem has not changed very much in our days with the strong currencies of the rich nations and the weak currencies of the poor ones.

special chapter to the question of how the brothers should deal with money (cf. RegNB 8). The addition of this chapter shows very clearly the intensity and depth of the brothers' struggle to keep themselves free from Assisi and its interests, and to strive after the realisation of a different economic model. They strive to create a brotherhood where the brothers do not wish to have anything from the whole world other than the food and clothing they need (RegNB 9:1) and which, they hope, will always be available to them, either as remuneration for their work or, if this is not given to them, by begging alms (RegNB 7:7–8; Test 22); a brotherhood which receives with kindness whoever comes, friend or foe, thief or robber (RegNB 7:14) and shares with them the goods of creation at the table of the Lord (Test 22);and a brotherhood, finally, which makes an exception by allowing the brothers to ask money for the lepers so that they may receive what they need and to which they have a right—a right that Assisi all too often refuses them (RegNB 8:10; 9:8).

The fact that the brothers wish to establish such a brotherhood proves convincingly that their decision to leave Assisi does not mean that the brothers choose poverty in the sense of lack of the necessary material goods, of destitution. In truth, they do not.[56] They are encour-

[56] With Flood, we emphasize that Francis and his first brothers were very clear in their mind about what they wanted. We differ here considerably from Armstrong when he writes: "Francis of Assisi lacked jurisprudence or legislative ability. His writings, even his rules, are filled with contradictions. On one hand, we find him insisting that a young man sell all his goods and give the proceeds to the poor before entering the fraternity; on the other hand, we are confronted with his concession that the brothers may have breviaries, an expensive proposition in the thirteenth century when books were written by hand and on parchment. At times we find him insisting that the brothers have no place or church that they can call their own; at others, we read his advice to open their houses to everyone and to decorate their churches in precious ways. Francis comes across to us—at least through his writings—as a bundle of contradictions, as an idealist who has little or no idea of practicalities." *St. Francis of Assisi. Writings for a Gospel Life*, New York, 1994, 152–153. And in an earlier article, he wrote: "Perhaps no phrase presents this ambiguous understanding of poverty more clearly than the permission that the brothers may have tools and instruments that are suitable for their trades, an allowance that has been used and abused since it was first written." Prophetic Implications of the "Admonitions," *Laurentianum* 26 (1986) 441. Rather than approach Francis with an a priori notion of poverty and accuse him of contradictions and ambiguous understandings, it would have been much better to start with the assumption that, after much reflection and discussion, Francis and his

aged to work to supply their own needs and the needs of others; they possess the tools of their profession; they have food and clothes; they have a place to stay and, what is most important, they have each other's support, especially when they are sick. They cannot possibly be considered poor, nor do they have any intention of allowing Assisi to drive them the way of the poor, as is clear from the various measures they take.[57] Looked at from this perspective, the brothers have no knowledge of an ideal of poverty. Such an ideal simply cannot and does not exist for them.[58] For the poverty of destitution and exclusion, of oppression, of

---

brothers came to a coherent view on poverty, even if this view does not fit our own legal view. Why does Armstrong not acknowledge that Francis and his brothers had certain insights, based on their experiences, which differ from the traditional understanding, and examine them as such, as different, on their own merits without already beforehand qualifying them as the rather unpractical views of an idealist, which we need not take very seriously in their historical concreteness? Here it becomes evident what the consequences are of a lack of contextualization and how this almost necessarily leads to a rather spiritualized and individualized understanding of poverty without little or no attention for the liberative and transformative challenges of Francis' view to the society and its economics. For in what continues, Armstrong speaks about "three distinct levels on which [Francis] would have us examine what we make our own. These are the areas of our inner selves, our relations with one another [especially in the area of becoming angry at the sin of another and of obedience], and, finally, our relationships with God" (154–155).

[57] A passage from Flood is worth to be quoted here in full: "Francis and his friends had what they needed for their life. We have to rid our minds of the later stories about Francis' poverty. We do it best by establishing that Francis was *not* poor. In his *The Poor in the Middle Ages* (1986; 1978 in French), M. Mollat sums up recent study on medieval poverty. As he sets out, early in his book (page 5), he offers a notion of poverty: 'A pauper was a person...' The notion ends up a highly phenomenological one, and means: A pauper was a person without social supports. That is precisely what Francis *did* have, and every member in the fraternity as well. In truth, they had social support far beyond what the rich burghers of Assisi could rely on. The brothers had so much social support that they were extending it to lepers and needy and drawing them back into the human community. The social support of the brothers included food and clothing as well as sick care and certainly brotherly encouragement" (32). See also 41–42.

[58] "In what does this poverty consist? To answer the question we might turn to the ways in which Francis speaks of poverty. Rarely do we find him using the word 'paupers.' In fact, we find the word only twelve times in his writings to refer to a condition or state of life. Nowhere does he write of living *sine rebus mundi*, with-

sickness and early death, which Francis encounters in the society of his days, is in the eyes of Francis and his brothers nothing but the consequence of sin: a grave injustice which Assisi commits against the poor and the oppressed for whom there is no place within its system.

It was precisely this sin which Francis and his brothers wished to counteract with their choice for a new economic system in solidarity with the poor. Not wanting to appropriate goods to themselves and thereby to exclude others, they intended to develop an alternative which would give all people access to the goods they needed but were often denied to them.[59] Hence, by their non-appropriative, sharing approach to the goods of creation, they wished to undo the division and exclusion

---

out the things of this world, or in destitution. Francis, however, usually writes of living *sine proprio*, without anything of one's own, without anything that is proper to one. He continually raises the question, therefore: What can I call my own? This becomes the central issue of the embrace of poverty. Material poverty is no doubt the first step in answering the question, but the more seriously and authentically it is embraced, the more it frees us to move into the uncharted depths of our lives where we discover what we really call our own." Armstrong 153. Unfortunately, Armstrong does not speak any further about what material poverty is, except for saying that "material poverty is an outward sign [a sacrament] of a much deeper, interior poverty. It is symbolic, in other words, of an unseen, more penetrating reality. At the same time, material poverty—like the outward signs of the sacraments, water, bread, wine, the laying on of hands, and so on—leads us more effectively to that inner poverty and enables us to grapple more freely with letting go of all those things that prevent us from embracing God totally" (154). One notices immediately the spiritualizing and individualizing tendency to which we referred in note 8 as the necessary consequence of an a-historical, a-contextual approach and which makes Armstrong concentrate on the three levels mentioned there without taking seriously Francis' confrontation with the sin of Assisi and his efforts to undo its consequences. This is further confirmed by Armstrong's stress on "a much deeper, interior poverty" which implies that our stress on Francis' understanding of poverty as a liberative and transformative force, leading to an alternative society, is less deep and hence also less valuable, not really worth pursuing.

[59] Both my approach and my conclusion differ also from Nolthenius.' She summarizes Jesus' approach by saying that "not having possessions in the Gospel is much more a 'no' against Mammon than a 'yes' to deprivation, let alone a 'yes, please." Nowhere in the Gospel is poverty an aim in itself; on the contrary, the alleviation of the poverty of one's neighbour is an aim." She then continues: "Francis' glorification of Lady Poverty is far removed from this mild and perfectly sensible attitude. His passion for hunger and cold borders self-destruction. Whoever only lifts

inherent to the property-centred system, and so free the poor from their poverty by seeing to it that they would receive what, according to the deepest conviction of the brothers, rightfully belonged to them. Francis and his brothers elaborated their views in their theology of alms which they developed in chapter 9 of the Rule of 1221 and which they briefly summarized in the thesis: "alms are a legacy, an inheritance and a just right due to the poor, which our Lord Jesus Christ acquired for us" (RegNB 9:8).[60]

Chapter 9 of the Rule of 1221 found its origin in the brothers' experience of opposition after they broke with the world of Assisi. The people of Assisi especially refused to accept the fact that, although the brothers were very capable men, they kept rejecting certain responsible posts which Assisi offered them, and rather preferred to share the life of people who were considered to be "of little worth and who were looked down upon, of the poor and the powerless, the sick and the lepers, and the beggars by the wayside" (RegNB 9:2); they were not even afraid to go begging themselves! Because of this, the brothers had many insults

a finger and touches a coin (2 Cel 65), or dares to think that a beggar in his heart would like to be rich (LegPer 114), makes Francis get beyond himself with anger. There are more voluntarily poor people who show signs of such fanatism. Usually, by acting in this way, they react against a church that has become too rich. This cannot be shown to have been the case with Francis. He presents his poverty stubbornly as a following of Christ. He knew the gospels by heart. He *must* have known that he exaggerated them on this point. The time in which he lived, must have influenced this view" (235). Whereas we agree with Nolthenius that Francis was passionately concerned about poverty and incidentally may have been angry with his brothers who did not observe poverty, we disagree when she uses somewhat tendentious stories about certain incidents in order to conclude that "Francis' glorification of Lady Poverty was far removed from the mild and perfectly sensible attitude" of the gospels in which "poverty is nowhere an aim in itself," but rather "the alleviation of poverty." Why does she place so much trust in those stories, without even asking about their origin and purpose, rather than carefully analyse Francis' writings in order to determine the meaning Francis gave to poverty in the everyday life of the brothers and so to define the place it occupied witnin his spirituality and the spirituality of the brotherhood? To put it somewhat exaggeratedly: the stories must not lead us in our interpretation of the writings; rather the writings must provide the framework within which to interpret and to evaluate the stories.

[60] See Flood 40–44, where he gives an excellent analysis of RegNB 9.

thrown at them: "You have left your own possessions and now you want to eat at the expense of others." Even their parents and relatives persecuted them, while the others, great and small, men and women, derided them as madmen and fools (AnPer 17b–c; 3 Comp 35). In short, the people "shame the brothers and refuse to give them alms" (RegNB 9:6). As a result, some of the brothers experience it as a real burden when they have to go out to collect alms (RegNB 9,9). They suffer under the humiliations they have to undergo. Due to the social pressure of Assisi, they have difficulty with the worthless place assigned to them on the edge of social life of Assisi. They even start feeling ashamed of what they have set out to do (RegNB 9:4).

It was in such a situation that Francis and his brothers felt the need to admonish and support one another; they were not to allow Assisi to interfere with and determine their vision and their identity. They did so by telling each other the story of the poor and humble Jesus.[61] But especially they "recalled that in similar circumstances our Lord Jesus Christ, the Son of the living and all-powerful God, set his face like flint and was not ashamed" (4). As hard as stone, Jesus resisted the social pressure of the people. He fought the social exclusion and the humiliation he

[61] The importance of storyteling in relation to virtues is underlined by Catherine M. Wallace, *Storytelling, Doctrine, and Spiritual Formation*. She writes: "Our lives, even at their best, are not tightly focused and elegantly coherent. Real lives are awash in chaos and ambiguity and un-certainty, in suffering and pain and fear. That is why we need stories, I suppose, because stories let us escape the chaos of life for a while; stories help us to survive the mayhem and the drudgery; stories help us to imagine some order and some meaning within the tedious uproar of the ordinary week. In our stories, we can create worlds in which it is clear that people are kind, or that fortitude and hard work pay off, or that we have resources of strength and courage that we never knew we had. Or, of course, we can tell stories in which everything is always terrible and hopes are always disappointing and needs are never met. I know people who always tell that kind of story. I bet you do too. And that's why we are profoundly blessed by stories that encourage us in the face of disaster, that make sense of our lives in the presence of pain, and that connect us to vital and life-giving traditions. Alasdair MacIntyre *(After Virtue)* argues that whatever counts as virtue in our lives, whatever counts as true, as noble, as worthwhile, as reliable and as certain—these virtues are defined and preserved in our storytelling or they are lost. There is no "scientific' proof of the objective value of fidelity or integrity or kindness. There are no double-blind controlled studies statistically proving the value of courtesy or forgiveness or courage. There are no rigorous philosophic demonstrations, no toughminded proofs. There are

had to undergo, because he wanted there to be room for everyone. He refused point-blank to accept the shame the people wanted to put on him. For he was convinced that, if there was any shame in his living on alms, it had to be credited not to him who suffered it, "but to those who caused it" (7). The image of "Jesus setting his face like flint" does not fit very well the traditional interpretation of Francis' view on Jesus. It does show, however, the character and the degree of opposition the brothers in their following of Jesus should mount against the way the people of Assisi were treating them. The brothers should prepare themselves for a hard fight in which the example of Jesus' hardness, of his strong resistance should be a source of inspiration and strength to them. Under no condition should they allow themselves to be disheartened by the accusations of the people, however humiliating they might be. Rather they should harden themselves and continue on the road they had chosen.

---

only stories, stories that testify to the dignity and the hope and the humanity of virtuous lives. It is in telling such stories about our own lives that we discover what our lives mean, what our values are, what differences our virtues make, and how we are connected to the past and to the community in vital ways. And it is in sharing our stories that we grow in the virtues that provide whatever we know of honor and serenity and hope, because the virtues are sustained and transmitted and taught through storytelling and not by means of abstract, systematic argument. The world becomes a kinder place when you tell three other people about someone's kindness to you. The world becomes a more honorable place when you tell them about honest decisions you made or saw someone make. The world becomes a more courageous and cheerful place when you recount your troubles and how you nonetheless survived with your sense of humor intact. In short, stories change the world. The world changes in all of these ways because your story encourages me to act or to feel in certain ways by immersing me, just for a while, in a created world in which the power and the importance and the meaning of virtue are much clearer that they ever can be in 'real life.' Sandra Schneiders argues that when we hear a good story we are changed because we have experienced something that ordinary life does not commonly provide. We have come face to face with new possibilities, with new grounds for hope, with new support for the struggle of our own lives. When we leave the world of a story we walk out changed, she says, because now we will see our own lives in a new light. Our sense of life's possibilities can be permanently changed or enlarged... That dynamic informs our lives as believers no less profoundly. Church community, as a reservoir of stories and storytelling, can create a world in which God is stunningly real and present, in which grace is reliably given, in which growth is possible and hope has meaning." *Anglican Theological Review* 81 (1999) 39–59, here 53–54.

For, even if Assisi did not appreciate their way of life, yet the brothers ought to know that they were in good company. The suffering they had to endure at the hands of the people of Assisi should be a clear proof to them that they were on the right track with the choice they had made to leave the world of Assisi. They were really walking in the footsteps of Jesus! As Flood says, "they have become companions of Jesus on the long, long road towards a just new world."[62] Thus they succeeded in giving birth to Jesus in a new historical form within their society (2 LetFaith 53). Through their commitment to and their solidarity with the poor they brought Jesus back, as it were, to a world from which he had been effectively banned by sin. They offered him a possibility to continue his work of redemption for the liberation of the poor. Hence, by placing the shame that was caused them in a broader perspective, the brothers tried to overcome together the paralysing pressure of Assisi and to free themselves for their commitment to build a new society that was based on their knowledge (RegNB 9:7) that, in God's eyes, the poor are not without rights, but possess divine rights of inheritance as God's children (RegNB 9:8).

This knowledge formed the basis for the radical difference in vision that existed between the brothers, on the one hand, and the people of Assisi on the other. In Assisi the poor did not have rights. For the people of Assisi this was the most normal thing in the world. It had even officially been confirmed in the peace treaty of November 1210: only those who possessed money and goods were entitled to obtain civil rights. After having obtained them, they were obliged, as citizens, to promote the economic growth of Assisi with the help of all means at their disposal. The poor were, literally and figuratively, nowhere in this process. They simply did not count. The brothers, however, did know with great certainty that the relations between people were meant to be radically different from the way they had developed in Assisi. If the poor were without rights in Assisi, it was not because they did not have rights, but because Assisi had taken their rights away from them. It was precisely this policy which constituted the sin of Assisi, namely that its citizens appropriated to themselves the goods of creation, considered them their own and thus actually denied the poor the use of these goods, which in reality belong to God, who destined them for all people, including the poor.

[62] Flood 42.

By acting in this way, the people of Assisi repeated the sin of Adam, the sin of the beginning, through which the first man and woman were banned from paradise (Adm 2), where God, their Creator, had placed them (RegNB 23:1). Paradise, therefore, is the place where men and women truly belong in God's plan. In order now to put an end to the sinful situation due to which humankind is excluded from paradise, and to open the possibility for a new creation or paradise, "the just Father" (RegNB 23:1) has sent "his beloved Son from on high and has brought salvation in the midst of the earth." Hence, all men and women can "sing a new song for... the Lord reigns from the wood of the cross" (OffPass VII:3.5.9), the tree of life in the midst of paradise. The original order of paradise, which was radically destroyed by Adam's sin of appropriation, has been restored by Jesus' death. Thus Jesus has again acquired for the poor the right to share in the goods of creation. He has returned to the poor the inheritance which belongs to the poor as children of God, but which had been robbed from them by the economic system of Assisi (RegNB 9,8). The poor can sit again at the table of the Lord (Test 22), as children of the king, as royal heirs, who are entitled to a place at the king's table, for the inheritance rightfully belongs to them (AnPer 35b; 2 Cel 16).[63]

The fact that Jesus faithfully committed himself until his death on the cross to overcome the sin of the beginning and to restore the original order of paradise (RegNB 23:3) was at the same time meant "to leave us an example that we should follow in his footsteps" (2 LetFaith 11–13).

[63] My interpretation differs considerably from that given by Nguyên-Van-Khanh who writes in a commentary on RegNB 9: "The Lord had no place to stay. He did not have a fixed abode. For Francis, the Lord could not but be 'a poor man and a transient' *(pauper et hospes)*: a guest whom one receives, who 'lived on alms, he and the Blessed Virgin and his disciples.' And because the Lord was the beggar, all alms now belong to him, to him and to all who are poor like him." Unfortunately, Nguyên-Van-Khanh does not give any further explanation for his somewhat strange conclusion that all alms belong to Jesus because he became a beggar. After quoting RegNB 9,8, he then continues: "We note the theological depth of Francis. He does not only affirm that Christ was a beggar and a pilgrim, but also that he was a brother of all the poor. Because Christ, by becoming a beggar, appropriated to himself the alms of the world and subsequently willed this 'heritage' and 'this just right' to all the poor, they are not only linked to him by an external resemblance of poverty but, more profoundly still, by a bond of kinship: they are members of the same family as Christ, because they share the same heritage and the same right... Francis evokes once more the image of Christ, the

Hence, in imitation of Jesus, the brothers should devote themselves with their whole being to establish anew in their own society the original order which Jesus restored by his death on the cross. Concretely speaking, this implied that the brothers would make serious efforts to transform the situation of Assisi so that the poor would no longer, as people without rights, be sent off with a gift which some rich citizen of Assisi out of charity deigned to hand out to them if they humbly and submissively would ask for it.[64] On the contrary, the brothers were to commit themselves to build a society where the poor would have the rights won for them by Jesus acknowledged and where they therefore were to obtain their due share in the goods of creation. It is clear that in doing so the brothers not only strove after an entirely different socio-economic and political order, but also developed an entirely different language.

Beggar, for his brothers in the This Testament: 'Et quando non daretur nobis pretium laboris, recurramus ad mensan Domini petendo eleemosynam ostiati.' The honour of going out to collect alms cannot be expressed better, for the recourse to alms is called recourse to the table of the Lord. Because the Lord lived on alms so that his table was filled with what was offered him, to have recourse to his table means to go out to collect alms: by taking the same food as the Lord, namely alms, people become his table-companions." *Le Christ dans la pensée de saint François d'Assise d'après ses écrits*, Paris 1989, 76–77. We cannot accept Nguyên-Van-Khanh's view on the table of the Lord filled with the alms which people offer to Jesus, the Beggar, and which he then appropriates to himself and shares with the poor. In our view, the table of the Lord is the creation which God originally made for all and in whose goods all are to share according to God's plans. Unfortunately, God's plans were thwarted through the human sin of appropriation. The poor and humble Jesus undid the consequences of this sin through his life and death and so restored the original plan of God in which alms are a heritage and a just right due to the poor and not just a hand-out at the mercy of the rich.

[64] Referring to M. Mollat, *Les pauvres au moyen age. Etude sociale* (Hachette 1978), Reijsbergen describes this attitude: "In the twelfth century, a development in mentality took place which would lead to a new theology of poverty. Ingredients were... the authority of writers like Augustine, Ambrose and Gregory the Great who spoke frankly about the duties of the rich over against the rights of the poor, as well as the ethics of classical authors like Cicero, Horace and Seneca. As a result of these influences, a theology was developed in which the place of the poor was close to that of the rich. Taking as a starting point that both the poor and the rich were created by one and the same God from the same soil and that, in principle, the creation equally belonged to all people, medieval people created, in typical

They did use the same words as the people in Assisi, but these words obtained a radically new meaning among the brothers on the basis of their new vision of man and world, their different knowledge about God's plan of creation and redemption revealed in the poor and humble Jesus.

This is especially true with regard to poverty—a word that, as we noticed above, was absent from the brothers' first reflections, and entered only at a later date in chapter 9 of the Rule. At that time, as we have seen, problems about begging had arisen within the brotherhood due to Assisi's opposition to their way of life, and the brothers found it necessary to encourage each other by telling the story about Jesus' poverty and humility. In doing so, the brothers received new strength and courage to continue on the way they had chosen. However, they also became more explicitly aware that if there is a poverty that is sinful and degrading, there is also a holy, redeeming poverty, the poverty Jesus chose and lived in the fulfilment of his mission of redemption. It is this holy, redeeming poverty which will undo the consequences of the original sin of appropriation and bring back paradise.[65] The people of Assisi could not possibly understand this view. In their mind, paradise was a

---

fashion, an *ordo* for the problem of poverty, in which the role of the poor was to receive because it was the holy duty of the rich to give. The poor were thus privileged creditors who, however, had to wait for the fulfilment of their right in a subordinate, an inferior position, because the attention was focussed one rich, on those who were wealthy... [T]he place of the poor remained in the church portals, in the shadow of the heavenly reign that was portrayed above his head. There the poor preserved their humility, as a spiritual salvation in human form for the more wealthy and as a model of the inferior life after their social downfall" (137–138). Reijsbergen acknowledges thus that this description starts from the perspective of the rich. For Francis, however, the starting point is with the poor among whom he lived and who have a right, won for them by Christ. Therefore, Francis argues, to beg is not shameful at all. It is not a social downfall, as the rich want the poor person to believe. On the contrary, the shame lies entirely with the rich who exclude the poor and treat them as inferior, as people of lesser worth. In Francis' view, the poor do not belong in church portals where they can practise their humility for the benefit of the rich and their own, but they have their rightful place at the table of the Lord.

[65] This idea is worked out in much detail in the *Sacrum Commercium*. Esser and many others hold that this allegorical work was written in 1227 (see K. Esser, Untersuchungen zum Sacrum Commercium beati Francisci cum domina Paupertate, in *Miscellanea Melchior de Pobladura*, vol. I. Roma 1964, 1–33). Others,

place of abundance and wealth: the continuation and final legitimation of their present economic system, based on possessions and power. They could not therefore accept this strange interpretation of Francis and his first brothers. For the people of Assisi, there was nothing holy about poverty. In their view, poverty and paradise excluded one another.

They were supported in their view by several brothers, brothers who had joined later and were apparently not convinced by the theology

---

however, think that, because SC gives a complete and well articulated answer to the views of the secular masters in Paris, its date of composition has to be placed between 1250 and 1270, at the time of conflict between the secular clergy and the Mendicants at the University of Paris (see S. Brufani, in his introduction to *Sacrum commercium sancti Francisci cum domina Paupertate*, Assisi 1990, 1–55; id. *Fontes Franciscani*, Assisi 1995, 1700). Again others argue that the biblical character of SC is not typical of the scholastic style of argumentation used in the conflict at Paris and that there is no trace of the later acerbic rhetoric Hence SC seems, according to them, "to be more of an early encouragement ro follow the spirit of Francis' love of poverty and to avoid the failings of many who had seen poverty as an ideal but had compromised their vision," particularly with "the construction of the magnificent basilica in honor of Saint Francis carried out by Pope Gregory and Brother Elias." For these reasons, they are of the opinion that SC is written between 1237–1239, maybe by Caesar of Speyer. R. Armstrong, W. Hellmann, W. Short (eds), *Francis of Assisi: Early Documents. Vol. I: The Saint*, New York 1999, 525–527. According to SC. Lady holy Poverty's original abode is in paradise, "that most pleasant and beautiful place." There she rejoiced exceedingly and played before man all the time "for, possessing nothing, man belonged entirely to God" (25). It describes very well the situation at Francis' time when there were "among us those who were not of us." They said that they were poor, when they were not. They were still thinking like the world. They failed to leave Assisi and dragged it with them into religious life. They put on the habit without putting on the new man. They merely covered the old. They had no intention of entering holy Poverty's service even though they were wearing the signs of service, for they did not think poverty made any sense. In line with the dominant culture of their days, they called Poverty "lazy, rough, wicked, uncultured." Yet, they intended to stay, and to use the brotherhood for their worldly purposes. In short, they were "corrupt of mind and devoid of truth" (38). Taking advantage of their state of mind, Avarice, first disguised as Discretion (43), and afterwards as Providence (45), succeeded with the help of all kinds of arguments that sounded quite reasonable and were couched in religious language, to convince those brothers to leave their own vision on possessions and to start handling material goods again in conformity with Assisi's rules. They were recaptured by the system. And whereas before, as followers of holy Poverty, they were considered foolish and uncultured, now they were praised by the people of Assisi because of their asceticism and their

Francis and his brothers had developed in the Earlier Rule 9. In their eyes, poverty and its companion, begging, were an obstacle to the proper functioning of the brotherhood in church and society. Hence they were not prepared to just "lay down their office of preaching without any protest" (RegNB 17:4). For what was really the use of preachers laying down their office and starting to work with their hands instead? Wasn't that a waste of talents which could be much better used for the moral and religious uplift of the people, for the building up of the church? And why shouldn't the brothers have proper houses of study and books? Shouldn't those who join the brothers have the opportunity to study the word of God to become "ministers of spirit and life" for the people (Test 13.24)? Further, what was wrong with the brothers holding responsible jobs and receiving money for the work they were doing (RegNB 7:1.7)? If they had money or were in the possession of goods, wouldn't they be able to do much more good for poor people and lepers than by their manual work or their begging (RegNB 8:8–11)? The answers to these and other similar questions were rather obvious to them. Of course, they should use their God-given talents in the way that was most beneficial to the people and to the church. Of course, they should create the conditions favourable to study the word of God in order thus to enable the young brothers to become well-trained preachers. And of course, they should not refuse whatever money would be given to them for their work as it would give them the possibility to help the needy more effectively.

Evidently, the growth of the brotherhood was accompanied by a growing difference among the brothers as regards the understanding of poverty and its place within the brotherhood. Francis addressed this problem in the Later Rule 5–6. As followers of most holy poverty, the brothers may receive for their work whatever is necessary, just as in par-

holiness. For they used the goods they obtained from the people wisely and modestly within the system, not getting attached to them but doing good with them as it befitted holy men. This praise, however, was obtained at the cost of their prophetic witness against the world's handling of material goods which perpetuates the world's sin of appropriation and keeps humankind far removed from paradise where God placed our first parents and to which he restored us through the poverty and humility of Jesus. For an excellent commentary, see D. Flood, *Poverty's Condition. A Reading of the Sacrum Commercium*, Haversack Occasional Paper 2, Chicago 1990.

adise where our first parents did not suffer want but had whatever was necessary for a good and decent life. Having said this, Francis reiterated most forcefully the original ideal: the brothers shall not appropriate anything, whatever other brothers may advise them to the contrary. They will not even do so when this means that they will not have the necessities of life that are due to them for their work, and have to go begging. If this happens, the brothers must not feel ashamed. Rather, they must know that they are following the example of the poor and humble Jesus. Their poverty then is that holy, redeeming poverty which makes them heirs and kings of the kingdom of heaven that Jesus came to establish here on earth. They may be poor in things, but in possessing only holy poverty, they are rich in virtues. For whoever possesses one holy virtue possesses all of them (SalVirt 6).

It is clear that this understanding of holy poverty forms the basis of the critique of Francis and his brothers on the socio-economic and political situation, and of their vision of a new redeemed, liberated society in which the divisive and exclusive property system does not reign, but the non-appropriation of goods becomes the normative way of life whereby all without exception are given access to the goods they need at the table of the Lord's creation. Francis and his brothers hoped to realize this redeemed society first of all within their own brotherhood. At the same time, on their journey through the world they would do all within their power to win others to their vision, especially through their way of life (RegNB 14). For with their commitment to Lady holy Poverty, Francis and his brothers intended in the final analysis to liberate the world from the sinful "captivity" (RegNB 23:3) in which it is held, and to give back to all their rightful place in the restored paradise. There no one will appropriate anything at the expense of someone else and so continue the original sin which keeps humankind excluded from paradise. Rather, all will share together all of creation's goods, which God did not create for a happy few but for all people without exception, because all are created in God's image and likeness. In this way, not keeping anything for themselves as if it was their own, they will return all good things to God, from whom they come and to whom they belong (RegNB 17:17) and who has destined them to be shared by all at his table.

Therefore, when at the end of his life Francis admonished his brothers "to always love and be faithful to our Lady Holy Poverty" (TestSiena 4), this cannot refer to the poverty they had come to see and understand as a sinful condition. Rather, this admonition must be understood against the background of the situation which had arisen in the brotherhood where, precisely because of the consequences, several brothers were no longer faithful to the original ideal to leave Assisi and to live in joyful solidarity among the poor, especially among the lepers, not counting the cost (RegNB 9:2; cf. 1 Cel 104). It was in order to motivate those brothers to return to the choice they made at the beginning that Francis referred to the example of Jesus who, "though he was rich beyond all other things, willed to choose poverty in this world" (2 LetFaith 5) to make us rich through his poverty.

But what was the meaning, the content of the poverty which Jesus chose? For Jesus poverty was not an end in itself, but a means to fulfill his mission of redemption and to restore paradise. Jesus' poverty, whereby he emptied himself from his riches, not holding on to or claiming anything as his own, was thus first and foremost an act of solidarity with the poor by which he wished to redeem them from their poverty, their material condition of insufficiency and their basic lack of esteem and social support, and to make them "rich" with the riches they were supposed to have had if the first parents had not sinned and lost paradise. Indeed, Jesus fed the hungry, he healed the lepers, he made the blind see and the lame walk, and he incorporated them into a new community where the poor were blessed because they were no longe poor, but were heirs of the kingdom, not in some distant future, but already here and now!

Often the redemption from poverty, the being made rich by Jesus, is interpreted in a "spiritual" way. We need then to remember Francis' statement that through his life and death Jesus restored to the poor their right to alms, that is, to their fair and just share in the goods of God's creation. According to Francis, Jesus' poverty has thus what we would call a socio-economic and political dimension. It is this poverty, Jesus' holy and redeeming poverty, to which the brothers must be faithful, even when suffering and persecution become their lot because of the opposition of Assisi yo their alternative way of life. As Flood says: "Under poverty [Francis] understood the redemptive tactics of the Franciscan movement,"[66] by which Franciscan brothers and sisters

[66] D. Flood, The Domestication of the Franciscan Movement, *FranzStud* 60 (1978) 311–327, here 327.

attempt to confound the sinful and unjust structures of Assisi's economy and to establish an order that is in conformity with God's original design.[67] In these endeavours, Lady holy Poverty is their guide, their source of strength and encouragement, their God-given "portion," which will lead them into the land of the living (RegB 6:5).

With Your Sister, Holy Humility (v. 2)

Poverty and humility are also elsewhere mentioned together as essential characteristics of Jesus' life and that of the brothers. In fact, poverty and humility are used to summarize both Jesus' life (RegNB 9:1; RegB 12:4) and the life of the brothers (RegB 6:2), whereby Jesus' life serves as inspiration and example for the life of the brothers.[68] Their being mentioned together is not surprising when we consider that their counterparts, possessions and power, are the dominant forces in the world of Assisi. Of course, the brothers have left this world; yet they are continually being confronted with it and its forces on their going about through the world. And as we have seen, the possessions of the world exercise such attraction on the brothers that some of them forget about the original ideals, especially when they prove difficult to realise. The same holds good for the power of the world which keeps enticing the brothers, for they are humans too. And so there are brothers who want "to appropriate to themselves the ministry of the brothers and the office of preaching" (RegNB 17:4), because they give them power and respect among the brothers and in the world—possession and power find each other here within the brotherhood as they do in Assisi! But what can be done about this alliance, when the highest authorities in the church are keen that the brothers take up positions of authority and power and even

[67] "We may not reduce Francis' doctrine of the virtues to a personal ascetical attitude. We must allow the entire project of life of Francis and his first brothers as it found expression in the Rule, to resonate as background. In the first brotherhood poverty and humility also have a social significance. As a community the brothers wish to unmask, to expose the ideals of their society as a false way of salvation. Their concrete life as brothers, that is their social choices regarding labour, salary, position and housing (RegNB 7), was meant to demythologize the new merchant society that was developing in Assisi." A. Jansen, Lofzang op de Deugden II, *FL* 75 (1992) 173.

[68] The combination occurs even more frequently in the writings of Clare: 3 BrAgn 4 and 24; RegClar 8:2; 12:13; TestClar 46 and 56.

try to convince them to do so by appealing to the need of the church (2 Cel 148)? And this is but one instance of possession and power trying to encapsulate the brothers. There are many others, as we will see in what follows. Lady Humility is therefore in danger among the brothers and Francis prays to the Lord for her, that the Lord may save her together with the other virtues that are vital to the brotherhood.

Humility has various synonyms in the writings of Francis, like *minoritas*, being subject, service, etc. And although we wish here to concentrate on the word "humility," it does not seem possible to understand completely the meaning of humility without taking into account its various synonyms. We have already mentioned that Assisi is not prepared to accept the brothers' opposition to its economic system. Notwithstanding the brothers' refusal to cooperate, the citizens of Assisi keep on trying to win the brothers over to the world of money, status and power. They offer the brothers posts as financial administrators in charge of accounts or as an officials of the commune supervising its service institutions (7:1).[69] For the brothers are hard working, honest and completely trustworthy. They are the right persons for such responsible posts. Yet they do not want to accept them. For by accepting them they would become part of the system that recommends an economy of growth and thus divides people: the rich—the winners—against the poor—the losers. The brothers would not bring peace—as they want to,

[69] Something similar happened in Milan with regard to the Humiliati. Basing himself on a study of Manselli, Flood writes: "Manselli explained how officials in Milan entrusted the Humiliati with delicate tasks of communal importance... They served as tax assessors and collectors, as weight controllers for corn and flour and bread and as city treasurers. They were entrusted with these tasks because they were honest and industrious and innocent of party politics. The people of Assisi had such an idea in mind when they offered the brothers work in finance and in records (*camerarius* and *cancellarius*). One role required civil honesty, the other professional competency... In their offer to the brothers, the Assisians recognized their abilities. More important, the Assisians interpreted their Christian commitment. In their refusal, the brothers refused the Assisian interpretation of their 'rule and life.' They said in sum: 'Do not use the story of the Humiliati to explain to yourself what we are doing and what it means.' Historians do precisely that. They put Waldensians, Humiliati, and Franciscans together in one category. They explain them as the moral prophets of their age. Yet in this passage the brothers excluded as contrary to their life an economic function in Assisi similar to the one exercised by the Humiliati in Milan. In other words, they distinguished themselves economically from Assisi. They were not

for the Lord himself has given them this task (Test 23; RegNB 14:2)—but division. Hence, they make a clear decision: they will be "the lesser ones and subject to all who are in the same house" (7:2).[70] Making this choice in the Spirit of the Lord, they break with the system of Assisi, based on power and oppression, and commit themselves to building an alternative structure, based on humble service and brotherly solidarity with the poor and oppressed. They do not want to be *domini* and *maiores*, but *fratres* and *minores*. Thus they hope to create the conditions for putting an end to the divisions and establishing true peace, the fruit of the Spirit of the Lord (17:15).

This liberating insight, which enables the brothers to bridge the divisions and to experience true peace in brotherhood, is good news in a world that knows so much oppression and exploitation, and is involved in numerous wars between cities, between pope and emperor, between Christians and Muslims. The brothers cannot keep this good news to

---

merely honest and modest; they were different in the way they related to things and to people. In the difference lies the story." *Francis of Assisi and the Franciscan Movement*, 21–22.

[70] "... to live as a subject is from the very beginning one of the characteristics of the life of Francis and his brothers (Test 19). In this way they indicate their place in the society of their days," not only in the world of work (RegNB 7:2), but also with regard to the Saracens and other nonbelievers (16:6). Francis expresses himself most radically in the Salutation of the Virtues, where he speaks about being subject "even to all beasts and wild animals" (16–18). See Sevenhoven, a.c. 203–204. "To be subject... was for Francis not a specific virtue which was to be realized separately and constituted an addition to his real resolve. Rather, it was a part, even the central part, the very heart, of the *Vita evangelii*... His concern is the imitation of the historical Christ of the gospels as the earthly-human, visible, tangible form of the Son of God who appeared to us in humility." K.V. Selge, Franz von Assisi und die Römisch Kurie, *Zeitschrift für Theologie und Kirche* 67 (1970) 129–161, here 149 and 151. Within the context of his article, Selge speaks only about being subject to the ecclesiastical authorities. He does not however research the origin of Francis' vision: that the Lord, and no one else, revealed this original form of evangelical life to Francis after he had left Assisi. It is precisely this origin which gives a totally different accent to Francis' wish to be subject. As will be shown in the following pages, Francis and his brothers see their "being-subject" first and foremost as an alternative way of life and as a protest against the use of power and violence in church and society. This original Franciscan interpretation, which Francis repeats in his Testament, should also be taken into account when interpreting the implications of the more legal, and not typically Franciscan, but rather common ecclesiastical expression "always to be subject and prostrate *(subditi et subjecti)* at the feet of

themselves, nor would they want to. Rather they feel the urge to share with others their vision of a new world which confounds the old one (SalVirt).[71] Thus Francis insists that his "brothers who, by divine inspiration, go among the Saracenes... do not engage in arguments or disputes but are subject to every human creature for God's sake" (RegNB 16:3.6; cf. 1 Pe 2:13). By their "being subject," they are to extend their peace mission beyond the borders of the Christian world into Muslim lands to counteract there the evil done by the crusades. They are not to join the power and might of the crusaders' army against the Muslims. They are not even to use the verbal violence of arguments and disputes against them. Rather, they are to live among them in humble service and so extend to them Jesus' greeting of peace, not only in words but in deeds (RegNB 14.2; Test 23).[72] And in his Second Letter to the Faithful, Francis invites all men and women who want to lead a truly Christian life to join the brothers and "never to desire to be over others; rather [they] must be servants and subject to every human creature for God's sake" (47–48; cf. 1 Pe 2:13). Together then with all people of good will, the brothers are, through their life of service in solidarity with people, everywhere in this world, to unmask the evil consequences of power and might and to build a new society, where there is peace for all.

As the text quoted from the First letter of Peter shows, Francis and the brothers commit themselves to this mission "for God's sake."[73] For, as

---

the same holy church" at the end of chapter 12 of the *Regula bullata*. It will then appear that Francis and his brothers with their admonition to be subject to the Saracens for God's sake do not agree with the official church policy regarding crusades and Saracens, sanctioned by pope and council and aimed at the violent submission of the Saracens, but are rather following the form of the gospel which the Lord has revealed to them. See my *Francis and Islam*, 83–87.

[71] Flood 168–173.

[72] See my *Francis and Islam*, 71–87.

[73] This interpretation of the text of 1 Pe 13, though not the most common one, can be found already in a commentary of Haymo of Halberstadt (+ 853): "... propter Deum, qui nos docet, dicens: Discite a me quia mitis sum et humilis corde...; et iterum: Omnis qui se humiliat propter Dominum, exaltabitur a Domino" *PL* 183, 506–507. Closer to Francis is Ralph Ardent (+1198) who comments: "... propter Deum. Propter eum quippe solum nos ad invicem humiliare, et invicem nos subdere debemus, qui quod praecipit ipse fecit, ut later alteri ministraremus, et alter alterius pedes lavaremus..." *PL* 155, 1879–1880. See for this, M.A. Lavilla Martín, La sumision a toda criatura por Dios, propuesta por Francisco de Asis. Un pasaje de la historia exegética de 1Pt 2,13, *Antonianum* 74 (1999) 463–499, here 470–471.

we will see, they have developed a different understanding of God. God is not the God of power and might who is invoked to legitimize the existing economic system of Assisi or even to justify the crusades. On the contrary, focussing ever more intensely on the poor and humble Jesus, the brothers have come to see God as the God who came to us in the humble Jesus who lived among us not to be served but to serve, and so realized God's plan of redemption (cf. RegNB 4:6). It is for the sake of this God that the brothers know themselves to be called to be subject to every human creature, not in order to perpetuate the system of Assisi with its sinful humiliation and oppression, but rather to break through it unto the redemption, the liberation of people. Thus, when Francis in the rule says that the brothers must be *fratres minores*, lesser brothers who are subject to all, he does not mean that they must submit again to the system of Assisi where the leaders rule over the people and keep them subject to their power.[74] On the contrary, Francis states very explicitly, on the basis of the gospel: "It shall not be like this among the brothers" (5:10). The system of Assisi, of lords and subjects, of people who have rights and people who do not, may in no way be continued. No one shall hold power or dominion over the other; rather they should become one another's minister and servant, washing one another's feet (5:9.11; 6:4).

It is evident that Francis and his brothers understand *minoritas* and "being subject" in a completely different way than the rich and power-

[74] I differ here from L. Lehmann: "Wherever a brother may go, among Christians or non-Christians, all claims to power, all arrogance are excluded. The Franciscan does not rule over others, he allows himself to be ruled by others. He does not impose new structures, but starts by submitting himself to the existing ones, in order then, if need be, to dissolve the unjust structures from within." "Main Features of the Franciscan Understanding of Mission according to the Rule of 1221," *FrancDigest* 2,1 (January 1992) 6. As I have explained, Francis clearly decides that he will *not* be subject to the system and, if need be, remove its unjust structures; rather, he radically breaks with it: "I left the world" (Test 3), and to take care that this world does not return: "it shall not be like this among the brothers" (RegNB 5:10). In their interpretation of Francis, many authors understand certain words very traditionnally in accordance with the dominant form of religious spirituality. They pay too little attention to the fact that Francis' break with Assisi and its value system results, among other things, in that several keywords obtain a completely different meaning in the brotherhood. For this see D. Flood, A Brief Survey of Early Franciscan History, *Haversack* 1, 5 (May–June 1978), 7–9.

ful. For the latter, these words imply a one-way traffic. The "being subject" is forced upon a group of people, the servants, who must be subject to their masters. And they are to accept this humbly, for it is God's will for them. In this situation, humility teaches the servants their lowly place within the hierarchically ordered structures of possession and power and teaches them to stay there. For Francis and his brothers, however, "being subject" is a matter of a two-way traffic, or at least an attempt towards it. Their "being subject" is not exacted from them; rather, it is freely chosen, negatively, as a criticism of and protest against the hierarchical structures and the inequality and oppression they actually lead to, but especially also positively, as an act of solidarity with the poor and, at the same time, as an invitation to the rich and the powerful. The latter are invited to leave their way of thinking and acting with regard to power and its evil, sinful consequences, and instead, through mutual submission and service, to lay the foundations for a society of equality, of brotherly and sisterly respect for each other and of true peace.[75]

Francis and his brothers are thus very explicitly concerned about a way of behavior that is mutual: the brothers must wash each other's feet (6:4). And it is through this mutual, humble service that they are to build a new world. Humility, then, together with poverty, is for Francis not so much an ascetic practice aimed at personal holiness, but rather the organising principle of the new society of equality, of the brother/sisterhood they want to establish in the name of Jesus and his gospel. This brother/sisterhood will be radically opposed to the existing society and its understanding of humility as a means to keep the poor and oppressed in their place.[76] Obviously, the brothers cannot expect the whole world to

[75] The emphasis which Francis lays on submission and service may sound alien and alienating to people who in whatever way, individually or as group, are forced into submission. Indeed, we are dealing here with words that are historically and culturally loaded. However, Francis uses them as a challenge and a protest against the power politics of the rich and the mighty which he has experienced as sinful. This sin can only be destroyed and true peace established if the rich and mighty give up every sense of power, every feeling of superiority, for these exclude true sister- and brotherhood which are based on mutual service in a spirit of equality and respect for the other as other.

[76] Lavilla Martin reaches a similar conclusion: "Francis' social context raises a question: How is it possible that Francis proposed submission and service at a time when liberation movements of people who were dependent on or subject to others

be prepared to change its ways all of a sudden and to convert to the ideal of the gospel. Someone must take the initiative. Francis and his brothers are ready for it. They decide "to go about through the world" while proclaiming this good news of *minoritas* and *fraternitas*. In doing so, they make themselves extremely vulnerable.[77] Others may reject the invitation and in all sorts of ways try to put the brothers to shame. But then they

---

were active in central Italy? The answer is simple: because the submission Francis proposed was an evangelical submission which did not destroy people by turning them into slaves, but rather liberated people and brought them together as brothers and sisters, a submission which aimed at mutual service and love among people. On the other hand, the majority of the people who were dependent did not profit from the process of liberation. Even the suppression of the personal bondage of serfs who were owned by their masters was in many cases an outward appearance only, because it was replaced by other kinds of bondage which were even much harsher for the people involved. It cannot be established to what extent Francis was conscious of the implicit denunciation present in his proposal. However, it is evident that he offers two models of relationship to his brotherhood and to the society in general: the model of servitude, of submission and that of the family. It might seem as if these two types of relationship between people cannot be reconciled with one another. Not so for Francis and the word of God from which he derived his inspiration! These two models are not opposed to each other; they rather complement each other. People have to be little, submissive, ready to serve and subject to all in order to be brother or sister to all (and within his brotherhood: mothers and sons of each other). In this way, Francis gathered the aspirations of the people of his time through a movement toward greater solidarity, through the creation of equal relations among people, but not in order to form closed groups that would dominate others, as it frequently happened, and through the establishment of family relations based on mutual submission and service, and not on power of some over the others. This ideal of Francis is closely connected with his concept of authority and government. He wished that they be of service to others and not dominating, caring and not possessive, without falling into idolatry of themselves nor into the denial of their necessity and validity for human relations" (498–499).

[77] The essential importance of this attitude of vulnerability for the dialogue with people of other religions and cultures, see J. van Gerwen, Christian Faith and (In)Tolerance, *Louvain Studies* 16 (1991) 220–241, here especially 239: "Real tolerance presupposes unconditional love, rather than calculation, because one has to be ready to accept the risk of being misunderstood, hurt, or even killed by the other, before a common basis of understanding will be reached. I need to risk myself (my identity) honestly and unconditionally, hoping (not being sure) that the other will do the same to me. It is necessary that I make the first move, not waiting for the other's opening."

will encourage one another by referring to the example of Jesus' humility (9:1) , which proves that there is a holy and redeeming humility in sharp contrast to the enforced, sinful humility which the mighty and powerful impose on the poor and powerless.

Differently from the example of Jesus' poverty which he hardly elaborates in his other writings, Francis pays more attention to Jesus' humility, especially when speaking about the Eucharist and the Incarnation. The ideas which he develops on these two subjects confirm and deepen what I have said so far. The Eucharist is for Francis the sacrament of God's humility. However, as the First Admonition indicates, this truth about the Eucharist, like so many other basic truths, is no longer seen by some of the brothers. This situation prompts Francis to write his Admonition to warn them of the grave consequences of their wrong vision and to place before them the example of Jesus' humility in the Eucharist in order to motivate them to abandon this wrong vision and instead to follow Jesus' example. The First Admonition is therefore a privileged place to study Francis' understanding of humility within the context of the developments within the brotherhood, and especially to learn about the conditions of possibility for such understanding.[78]

The central question of Francis' First Admonition is formulated in verses 14–15: "Therefore, O sons of men, how long will you be hard of heart? (Ps 4:3). Why do you not recognize the truth and believe in the Son of God? Starting from the presumption that Francis wrote his Admonitions to address problems the brothers were facing, I interpret Francis' question as a reference to the fact that there are apparently brothers who are hard, or rather heavy of heart (*gravi corde*) and who do not recognize the truth about the Son of God, Jesus Christ, who is the way, the truth and the life (1). Who are these brothers? The Earlier Rule 9:14 can probably shed some light upon this question.[79] There we read: "And let them recall what the Lord says: Take heed that your hearts do not become heavy *(ne forte graventur corda vestra)* through intoxication

[78] For this and what follows, see my article: "Eucharist and Priesthood according to Francis. With Special Reference to his First Admonition," *FrancDigest* 7,2 (December 1997) 13–27.

[79] I borrow this reference from G.P. Freeman, "Usquequo grave corde?" Zur Deutung der 1. Ermahnung des Franziskus, *Laurentianum* 29 (1988) 386–415. Unfortunately, Freeman himself does not elaborate this reference.

and drunkenness and the cares of this life *(curis huius vitae)* for that day will come upon you unexpectedly; for like a trap it will come upon all who dwell upon the face of the earth (Lk 21:34–35)." Speaking about those who are heavyhearted because of the cares of this life, Francis explains in his the Second Letter to the Faithful: "[They] are deceived by the devil... they are blind because they do not see the true light, our Lord Jesus Christ. They do not have spiritual wisdom because they do not have within them the Son of God who is the true wisdom of the Father... They see, acknowledge, know and do evil, and, knowingly, they lose their souls. See, you blind ones, [you who] are deceived by our enemies, the flesh, the world and the devil" (63–69).

These two texts indicate clearly that those who are heavy of heart and cannot know the truth about Jesus are those brothers who have been deceived by the flesh, the world and the devil. They see and know evil, but they do not or rather cannot see the true light. For they do not have the wisdom of the Spirit. On the contrary, they have the knowledge of the flesh. We have here a clear reference to two possible ways of seeing, two possible ways of knowing which Francis deals with more explicitly in the First Admonition. There he clearly distinguishes between seeing in the lifegiving Spirit *(in Spiritu videre; videre secundum Spiritum et divinitatem; oculis spiritualibus contemplantes*, 6.8.9.20) and seeing according to the flesh, which is of no use *(caro non prodest quidquam; videre secundum [carnem et] humanitatem; intuitu carnis*, 6. 8.20). This dialectic leads inevitably to two different and even opposed groups: the brothers who by divine inspiration (RegNB 2:1; 16:3) have left the world to live in the Spirit among the people, even among the Saracenes *(spiritualiter conversari*, RegNB 16:5) and the brothers who have returned to the world of Assisi which is dominated by the cares of this life *(curis huius vitae)*, the cares of possession and power, and hence have become so heavy of heart that they are no longer able to see with the eyes of the Spirit, but only with the eyes of the flesh.

It is evident that the two ways of seeing have everything to do with the place where the brothers are. Their social location strongly influences their perspective and thus creates the conditions which make it possible to see certain realities or not to see them at all.[80] And so it hap-

[80] Cf. what the sociology of knowledge says about perspectivism, "i.e. a recognition that social location profoundly influences our sensibilities, attitudes, priorities, moral commitments, etc." And in turn one's "concrete commitment to solidarity

pens that the brothers who have returned to the world of Assisi lack the proper perspective to see the truth of the Eucharist precisely because of their return. Heavyhearted and blinded as they are, they see Jesus only according to his humanity, or rather they see him only with human, carnal eyes (*secundum humanitatem* as opposed to *secundum Spiritum et divinitatem*). And because of their way of seeing, because of their socially and geographically determined perspective, they cannot see with the eyes of the Spirit how this Jesus in his humanity, i.e. in his poverty and humility, truly is the Son of God (8). For them God is first and foremost a God of greatness and power; the guarantee of the structure of Assisi based on possession and power. A God who is humility (PrGod 4) is for them unthinkable. Hence they cannot look at Jesus from the perspective of such a God and discover in the poor and humble Jesus the Son of God who is for them "the way, the truth and the life" (1; cf. Jo 14:6) and who invites them to follow this way and so to find God.

In the same way they cannot see how bread and wine, these humble gifts, are truly the body and blood of our Lord Jesus Christ who daily comes to us in humble form (9; 17). The Eucharist as sign, as sacrament of God's humility which in Jesus becomes visible among us, is beyond their understanding. It signifies in reality the complete subversion of the world of possessions and power in which they believe. However, because of their spiritual blindness, preoccupied as they are with the cares of this age and not with the things of God (cf. LetClergy 7), they fail to see this truth. For them the solemn celebration of the Eucharist and the carrying about of the monstrance with great pomp and splendour in a procession (1 LetCust 4) have a completely different function than to remind them of the humility of God and to invite them to the imitation of this humility as the principle of organisation for a new and different society in conformity with God's original plan. Rather, they are to them a show of power and might in support of the existing hierarchical order of the present age, not a challenge to leave this age (Test 3), to set aside the

---

places one in a social setting more conducive to understanding the suffering of the poor, the current ideological legitimations of poverty (including those that are theological), and our responsibility for engaging in 'liberating praxis.'" Stephem J. Pope, Proper and improper partiality and the preferential option for the poor, *TheolStud* 54 (1993) 247. Cfr. also the so-called "hermeneutics of dislocation." Michael Warren, "The Local Church and Its Practice of the Gospel: The Materiality of Discipleship in a Catechesis of Liberation," *Worship* 67 (1993), 452.

cares of this age (LetRulers 4.6; RegNB 22:26) and to restore the original order of God's age, Gods' reign,[81] where all are brothers and sisters, children of one and the same Father in heaven, all sitting at the one table of the Lord and humbly serving one another in love!

After warning those brothers who have been enticed to go back to Assisi of the consequences of their failure to see with the eyes of the Spirit and to recognize the truth revealed in Jesus, the Son of God, and in the Eucharist—they will eat and drink judgement unto themselves (12–13)—Francis proclaims once again his vision of the Eucharist in a short hymn. It is a final attempt on his part to open the eyes of his brothers to the beauty he has discovered in the Eucharist and to make them return from their ways. "See, daily he humbles himself as when he came from the royal throne into the womb of the Virgin; daily he comes to us in humble form; daily he descends from the bosom of the Father upon the altar in the hands of the priest" (16–18). In this hymn Francis sees the Eucharist as the continuation of the Incarnation, of God's descent, a continuation that does not occur only at some very special occasion, but daily. Francis is deeply touched by this act of generosity on God's part,[82] so much so that up to three times at the beginning of each verse he repeats "daily." It looks almost as if Francis can hardly believe it himself and has to keep reminding himself. Yes, it is true: in the eucharistic Jesus God daily humbles himself to be with us, even to the end of time (22). And in his Letter to the Order he exclaims: "O sublime humility! O humble sublimity! That the Lord of the universe, God and the Son of God, so humbles himself that for our salvation he hides himself under the little form of bread!" (27). God's humility in Jesus: it is God's "stupendous favour" (*stupenda dignatio*, 26) towards us, for our salvation!

It is this stupendous favour which is also very much in Francis' mind when, at the beginning of the Second Letter to the Faithful, he gives a description of the way he understands Jesus. Francis sees Jesus as the Word of the Father (3). And the Word that the Father speaks in Jesus,

[81] For this idea, see also below under IV B f.

[82] "The humility of the incarnation and the charity of the passion occupied Francis' memory particularly, to the extent that he wanted to think of hardly anything else" (1 Cel 84). "Brother, every day I find such sweetness and consolation in recalling to mind and meditating on the humility the Son of God manifested while he was on earth that I could live until the end of the world without hearing or meditating on any other passages from the Scriptures" (LegPer 38).

loud and clear, is the word of descent, of going down. This is evident in the choice Francis makes in his enumeration of the important events of Jesus' life where Francis limits himself to the incarnation and birth of Jesus, the eucharist, Jesus' agony in the Garden of Gethsemane and his death, and does not mention at all Jesus' preaching, his miracles and his resurrection (4–9). This choice manifests a definite one-sidedness which, without any doubt, points to Francis' being deeply impressed by Jesus' descent, his humility. This movement of Jesus' descent starts in verse 4 with the most high Father in heaven and ends in verse 9 when his sweat as drops of blood falls on the earth. It is the lowest point of a life of continuous descent. Not only did Jesus come down among us and share our humanity and fragility, he also wanted above all to choose poverty, even though he was rich. He did not want to appropriate anything to himself, but emptied himself ever more, until he could not go any further, any lower. Once Jesus has reached this lowest point, and his aversion from this suffering and his fears have surfaced, he is able to surrender his will to the will of the Father and to accept his death. This surrender and acceptance constitute the turning point. From that moment onward, everything starts moving upward again. In fact, Jesus' crucifixion is for Francis already the beginning of his glorification, his exaltation. This upward movement and the perspective it opens show that the way of descent, of going down, of humbling and emptying oneself, is not meaningless. On the contrary, it is the way to new life, a way that Jesus went, leaving us an example that we should follow in his footprints (13) and so be saved through him (14).[83]

In this light, God's humility in Jesus can best be described as an act of solidarity with humankind whereby God, who is king, sitting on a royal throne, leaves behind all power, descends among us, shares our humanity and fragility, chooses poverty above riches and, in the end, empties himself totally so that by this sublime act of humility the humble, and the lowly may be exalted (cf. Lk 1:52). It is just like in the case of Jesus' poverty which he chose that we might be rich. It is clear then that we have here again an instance where a well-known and often used concept gets an entirely different meaning in Francis' writings. For Jesus' humility has nothing to do with the humility as understood within the dominant culture. Rather, it stands in profound contrast to the attitude

[83] See G.P. Freeman, The Word of the Father. A commentary of Francis' Second Letter to the Faithful, verses 2–15, *FrancDigest* 9,1 (March 1999) 19–27, here 22–26.

of humble acceptance and subservience which the mighty and the powerful within the power structures of Assisi expect from the poor and weak and defenceless. In short, Jesus' humility is not humiliating and degrading, depriving people from their dignity as human persons. On the contrary, it is holy and redeeming; it does not put down, but exalts the lowly.[84]

This salvation, this exaltation, however, does not happen automatically because Jesus humbled himself dying on the cross. The situation of the world in Francis' days was ample proof of this. The brothers will have to identify themselves personally with Jesus' humility so as to make it bear fruit unto the exaltation of the lowly in their own world. Thus in his Letter to the Order, after having expressed his admiration for God's sublime humility in Jesus, Francis admonishes his brothers, insisting that they must "look at the humility of God" in Jesus and "humble themselves," making God's humility their own (28). And in the passage from the the Second Letter to the Faithful, which we just commented upon, Francis ends by saying that Jesus left us his way of humility as an example that we should walk in his footsteps and so find salvation for ourselves and for others. And further on in the same letter, Francis makes this very concrete in the text quoted earlier: "We must never desire to be over others; rather we must be servants and subject to every human creature because of God" (47; cf. 1 Pe 2:13) who humbled himself in Jesus becoming our servant. The brothers then must translate God's humility in Jesus by their "being subject" to all people and so renew God's redeeming action unto the salvation of the world (cf. 53).

This call to translate God's humility in their actions is most evident in the celebration of the Eucharist. For in the Eucharist, the brothers who see with the eyes of the Spirit daily celebrate God's humility (Adm. 1:16–17), that is, God's loving act of redeeming and exalting solidarity in Jesus who is for them "the way, the truth and the life" (1). Hence, the celebration of the sacrament of God's humility is not a mere remembrance of the past. Rather, it is meant as a celebration through which the brothers daily over and over again unite themselves with the humble Jesus and resolve to follow him in his humility as the way to true life. Thus, daily living like Jesus in a solidarity of humble service with the marginalised of society, they hope to find life for themselves and for others in

[84] See for this also the view of Lavilla Martin, quoted above in note 76.

God's kingdom. The Eucharistic celebration then is for the brothers a continuous invitation and challenge to identify with Jesus through their humble way of life, that is, through their solidarity with the victims of the power structures, and so to confound the mighty and powerful, the proud and self-exalted in this world (SalVirt 12; cf. RegNB 17:5), to undo the sinful, humiliating structures of might and power, and to transform society into a true brother/sisterhood where no one is put down but all are equal and are ready to wash one another's feet (cf. RegNB 6:4) after the example of the humble Jesus who did not come to be served but to serve and so to establish his Father's kingdom.[85]

To follow the example of the humble Jesus is not an easy task nor is its goal, the transformation of society, quickly achieved. It is not without reason then that Francis often links humility with patience. In Francis' mind, however, this link is not only experiential, based on his observation of reality. It goes much deeper in that the link refers to the way God operates in this world. In other words, the link is essentially theological, as is evident in that both are mentioned together in the Praises of God as attributes of God (4) and are also joined together as fruits of the Spirit of the Lord (RegNB 17:15). And indeed, in the incarnation God does not use his power and might to force people, to overpower them, in order thus to establish his kingdom, his rule, in an instant. Rather, becoming one of us in the humble Jesus, God invites people, and continues to invite them through the example of Jesus' life of poverty and humility to accept his message and to follow his way, all the while not forcing them but respecting their freedom of choice. The gospel image is that of the sower who sows the seed—the word of God—and after it has fallen in good soil waits patiently for it to develop slowly but steadily and finally to bear fruit (cf. RegNB 22:11–17).

It is this divine way of operating in and through Jesus which the brothers have to make their own under the inspiration of the Spirit of

[85] A similar idea, though not clearly elaborated in a concrete historical fashion, can be found in R. Armstrong, *St. Francis of Assisi. Writings for a Gospel Life*, New York 1994, 130: "[Francis] reminds us of the humility of the Son of God who empties himself... He teaches us of the all-powerful God who continues to take the initiative in coming to us in ways that speak of lowliness, poverty... Only by identification with the Eucharist does Francis discover the way in which we human beings can undo the ravages of sin and respond to the dignity of the divine call"—and we would add—to redeem the sinful world and transform the society after the example of the poor and humble Jesus, not on the basis of power, but of humility.

the Lord (RegNB 17:15; RegB 10:8). Moved by the Lord's Spirit, the brothers abstain from any and all use of power, violence, or arms to rule over people (cf. RegNB 5:11). Instead they place themselves humbly and patiently at the service of others, trying to convince them by their example and to draw them to their way of life. Thus whenever they see or hear someone speak evil or act in an evil way, they will speak well and act well (cf. RegNB 17:19). This humble, non-violent, inviting way of behaviour appealed to many, as is clearly shown by the growing number of those who join the brotherhood to follow the way of the humble Jesus. Just like Francis at the beginning of his conversion and all throughout the rest of his life, these brothers too meet with opposition and even persecution because of the choice they have made. Many remain faithful to their choice and are able to bear much fruit in patience (cf. RegNB 22:17). But, as we have already mentioned several times, there are also brothers who do not have the courage and the patience to continue on Jesus' way and to persevere until the end. Confronted with this situation, Francis admonishes his brothers: "let the brothers pay attention to what they must desire above all things: to have the Spirit of the Lord and his holy operation, to pray always to him with a pure heart and to have humility, patience in persecution and sickness, and to love those who persecute us, find fault with us, or rebuke us, because the Lord says: Love your enemies, and pray for those who persecute and slander you (Mt 5:44). Blessed are those who suffer persecution for the sake of justice for theirs is the kingdom of heaven (Mt 5:10). Whoever perseveres to the end, will be saved (Mt 10:22)" (RegB 10:8–12).

Those who bear fruit by patiently following the example of the humble Jesus even in times of persecution know that it is not their own doing. Yet, there are brothers who "exalt themselves over the good things which the Lord says and does in them" (Adm 2:3). Francis begs them "not to glory or rejoice in themselves or to exalt themselves inwardly because of the good words and works, or indeed of any good that God sometimes does or says or works in them and through them." Rather they should "strive to be humble in all things" (RegNB 17:5–6). In this context humility has the meaning of true self-knowledge of the human creature before God. Humility then is the humble recognition that all good things, including the virtues, come from God (ibid. 17; SalVirt 4) and that "nothing belongs to us except our vices and sins" (ibid. 7). We stand therefore empty-handed before God, or worse still, as debtors.

To humbly accept this basic truth about our human existence that we are what we are before God and nothing more (cf. Adm 19:2) is difficult, even for some of the brothers. In line with the value system of Assisi, they rather want to possess something of their own to be proud of. To this end they even appropriate to themselves the good that belongs to God. For possessions and the power that goes with them make them someone in the eyes of the world, someone to be counted. But once they have been placed in a high position, they do no longer wish "to descend from there of their own accord" and to be "under the feet of others" (ibid. 3–4). They have forgotten the example of the humble Jesus who "daily descends from the bosom of the Father" (Adm 1:18). They have been blinded to the true meaning of their existence as humans and as followers of Jesus and his gospel. For although they stand empty-handed before God, God needs them in order to do and say and work good in this world in them and through them (RegNB 17:19). They are not to do this by power and might, but by patiently practising, after the example of Jesus, the virtues of holy and redeeming poverty and humility in solidarity with the poor and lowly in order thus to liberate and exalt them (cf. Lk 1:52) and to give them a place within paradise that was lost but has now been regained.

Lady, Holy Charity

God has many names, but the name which stands out is *caritas*, charity, love. In fact, on four other occasions Francis speaks about "the love which God is" (*caritas quae Deus est*, 1 LetFaith 2:19; the Second Letter to the Faithful 87; Earlier Rule 17:5; 22:26). On those occasions it is for the sake of this love which God is and in answer to this love that Francis asks his brothers to act in a particular way. In other words, the love which God is and which became, in a special, unique way visible in the person and in the life and love of Jesus, becomes for Francis the outstanding motive for choosing and following a particular way of life.

In the great Admonition in chapter 22 of the *Regula non bullata* Francis begs all his brothers "in the holy love which God is to remove every obstacle and put behind them every care and anxiety, and in the best way they can to serve, love (*amare*), honor and adore the Lord God with a clean heart and a pure mind" (26). The love which God is demands thus first of all that his brothers love and serve God with a heart and a mind that are cleansed and purified from all worldly care *(cura et sollicitudine)*, through which Satan may wish "to blind a person's heart" (20; 2 LetFaith 69). Or as he writes in the Prayer Inspired by the Our Father: God, "our most holy Father, our creator, redeemer, consoler and savior," you are "inflaming [the saints] to love because you, Lord, are love" *(inflammans ad amorem, quia tu, Domine, amor es*, 1–2). And a little further: "may we love *(amemus)* you with our whole heart by always thinking of you, with our whole soul by always desiring you, with our whole mind by directing all our intentions to you and by seeking your glory in everything and with our whole strength by spending all our strength and our affections of soul and body in the service of your love and of nothing else" (5).

And in the great Prayer in chapter 23 of the *Regula non bullata*—the Franciscan Proclamation, as Flood calls it—after having mentioned all the various groups of people and all nations everywhere on earth "who are and who will be," Francis proclaims: "Let us all love *(diligamus)* the Lord God with all our heart, with all our soul, with all our mind, with all our strength (cf. Mk 12:30) and fortitude, with all our understanding (Mk 12:33), with all our powers (cf. Lk 10:27), with all effort, all affection, all emotion, all desire and will: the Lord God who has given and gives to each one of us our whole body, our whole soul, and our whole life; who has created us and redeemed us and will save us by his mercy alone; who did and does all good things for us who are miserable and wretched, rotten and foul-smelling, ungrateful and evil.., who is the fullness of good, all good, the true and supreme good" (8–9).

It is evident that Francis cannot find words enough to express his admiration for the goodness and love which God has manifested towards us in our creation and redemption. Struck by this ineffable and unfathomable goodness and love of God (cf. 11) Francis feels he cannot stress sufficiently that we have to answer this goodness and love with all that we are and all that we have. Here too he cannot find words enough to impress upon us the greatness and seriousness of our duty to love God. He joins the words of Jesus' answer to the question about the greatest commandment to those of the scribe's confirmation, as he finds them in Mark 12:30 and 33; next he adds an expression from the parallel text in Luke 10:27, and then, as if this is not yet enough, he adds still another five expressions, all of them accompanied by "all" *(totus)* so as to exclude the possibility of keeping anything behind for ourselves. God's goodness and love, through which we received and continue to receive all good things, demand our unconditional and total response.

But what does this total response actually imply? How is this total response to be given concretely in the situation of our daily lives? How are we to love God in our going about through the world? If we want to love God, who in his love created us and formed us to the image of his beloved Son according to the body (cf. Adm 5:1), and through the holy love with which He loved us, willed to redeem us through Jesus' cross and death (RegNB 23:1 and 3), it is obvious that we cannot do this except by walking in the footsteps of Jesus, for it is in his image that we are created and by his cross and death that we are redeemed. This Jesus, therefore, is for us "the way, the truth and the life": the life he lived from his birth in the crib to his death on the cross is for us the true way to true life (cf. Adm 1:1). Following that way, we are not alone for in the eucharist he is always with his faithful to the end of time (22).

It is in light of this brief description of Francis' view on God's love and on our creation and redemption, that we have to read the admonition Francis gives to his brothers in the Earlier Rule 17, the original ending of the rule. Recalling the love which God is[86] and which has been made visible among us in Jesus' humility, he reminds them once more and with great urgency how they have to answer this love of God. He writes: "In the love which God is, I beg all my brothers, those who preach, those who pray and those who work, whether cleric or lay, to strive to humble themselves in all things, not to pride themselves nor to rejoice in themselves nor to exalt themselves interiorly about their good words and works, in fact, about any good which God sometimes does, says or works in them and through them" (RegNB 17:5–6). Rather they must follow the promptings of the Spirit of the Lord, the Spirit of Jesus who "strives for humility and patience, and the pure simplicity and true peace of the Spirit, [and who] above all things longs for the divine fear

[86] "...the sentence: 'God is love' (1 Jn 4:.8.16)... is quoted nine times, not literally, but in an own, independent formulation: "In the love which God is, I beg..." "It is a sentence which has the value of an autograph, of a personal seal of Francis of Assisi. He uses it in order to request those things which are close to his heart and which represent his most inner and most high desires (W. Viviani)." A. Rotzetter, *Franz von Assisi. Ein Anfang und was davon bleibt*, Zürich 1981, no. 38.10. (English translation: *Gospel Living Francis of Assisi Yesterday and Today*, St. Bonaventure, New York, 1994).

and the divine wisdom and the divine love of the Father, and of the Son, and of the Holy Spirit" (15–16).

This text or parts of it have been quoted before when dealing with the other virtues. This repetition clearly illustrates how the virtues cannot be treated one apart from the other. They are all interlinked, one supposing the other, so that a brother who possesses one, possesses all (SalVirt 6). If a brother truly understands God's love in Jesus and wishes to answer it by loving God in return, following Jesus' example, such a brother will necessarily be humble and poor as Jesus was. That is: his actions will be opposed to the dominant values of society: pride and possessions.[87] He will not proudly appropriate the good words and works which God sometimes does, says or works in and through him. On the contrary, with patience—also in the sense of being ready to suffer for the choices he has made—he will in all pure simplicity, keeping himself from all rationalisations, continue on the way he has promised to go. Not claiming anything for himself, but rendering all good back to God (17) by sharing it with all his brothers and sisters in accordance with God's purpose of creation, he will lay the basis for the true peace of the Spirit: not the peace of Assisi which is built on possessions and power which divide people and therefore is a false peace not deserving its name, but the true peace that is based on sisters and brothers humbly serving one another.

It is upon such men and women who have persevered in doing what they have promised that the Spirit will rest (2 LetFaith 48); it is among them that the Spirit will see his longings fulfilled. For in the hearts of such men and women dwell the divine fear of the Father, i.e. the Father protecting the divine love in the human heart out of fear that otherwise the enemy may enter, blinding the heart and turning it away from God (Adm 27:5; RegNB 22:19); the divine wisdom of the Son, and the divine love of the Holy Spirit.[88] Unfortunately, however, there are brothers who

[87] "Love, which is a mark of God, is shown to be real when we adopt a logic and way of life opposed to the values of society. This was the path pointed out by Christ." G. Miccoli, Francis of Assisi's Christian Proposal, *Greyfriars Review* 3,2 (August 1989) 144.

[88] For this interpretation of the divine fear, see A. Jansen, Words of Salvation of Saint Francis. A Commentary on Admonition 27, *FrancDigest* 4,2 (December 1994) 1–24, here 4–6; see also 23–24, where Jansen also refers to RegNB 17:15–16 and to the Second Letter to the Faithful 48. It is a pity that Jansen interprets the admoni-

have been misled by the spirit of the flesh (9); they have been blinded again by "our enemies, the flesh, the world, and the devil" (2 LetFaith 69). By giving in to the spirit of the flesh and allowing the devil to enter (Adm 27:5), they have made it impossible for God to dwell in them and so lost the divine fear, the divine wisdom and the divine love! As a result they miss the *sancta operatio* (RegNB 17:11) through which they are to transform the world. On the contrary, they remain caught in a world where there is only an appearance of religion and holiness (ibid), but where God cannot dwell.

For the same reason, namely that "in the love which God is" the brothers should be humble and not appropriate to themselves any good the Lord does, says or works in and through them, Francis admonishes his brothers who are priest in his Letter to the Order: "If there should be several priests in a place, for love of love *(per amorem caritatis)* let one be content to assist at the celebration of the other priest" (31). For through this one celebration "the Lord Jesus Christ fills both those present and those absent who are worthy of him" (32).[89] When therefore a brother-priest celebrates the eucharist privately, such celebration is not needed to render Christ present and to enable him to fulfill his redemptive work among the brothers and, through them, in this world. Hence, by celebrating the eucharist privately the brother-priest concerned does not place himself at the service of Jesus Christ; rather, he holds his priestly ministry (24) as it were for himself to serve his own interests. In other words, he appropriates the priestly ministry to himself and uses it in one way or other to promote his own glory, to enhance his own status, thus posing a threat to the brotherhood as well. He is not humble, as

---

tion almost exclusively within the context of the religious, Christian growth of the person, and not within the context of the struggle within the brotherhood, as Flood does for whom the "where" *(ubi)* of the Admonition refers precisely to the brotherhood.

[89] The passage finds its origin in the papal bull *Quia populares tumultus*, issued by Honorius III December 3, 1224. With this bull, Honorius allowed the request of the brother-priests to celebrate the eucharist in all their places and oratories on portable altars. This led to a situation in which more and more brother-priests started celebrating their own private mass—a practice which Francis apparently did not agree with, even though pope Honorius allowed it in favor of the brother-priests. For a translation of this bull, see Armstrong, Hellmann, Short 561–562. However, their translation: "... celebrate solemn Masses with a portable altar, as well as the other divine offices..." seems not correct.

would befit him being a minister of the sacrament of God's humility (28). Rather, by insisting that he exercises his priestly function unnecessarily, he places himself in the foreground; he thinks himself more important than his non-ordained brother who can only assist at the eucharistic celebration. And so he exalts and prides himself on account of the good which the Lord has chosen to work through him (cf. RegNB 17:4–6).[90]

By acting in this way the brother-priest denies the deepest essence of the eucharist. For in the eucharist Jesus gives himself totally out of love (LetOrder 29), humbling himself for our salvation (27). For love of this love of Jesus, Francis requests his brother-priests to look at the humility of God, to humble themselves and to hold back nothing for themselves, including their priestly office (28–29). They should therefore be ready to forego their own private celebration and be content to assist at the celebration of another brother-priest in the same way as their non-ordained brothers, rather than unnecessarily celebrating the eucharist

[90] A survey of the different interpretations of this controversial passage, which in the Dutch translation of Francis' writings as well as in the *Omnibus* has by far the longest footnote, can be found in O Schmucki, La "Lettera a tutto l'Ordine' di San Francesco, *L'Italia Francescana* 55 (1980) 245–286; translated into English under the title: St. Francis's Letter to the Entire Order, *Greyfriars Review* 3, 1 (April 1989) 1–33. See also Rotzetter, no. 117. More recently, Bernhard Holter discussed the question at length in his *"Zum Dienst bestellt." Die Sicht des Priesteramtes bei Franz von Assisi und die Spuren seines Diakonats in den "Opuscula"* Werl 1992) 148–155. Schmucki thinks that Francis advises against the celebration of several masses because of the stipends attached to them which could lead to the "acquisition of earthly goods" (cf. LetOrder 14). Rotzetter on the other hand is of the opinion that, with the somewhat enigmatic motive: "for love of love" (*per amorem caritatis*), Francis appeals to the brother-priests to forego the celebration of private masses out of a spirit of brotherly love and a desire for unity: "The eucharist may not become a place of dispersion; rather it should be the place where the brothers are gathered together." Holter agrees with Rotzetter. In his view, the daily eucharist has to be seen in close conection with what Francis writes concerning the brother priests. According to Francis, they should not hold back anything for themselves so that they may be received totally by the Lord who gives himself totally to them (cf. LetOrder 29). Thus, in Holter's view, Francis is concerned here about their total union with Christ in his sacrificial surrender. This union is not a private matter, but should also bring the brothers together. It would be a contradiction in itself when every priest would want to achieve this union with Christ in the eucharist all alone. This union with Christ can only then take place in all its fullness when it is realized among the brothers in their relationship with one

on their own, for their own purposes. Apparently, Francis' request had become necessary with the increase of the number of priests within the brotherhood. Francis discerned very well the mentality that was growing among them and he feared—or perhaps he already knew from experience—that this mentality was going to do great harm to and lead to divisions within the brotherhood. And, what was even more disturbing,

---

another. Most probably Francis was guided here by his own personal experience. In the beginning, when there were very few priests among the brothers, the brothers were practically forced to take part in the eucharist together. Thus Francis had discovered the significance of the common eucharistic celebration for the life of the brotherhood. When he wrote his Letter to the Order, the number of priests had greatly increased. If all of them were to celebrate the eucharist privately, the common eucharistic celebration was to come under considerable threat and therewith the life of the brotherhood as such (153–154). While agreeing with Rotzetter's and Hlter's emphasis on the importance of the common eucharist for the brotherhood, I would like to go still one step further and ask what it was precisely in the behaviour of those brother-priests that threatened the life of the brotherhood. More than their physical absence at the common eucharist, it was the mentality. with which they acted. Now, reading Francis' request in its immediate context where the love of Jesus in the eucharist is described in terms of humility and total giving, to which the brothers should respond by humbling themselves and not holding on to anything, the conclusion seems inevitable: Francis sees the unnecessary private celebration of the eucharist as the expression of a mentality whereby the brother-priests wish to hold on to the priestly ministry which is not given to them for themselves but for the welfare of the community which is not served by their private celebration. They suffer thus from an appropriative mentality, just as the brothers who do not want to give up the office of preaching when asked to do so (RegNB 17:4). In this way, they contradict the love of Jesus who daily gives himself totally in the eucharist, and deprive, in fact, the eucharist from its possibility to effectively challenge them as lesser brothers. For it is their mission as lesser brothers to commit themselves, out of love for Jesus' love in the eucharist, to making Jesus' humility and Jesus total self-giving the basis for a new world, symbolized and already realized in the eucharist. Along a somewhat different route, we reach thus the same conclusion as David Flood who writes: "[In his letter to the Order, Francis] handled several questions raised by the presence of priests in the Order. After addressing all friars and pleading for reverence to the blessed sacrament, Francis spoke directly to the ordained brothers. They should not celebrate mass for earthly advantage or esteem (14). They should not pursue any worldly interest with the eucharist (25). Francis corrected the clerical demeanor whereby an ordained brother profited socially by his capacity to function as a priest. He described the fault specifically as one of social relations. Francis addressed a group in the Order in the interest of the movement's ethos,

it made the brother-priests forget their original calling as lesser brothers. More concerned about their identities as priests than about their identities as brothers, they were less open to the challenge which the eucharist as sacrament of God's humility posed to them. For the eucharist challenged all the brothers, whether cleric or lay, to continue Jesus' lifegiving mission by building a society which is not based on possessions, on proudly holding on to things which they consider their own, whereas in fact they belong to God, but where humility becomes the new organising principle, that is, the redeeming, liberating humility which, in light of Jesus' incarnation and of his daily coming down to us in the eucharist, can be defined as an act of solidarity, through which especially the victims of the sinful social structures are exalted and set free to become part of a new world, symbolized and already realized in the eucharist, and to join in a table-fellowship where all without distinction have their rightful place at the table of the Lord and can equally share in the goods of God's creation.[91]

Whereas in the Earlier Rule 17:5 Francis sees humility and the non-appropriation of the good which God works out in the brothers as their concrete answer to "the love which God is," he makes a somewhat wider application of this expression at the end of both versions of his Letter to the Faihtful. In the First Letter to the Faithful we read: "In the love which God is, we beg all those whom this letter reaches, with divine love kindly to receive these fragrant words of our Lord Jesus Christ written above" (2:19). This text is somewhat enlarged in the Second

---

not individual clerics in the interest of their private virtue. He told them not to match the public expectation extended to priests. He warned them off from playing the clerical role... In the letter's next development, Francis asked that one mass be celebrated though several brother priests reside together (30–33). Within the movement, he wanted the ordained friars to subordinate their identities as priests to their identities as brothers. He did not want them to function as priests when unnecessary. Very clearly, Francis contended with clerics who thought of themselves as clerics to the detriment of the brotherhood." The Domestication of the Franciscan Movement, *FranzStudien* 60 (1978) 321.

[91] For the eucharist as sacrament of God's humility and its challenge to the brothers, see our commentary on the virtue of humility, under II C e. See also my article: Eucharist and Priesthood according to Francis, with special Reference to his First Admonition, *FrancDigest* 7,2 (December 1997) 13–27.

Letter to the Faithful[92] where it becomes a much stronger, even emotional personal appeal on Francis' behalf: "I, Brother Francis, your lesser servant, ask and implore you in the love which God is and with the desire to kiss your feet, to receive these words and others of our Lord Jesus Christ with humility and love and to work them out and observe them" (87). Whatever Francis has written, are thus not his own words, but Jesus'. Francis is only a channel in God's hand. He passes on to the readers what he himself has received: the words that the Lord, and no one else, spoke and continues to speak to him in the gospel. But he could only receive these words and hear what the Lord was saying to him after he had left Assisi and had found a new place among the poor and the lepers.[93] And he begs his readers to do the same: to open themselves for God and to receive Jesus' words "with humility and love." Indeed, this is the only way to truly hear and receive the words of Jesus, for as long as people are proud about their own achievements, which are not really theirs, and concerned about their own interests, instead of the Lord's, they are simply not in a position to hear and receive the Lord's words and be challenged by them to live a life according to the gospel. The Lord's revelation passes them by, as they do not allow it to enter their hearts and make its home there. However, those who receive the words of the Lord will, with that same humility and love, be eager to put them into practice and make them the leaven of a new society.

Francis uses here the word *operari*, "to work" (87). This leads us back to the beautiful passage in the same letter which we quoted earlier, about

[92] Or is the so-called first version, contained in codex 225 of the Bibliotheca Guarnacci in Volterra, to be seen rather as a series of excerpts from the so-called second version, as Flood thinks? Flood's main argument is that the Volterra manuscript "contains a passage which betrays an incomplete transposition of its source. In that passage, the text describes an individual's death without having first introduced the individual... The complete text explains what happened" (The Commonitorium I, Introduction, *Haversack* 3, 1 (1979) 22–23). See also L. Lemmens in: *Opuscula Sancti Patris Francisci Assisiensis*, Quaracchi 1941, 182, note 1.

[93] Something similar happened to Francis when he stayed among the Saracens. This new place and the learning process he went through while being in their midst, made it possible for him to feel himself personally addressed by Jesus' words with which he chose to open RegNB 16: "Behold, I am sending you as sheep in the midst of wolves." In these words he recognised himself and his mission of peace whereas he failed to do so in a more explicit missionary text like: "Go, therefore, teach all nations..." with its heavy emphasis on teaching and preaching. See my *Francis and Islam*, 61–65.

the *sancta operatio*: the liberating, transforming activity in the Spirit of the Lord through which men and women who carry Jesus in their heart and body through love *(amorem)* like mothers give birth to Jesus again, give him a new existence in history (53). This passage starts with the admonition: "We must not be wise and prudent according to the flesh: rather, we must be simple, humble, and pure... We must never desire to be over others; rather we must be servants and subject to every human creature for God's sake" (45 and 47). And although there are many other words in his Letter about the love of God, about the sacrament of penance and the eucharist, about fasting, I would not be surprised if in asking the brothers to put the Lord's words into practice Francis had this passage especially in mind, for it forms the heart of the letter together with the acclamation to the Father and to the Son and Brother (54–56), which ends with the Son praying to the Father to bless and sanctify the brothers that they may be holy in being one as we are (57–60). Apparently, when writing his Letter, Francis is deeply concerned about the unity of the brotherhood which is in jeopardy because there are brothers who are going back on what they have promised the Lord. They follow the wisdom and prudence of the world; they desire to be over others. It is clear which brothers are meant here. It is to them that Francis addresses his urgent request "in the love which God is," that they may again receive the words of Jesus and do them with humility and love, thus bringing Jesus to life again in their own world. In this sense the request of the Second Letter to the Faithful, although more generally formulated, comes close to that of the Earlier Rule 17:5–7, where the word *operatio* is also mentioned, albeit that is here considered to be absent in those who are under the influence of the flesh (11).

From the various texts in which Francis motivates his often urgent request to the brothers with the expression "in the love which God is," it is clear that he gives his own personal interpretation of the way in which the brothers have to make concrete their answer to the love of God. As he is deeply impressed by the love of God as revealed to us in the love of the poor and humble Jesus, Francis emphasizes that the brothers must love God with their whole person, mind, heart and body, by being humble and by not appropriating the good that God works through them but rendering it back to God from whom all good comes. Basically it comes to this—the brothers must love God by walking in the footsteps of Jesus in poverty and humility. So they are to continue Jesus' mission, entrusted to Him by his Father, who "through [his] holy love with which [He] loved us *(per sanctam dilectionem, qua dilexisti nos)...* willed to redeem us captives through [Jesus'] cross and blood and death" (RegNB 23:3). The love which God is invites the brothers thus to join Jesus in his redeeming, liberating love which he lived in a life of poverty and humility in view of setting us free from our captivity and so restoring the Father's original plan for humankind: paradise, where God "placed" us and where we therefore belong, where we have our true home (1).

The love of God as revealed in the life of Jesus is also Francis' norm for the love of enemies. The love of enemies figures rather prominently in Francis' writings. At least five times he refers to Jesus' word about the love of enemies in Mt 5:44: RegNB 22:1; RegB 10:10; Adm 3:8; 14:4; the Second Letter to the Faithful 38. If we presume—rightfully, I think!—that Francis' writings always have some relation with his life experiences, the frequent quotation of this text points to the fact that, although Francis and his brothers wished to bring to all people Jesus' greeting of peace (RegNB 14:2; RegB 3:13; Test 23), they must have made quite a number of enemies when going about through the world on their peace mission. Interesting here is the story which can be found in 3 Comp 37: "The people they met were extremely surprised because in dress and manner of life they were so different from all others, and appeared almost like men of the woods. Whenever they came to a town or village or castle or house, they spoke the words of peace, comforting all, and exhorting men and women to love and fear the Creator of heaven and earth, and to observe his commands. Some people listened gladly; but others only mocked them as fools and humbugs, and refused them admission into their houses for fear they might be thieves and make off with something. Thus in many places they suffered innumerable trials and insults, and, finding no hospitality, they were driven to take shelter under the porticoes of the churches or houses" (see also AnPer 19). And in the Legend of Perugia 67 we read: "In the early days of the Order, when blessed Francis was travelling about in the company of a brother who was one of the first twelve, the latter greeted men and women on the roads and in the fields by saying to them: 'May the Lord give you peace!' The people were completely astonished for they had never heard any other religious greet them that way. Moreover, a few men asked in an offensive tone of voice: 'What is the meaning of that kind of greeting?' The brother was ashamed and said to blessed Francis: 'Brother, allow me to use a different greeting.'"

Confronted with such a situation, the brothers should not try to escape from their enemies. On the contrary, following the example of Jesus, who "called his betrayer 'friend' and freely gave himself up to those who crucified him," the brothers must consider friends "all those who unjustly inflict upon [them] trials and anxieties, shame and injuries, suffering and torments, martyrdom and death" (RegNB 22:2–3); and they must submit themselves to them in obedience "so that they may do with [them] whatever they want inasmuch as it has been given to them from above by the Lord (SalVirt 18). Briefly, the brothers must imitate Jesus in his love and obedience, especially at times of trial and persecution. They must "remember that they gave themselves and abandoned their bodies to the Lord Jesus Christ. And for love of him, they must expose themselves *(se exponere)*, making themselves vulnerable to their enemies, both visible and invisible, because the Lord says: Whoever loves his life for my sake will save it in eternal life" (RegNB 16:10–11). How should the brothers do this? How should they love their enemies and persecutors?

Enlightening in this context is the ninth Admonition where Francis connects the love for one's enemies explicitly with the love of God. After referring to the word of the Lord in Mt 5:44, Francis continues: "That person truly loves his enemy, who is does not grieve over the injury which the other does to him, but, out of love of God, burns *(uritur propter amorem Dei)* [with pain and sorrow] at the sin of the other's soul" (2–3). What is really important is not the injury which a person receives but the sin which the other committed against God. For by injuring his neighbour, his brother, the other person has violated the love of God for humankind as shown in Jesus and frustrated God's plan for a redeemed, a liberated world in which all people live together as brothers and sisters. It is clear then that "out of love of God" and of God's plans, the injured brother is first and foremost to be concerned about the defeat of God's plans through the other's sin and to feel a "burning" pain and sorrow on account of this.

It is also clear that the only way left to him to undo this defeat does not consist in trying to get his right by whatever means possible (cf. RegNB 14:4–6). For such an action divides the injured party and the sinner instead of bringing them together as brothers. Rather, "out of love of God," the injured brother is "to show [the sinner] love by his deeds" (4). He is not to treat him as an enemy but to be good and merciful and loving to him as a brother. Francis confirms this way of behaviour once more in a moving passage in his Letter to a Minister: "there should not be any brother in the world who has sinned, however much he may have possibly sinned, who, after he has looked into your eyes, would go away without having received your mercy, if he is looking for mercy... And if he should sin thereafter a thousand times before your very eyes, love him more than me so that you may draw him back to the Lord" (9–11). Such mercy toward sinners and love of enemies, Miccoli observes, are "based on the invitation to return to a logic which is the complete reversal, totally at odds with that which dominates ordinary relationships among people."[94]

Here we touch on Francis' way of dealing with evil and of overcoming or "confounding" it through "virtue" (SalVirt 8). Francis briefly summarizes this way of action in the very last admonition he gives at the original end of the *Regula non bullata*, after he has admonished his brothers to return all good things to God: "And when we see or hear [someone] speak or do evil *(malum dicere vel facere)*, or blaspheme God, let us speak well and do well *(bene dicamus et bene faciamus)* and praise God who is blessed forever" (17:19). Francis does not want his brothers to repay evil with evil, violence with violence. He wishes them to proceed in a non-violent, peaceful and understanding way, appealing to the good that lives in every person through their goodness, their humble, loving service towards them. We find an illustration of this in the delightful story about the conversion of the robbers in the Legend of Perugia 90. The brothers address the robbers from the very beginning as their "brother robbers" and treating them as such by "bringing them some good bread and some good wine," and in addition to them the next day "some eggs and cheese," while at the same time proposing the words of the Lord to them." In the end, "the Lord in his goodness will inspire the robbers to be converted because of the humility and charity that [the brothers] have shown them."

"For the love of Jesus exposing themselves to their enemies," "for the love of God showing their love in deeds to those who injure them": these words clearly confirm once again that the love which God is and which has been revealed to us in the love of the poor and humble Jesus, giving his life, his body for our liberation, constitutes for Francis and his brothers the most important motive for their love of enemies. And as

[94] Miccoli 145.

with Jesus' love, so also the love of the brothers for their enemies which becomes concrete and visible in their humble, loving service is directed towards liberating humankind from the enmity in which it is held captive and inaugurating a world in which God's original plan is fulfilled and past enemies live together in brotherly peace in accordance with God's logic. And since the imitation of Jesus' love urges them, the brothers cannot refuse: just like Jesus, they must remain faithful to their liberating mission, never mind the consequences this may entail for them. And even if the enemies are not converted through their humility and love, but turn against them and persecute them, the brothers need not be afraid to expose themselves to them for love of Jesus. For the Lord says: Whoever loses his life for my sake will save it in eternal life (cf. RegNB 16:11).

With Your Sister, holy Obedience (v. 3)

Of the six foundational virtues of the brotherhood mentioned in *The Salutation of the Virtues*, obedience is the virtue which occurs most frequently in Francis' other writings. In fact, obedience occurs 42 times, which is more often than poverty (13 times) and humility (15 times) together.[95] In *The Salutation of the Virtues* obedience occupies a special place: in verses 15–18 Francis breaks through the well-balanced structure of *The Salutation of the Virtues* to pay attention to certain problems of obedience that had arisen within the brotherhood.[96] As it is the only virtue treated in this way, it is evident that the virtue of obedience was of more than ordinary importance to Francis, who not only spoke very frequently about obedience but apparently went out of his way to save and protect this virtue when its place in the brotherhood was being threatened.

Holy Obedience is introduced as the sister of Lady Charity. The link between these two virtues is affirmed in two other important texts on obedience: the Earlier Rule 5:14–17 and Admonitions 3. In the Earlier Rule 5:14, which belongs to the brotherhood statute in which the relationships within the brotherhood are regulated,[97] we read: "through the

[95] For the precise figures, see above II, note 15.

[96] See our commentary on these verses in chapter V.

[97] See A. Rotzetter, *Die Funktion der franziskanischen Bewegung in der Kirche*, Schwyz 1977, 130–140.

love of the Spirit (*per caritatem spiritus*), the brothers should willingly serve and obey one another."[98] And Admonitions 3:6 speaks about: "loving obedience" (*caritativa obedientia*). The link which Francis makes in these texts between love and obedience points to a basic difference between the traditional and the Franciscan understanding of obedience.[99] In the monastic tradition, obedience is connected with humility, of which it constitutes the first degree.[100] This has everything to do with the fact that in monasteries obedience refers only to the relationship between the individual subject and his superior, his abbot, or, even where the rule of Benedict speaks about "mutual obedience," to the relationship between an inferior and his elder.[101] Monastic obedience, then, is the act of the subject—the inferior—by which he surrenders himself and his will into the hands of the superior. It presupposes a hierarchical order where humility represents the obvious attitude of the subject, the inferior, towards the superior, and as such it fits very well within the social context of the dominant feudal culture.

It is also clear that within such a relationship there can be no question of a brotherhood with its basic characteristic of equality: subjects never become brothers, they will always remain subjects. Francis, on the other hand, has left this feudal world and its hierarchical authority structures behind to form a brotherhood together with the brothers which the Lord, and not the cultural model of his time, gave him (Test 14). In this brotherhood, "all the brothers are not to have power or domination, least of all among themselves. For, as the Lord says in the gospel: The rulers of the peoples lord it over them and those who are the greater exercise power over them (Mt 20:25). It shall not be so among the brothers" (RegNB 5:10). This implies that, when Francis in the next verses speaks about obedience as regulating the relations among the brothers, he does not mean the traditional obedience as it fits within the feudal

[98] In his *The Birth of a Movement*, Chicago 1975, D. Flood translates incorrectly, I think: "the brothers should serve and obey one another through the love of willing spirit."

[99] I rely here on Th. Desbonnets, *De l'intuition à l'institution*, Paris 1983, 61-62.

[100] See *Regula S. Benedicti* 5:1. For the Franciscan understanding of humility, see above, where it is clear that humility too is taken out of the feudal, hierarchical context in which it is seen as a one-way relationship of the subject who has humbly to submit himself to the superior, and transformed into a two-way, mutual relationship between brothers.

[101] Desbonnets 71.

authority structure, but intends a new understanding of obedience as an attitude of loving service among brothers.[102] The brothers are called by the love of the Spirit and in obedience to the strivings of that same Spirit to serve and obey one another. It is thus that they restore God's lordship as it was in the beginning.[103] Within this evangelical or even paradisiacal understanding of obedience, there is no place for abbots, priors or superiors (RegNB 6:3), but only for brothers, some of whom are called in a special way to minister to the needs not of their subjects but of the other brothers (RegNB 5:11).[104]

The central place of the brotherhood in Francis' understanding of obedience is evident from various expressions Francis uses. In the Earlier Rule 2:9, he speaks about a novice who may be received into obedience

[102] 1. We differ here from Reijsbergen who writes: "Medieval people will almost immediately have associated the term obedience with their fixed place within the social structure... Also in the world of the clergy, obedience was part of the foundation of the correct way of life. Besides on the *stabilitas loci*, Benedict had based his instructions on this virtue. It was precisely in the practice of obedience, that people abandoned their own will and could exercise the virtues of humility and poverty. Francis greatly appreciated this Benedictine heritage. Although he belonged to the new laymovement of poverty and apostolic preaching, he distinguished himself by joining his clear insight in the meaning of a truly evangelical life with the attainments of the Christian tradition" (145–146). See also Miccoli who stresses the originality of Francis' project of life: "Francis in effect lived a religious experience which, as far as its original core is concerned, had no link or reference to the ecclesiastical tradition of his time. Even his contemporaries and those after recognized this more or less obscurely... when they described him as the 'new man' *(novus homo)*" (131).

[103] The idea of God's lordship is very much stressed by Verhey: "The real, most profound meaning of obedience is that human beings overcome their egocentredness and self-willedness. which are hostile to God, and that they acknowledge God as Lord over their life.. The social function of obedience is not in the first place to bring order in the relations within the community, but rather to establish God's lordship among the people in so far as God manifests his will through human authority" (130). It is a pity that Verhey explains this very valuable insight within the context of the traditional relationship between authority and subject and has no eye for the new, more evangelical context of obedience within the brotherhood where obedience is mutual service and so restores God's original plan with humankind in which, under God's lordship, people live together in peace and harmony, no one lording it over the other.

[104] See J. Hoeberichts, Ministry to the Friars in the Writings of Francis and the Early Biographers, *FIA Contact* 5,4 (1984) 22–31.

(*recipiatur ad obedientiam*) at the end of his year of probation; and in the Earlier Rule 5:16–17 he observes that the brothers who faithfully observe what they have promised the Lord should know (*sciant*) that they abide in true obedience (*in vera obedientia stare*), while those brothers who turn away from the commands of the Lord are wandering outside obedience (*extra obedientiam evagaverint*). Obedience is here presented as a space, as a kind of home for the brothers who do not own a home or a place and who as pilgrims and strangers in this world serve the Lord. The limits of this space are the limits of the brotherhood. The brotherhood is therefore the place where obedience receives its shape: brother serving brother, brother listening (*ob-audire*) to brother, through the love of the Spirit, which invites the one to willingly serve and obey the other in and through whom the Spirit speaks.[105] "And this," Francis adds, "is the true and holy obedience of our Lord Jesus Christ" (RegNB 5:15).

Francis interprets the obedience of Jesus to his most holy Father thus within the context of loving service and of listening. Inspired by the Holy Spirit of love, Jesus came to serve his fellow human beings in their needs rather than to be served by them; he came to listen to them and their concerns rather than to lord it over them (RegNB 4:6; 5:10–12). In this loving, listening obedience of service unto the very end, Jesus left all his followers an example how to walk in his footsteps and so cooperate with him in realising God's plan for the redemption of the world (2 LetFaith 13).[106] In other words, "placing his will in the will of his Father" (ibid. 10), ready to give even his life, so that "he might not lose the obedience of the most holy Father" (LetOrder 46), Jesus showed his followers how they could move away from that first disobedience and its fatal consequences for humankind and towards life as God had wanted it from the beginning. People would then no longer appropriate to themselves their will and claim themselves to be lord over the good that belongs to God (Adm 2:3) to the exclusion of others and so cause death to each other and to the world; rather, through their obedience they would restore God's original lordship, serving and obeying each other in love, thus putting an end to sin and death.

[105] See H. Sevenhoven, How obedience turns into love, *FrancDigest* 7,2 (December 1997) 1–11, here 3–5. Also A. Rotzetter, *Franz von Assisi. Ein Anfang und was davon bleibt*, Zürich 1981, no. 48.

[106] See G.P. Freeman, The Word of the Father, *FrancDigest* 9,1 (March 1999) 19–27, here 24–26.

This true and holy obedience after the example of Jesus' redemptive obedience can be realized in various ways, depending on the way in which the Spirit of the Lord inspires a brother and invites another to listen to what the Spirit says through him. Thus the minister is not to contradict (*non contradicat*) the Lord when a brother, inspired by the Spirit, wishes to do what the Lord tells him to do (*dicit Dominus*), and to go among the Saracens. On the contrary, the minister has to respect this divine inspiration, to acknowledge God's Lordship, and allow the brother to go, rather than put himself in the place of the Lord and try to dissuade his brother and to hold him back, even for reasons of official pastoral policy, approved by the ecclesiastical authorities. And if the minister does not allow him, he shall be bound to give an account to the Lord (RegNB 16:1–4).[107]

Another example of this obedience to the divine inspiration can be found in the short, beautiful letter of Francis to brother Leo, where he speaks to him as a mother to her son. Summarizing all that brother Leo and he have spoken about on the way, Francis advises him in the following manner: "In whatever way it seems best to you to please the Lord God and to follow his footprints and his poverty, do this with the blessing of God and my obedience" (3). Francis is thus more than ready to agree with whatever brother Leo, after careful reflection, has come to see as the will of God for him. He fully respects brother Leo's decision, because he believes it to be taken under the guidance of the Spirit of the Lord, to he, Francis, cannot but obey.[108]

This obedience to the Spirit working in the heart of a brother has its negative counterpart in that Francis forbids his brothers to obey their brother-ministers in those situations where the Spirit is clearly absent. Thus Francis writes that a brother "is not bound to obey" when his minister, apparently not guided by the Spirit of the Lord but rather blinded by the spirit of the flesh, "commands any of the brothers something that is contrary to our life or against his conscience" (RegNB 5:2; cf. 4:3; 8:9; RegB 10:3; 2 LetFaith 41). For if this minister were truly guided by the Lord's Spirit, he would be profoundly concerned about the right direc-

[107] See my study: *Francis and Islam*, 48–49; 67–69.

[108] See L. Lehmann, The Man Francis in the Light of his Letters, *FrancDigest* 2,2 (June 1992) 53–57. For a new revised translation of this letter, see A. Bortoli Langeli, *Gli scritti da Francesco. L'autografia di un illiteratus* in: *Frate Francesco d'Assisi* (SISF 21), Spoleto 1994, 101–159.

tion of the life of the brotherhood (*rectitudo vitae* 4)—a life according to the form of the gospel which the Lord himself had revealed to Francis (Test 14)—and show great respect for the conscience of a brother, because it is there that the Spirit speaks to him. But as it is evident beyond any doubt that the command of this minister is not inspired by the Spirit, the brother need not obey. On the contrary, obedience to the Spirit demands from him in this situation that "reasonably and diligently considering the actions of [his] minister and servant," he admonishes him in the hope that he will "amend his way" (RegNB 5:3–4).

A brother can therefore never consider obedience as a way to escape from his own responsibility and to hide himself safely behind the decisions or commands of his minister. Nor for that matter can he find an excuse in official church policies, however convincing the arguments in their favour may sound. This is quite clear from the story in the Second Life of St. Francis 148, where Francis refuses to accept the argument of the Lord of Ostia that the brothers, "poor and men of charity," would make good bishops, by pointing out their calling: "Lord, my brothers are called *minores*... Their vocation teaches them to remain in a lowly station (*in plano*) and to follow the footsteps of the humble Christ." It is even more evident from a very strong passage in the Testament, where Francis explicitly forbids his brothers, in the name of obedience to the Spirit, "to seek letters from the Roman curia... under the pretext of preaching," in order thus to be able to devote themselves better, so they think, to this aspect of the pastoral policy of the church, or in an attempt to escape from "the persecution of their bodies" (25). Every brother remains always and everywhere responsible for the right direction of the life of the brotherhood. Always and everywhere he has to be attentive to the voice of the Spirit and in obedience to that same Spirit to decide about the way he and his brothers have to live the form of the gospel in the world, even if this would lead to persecution.

These observations about the obedience of the brothers to their ministers apply also to the obedience to the ecclesiastical authorities. This is clear from the admonition in the Earlier Rule 19, where Francis writes: "And we should accept all clerics and all religious as our lords in all that concerns the salvation of the soul and does not deviate from our religion," i.e. from the way of life of our religious community (3; cf. RegNB 4,3).[109] Obedience is never a blind obedience in the sense of

[109] The English translations of Flood and Armstrong translate *nostra religio* as "our

"Befehl ist Befehl," "command is command." The brothers always have the responsibility to discern whether something is indeed not against the way of life which, guided by divine inspiration, they have promised the Lord to follow. For it is this way of life which they have recognized as God's will for them and which they therefore have to observe faithfully above everything else for the salvation of their soul. This understanding of obedience is presupposed in the Testament of Siena, where Francis admonishes his brothers: "Let [the brothers] always be faithful and subject to the prelates and all clerics of Holy Mother Church" (5); thus we must add here: "in all that concerns the salvation of their soul and does not deviate from the way of life of our religious community."

The fact, mentioned above, that Francis and his brothers on several occasions explicitly add the clause: "in all that concerns the salvation of their soul and is not contrary to their life" (RegNB 4:3) or something similar, is a clear indication that they are well aware of the conflicts that, at times, arise between brothers who want to be obedient to the Spirit of the Lord, and their ministers or the ecclesiastical authorities who, for whatever reason, ask the brothers to act in a way that is not accordance with the life according to the gospel which the Lord had revealed to them (cf. Test 14). It is also clear from these additions that, whenever such conflicts occur, Francis wishes to protect and support the brother who wants to be faithful to the way of life which he entered upon under under divine inspiration (RegNB 2:1). This support, however, seems difficult to reconcile with a passage from the Testament where Francis writes: "And I firmly wish to obey the minister general of this fraternity and another guardian whom it might please him to give me. And I wish to be so captive in his hands that I cannot go anywhere or do anything beyond obedience and his will, for he is my lord" (27–28). It seems as if Francis here completely abdicates his own responsibility and leaves everything in the hands of his guardian, who can do with him as he wishes.

---

religion." The German and Dutch translations, on the other hand, translate "our order," as they also do in RegNB 2:10; 13:1; 20:1; RegB 2:12; 8:1; LetOrder 2.38.47, where Armstrong, too, no longer translates *religio* as "religion" but as "order." Flood is more consequent in that he translates *religio* everywhere as "religion," because Francis never spoke about his brotherhood as *ordo*, as an "order." However, in present English usage, religion only rarely refers to "a religious group or community." To avoid any confusion, I translate *religio* here as "religious community."

If this were indeed the case, Francis would go against his own understanding of obedience within the context of the brotherhood where the minister or the guardian does not have the last word to which the subject humbly has to submit, but the Spirit speaking in and through the brothers, individually and as a community. Hence within the brotherhood, the obedience to the Spirit is the final criterion by which the obedience to the minister or the guardian is to be judged. This implies, given the fact that the minister general and the guardian are also fallible human beings, that in certain situations a brother, Francis not excluded, may have to do something "beyond obedience and their will" in order to remain obedient to the Spirit, and so may have to go against the very wish Francis expressed in the Testament. Of course, it is possible to read the text of the Testament in the presupposition that normally the minister or guardian will only ask something that is in conformity with the *rectitudo vitae.* In such a case Francis would definitely wish to obey his minister or guardian, and be a captive in his hands, even if his request were very difficult to accomplish. But what about the "abnormal" situations which cannot *a priori* be excluded from happening in the brotherhood, as Francis very well knows and has even experienced personally? Why does he not add here the same clause he did before in several places of his rules? However one turns the passage of the Testament, there seems to be a serious discrepancy between Francis' wish expressed in his Testament and the advice he himself earlier gave to his brothers on various occasions. I will return to this problem later.[110]

A similar discrepancy occurs with regard to the stories about obedience in the Second Life of St. Francis 151–152, where, at least at the beginning of 152, the same or an even stronger impression is given that an obedient brother is to abdicate completely his own responsibility than in the Testament. There Celano tells us there how Francis describes "the truly obedient man under the figure of a dead body" and concludes: "a truly obedient man... does not ask why he is moved, he cares not where he is placed, he does not insist on being changed elsewhere. Raised to an office, he retains his accustomed humility; the more he is honored, the more unworthy does he consider himself." In the final paragraph, however, Celano somewhat corrects this impression where he says that Francis

[110] See below where I deal with the discrepancy between the Letter to a Minister and the *Regula bullata* on the one hand, and the testament on the other.

thought that "that obedience was the highest and was without anything of flesh and blood by which one goes by divine inspiration among the infidels, either for the sake of profit for one's neighbors or out of a desire for martyrdom." The highest obedience is thus free from all concern about power and status, about the success of one's preaching or how one can avoid persecution—things which flesh and blood are concerned about—and is present there where the divine inspiration becomes the dynamic force in the life of the brothers, encouraging them to remain faithful always to the original ideals, not counting the cost.[111]

Besides through their ministers or through the ecclesiastical authorities, the Spirit of the Lord can also speak to a brother and invite him to obedience in and through the needs of another brother. In that case, obedience is present when a brother listens to his brother who "confidently makes known his need to him," and then goes out of his way "so that he may find what his brother needs and minister it to him." And Francis continues: "And each one is to love and nourish his brother as a mother nourishes and loves her son, in everything for which God gives them grace" (RegNB 9:10–11). Just as Francis takes his relationship with Leo out of the feudal, monastic sphere of fatherly or abbatial authority and places it within a motherly context of nurture and love in his Letter to brother Leo, so he does here with the relationship between the brothers. Once again Francis makes it clear that he does not want the brothers to lord over each other; rather, he wishes them to love and nourish and serve one another, especially in their moments of need.

And whereas in the sphere of feudal, hierarchical authority the relationship between father and son is largely governed by laws and commands, the relationship between the brothers stands under God's grace, which invites the brothers to love and service and, in case of need, goes even beyond the limits imposed by the law.[112] For as Francis writes at the end of the passage in chapter 9: "Likewise also, in a time of manifest necessity all the brothers should take care of their needs as the Lord gives them grace, for necessity knows no law" (16).[113] There is thus a higher obedience than the obedience to law and authority: the obedi-

[111] See Rotzetter, no. 46.

[112] A good survey of the difference between the Franciscan practice of authority and that in the surrounding society can be found in Flood, *Francis of Assisi and the Franciscan Movement* 120–126, under the title: Authority as Service.

[113] For this canonical axiom, see *Decretum Gratiani*, II, I, glossa ante c.40.

ence of the brother who, moved by God's grace, obeys God's voice which speaks to him in the needs of his brother and invites him to answer those needs through loving, nurturing service: a service where he does not feel himself bound or restricted by the limits of the law, but free to act in whatever way God graciously inspires him to respond to his brother's needs in the best possible way. Acting in this way under the inspiration of God's grace, this brother fulfills God's will because God does not want anyone to suffer need. Rather, God wants all people to sit at the table of creation, sharing all its goods which God meant to be enjoyed by all without exception.

A special place among the brothers is occupied by the brothers who are weak, either spiritually or physically, and hence are in need of special care: the brother who has sinned and the sick brother. As to the first, Francis writes: "And let all the brothers, both the ministers and servants as well as the others, beware not to become upset or angry at the sin or evil of another... but they should spiritually help the brother who has sinned as best they can" (RegNB 5:7–8). That is, they should help that brother to free himself from the power of the spirit of the flesh and bring himself again within the working sphere of the Spirit of the Lord. They should try to do so mainly by being merciful to them.

The Letter to a Minister has a beautiful passage in this regard: "...there should not be any brother in the world who has sinned, however much he may have possibly sinned, who after he looked into your eyes, would go away without having received your mercy, if he is looking for mercy. And if he were not to seek mercy, you should ask him if he wants mercy, And if he should sin thereafter a thousand times before your eyes, love him more than me so that you may draw him back to the Lord. Always be merciful to brothers such as these" (9–11), even if they behave so badly that they "want to lay hands on you" (2). Rather than considering them "an impediment" to the love of God, from which he needs to escape into a hermitage (4), or rather than "wishing that they be better Christians" (7) who would not trouble or lay hands on him, the minister should accept them as "a grace" of God (2), inviting him to love God by showing mercy to them, "because it is not the healthy who are in need of a physician, but those who are sick" (15; cf. Mt 9:12). And if the minister "desires that things be this way and not otherwise," i.e. if the minister acknowledges that God is graciously speaking to him through the need for mercy and forgiveness of the brother who sins, whether the latter recognizes this need or not, then Francis "knows full well" (*firmiter scio*), with that typical Franciscan knowledge, that the minister "by loving those who do these things to [him]" and not forcing them, performs an act of "true obedience to God and to [Francis himself]" (3–5), because he follows in the footsteps of Jesus, the truly merciful and compassionate One.[114]

True obedience to God, then, is not so much the observance of a clear-cut command, but listening to the spiritual need of the sinner and showing love and mercy to him as God has done and continues to do in Jesus, the divine physician, in the hope to heal him and "to draw him back to the Lord" (11). We touch here on Francis' evangelical approach to sin and evil, developed in *The Salutation of the Virtues*, to "confound" sin by practising the opposite virtue, to overcome evil by doing good (RegNB 17:19; Admonition 9:3–4).[115] In light of this, the severe, threatening texts like the Earlier Rule 13 and Testament 31–33 seem quite out of place with Francis' views and with the concrete proposals for a revision of the Rule which he makes in the second half of his Letter to a Minister and which can be found in the Later Rule 7 and 10:4–6. Such severe texts fit a feudal, authoritarian understanding of the relationship between superior and subject, but contrast sharply with the loving, merciful, more brotherly and even motherly approach of Francis expressed in the Letter to a Minister. Francis "knows full well" that this approach is "true obedience to the Lord God." Therefore, Francis once again confirms this approach in the Later Rule 10, where he completely reverses the commonly accepted feudal relationship between superior and subject, stating emphatically that the brothers should follow the opposite way: "The ministers on their part should receive these brothers [who cannot observe the Rule spiritually, because they have come again under the influence of the spirit of the flesh] with great kindness and love and should be so approachable that they can speak and deal with [the ministers] as masters with their servants; for this is the way it should be: The ministers shall be the servants of all the brothers" (4–6).

To explain this discrepancy between the Letter to a Minister and the *Regula bullata* on the one hand and the Testament on the other, I am inclined to agree with Flood who sees the passage in Testament 27–33

[114] See Lehmann 50–53.

[115] For a more extensive description of the meaning of the verb *confundere*, see my commentary on verse 8 in III B e.

either as an addition by others or—in case Francis actually used the words, which I personally consider less likely—as a regrettable lapse. He writes: "These are not the words of a dying man. Francis might well have uttered them on some occasion, or something similar to them, for they have a faint parallel in the Chapter Matter (Letter to the Entire Order, 44–46). They do not fit the moment of a testament, however. Nor do they fit the Testament's form. They are out of proportion, as an admonition with the other two admonitions (24; 25–26) [which] engage in sharp boundary maintenance [between the brotherhood and the surrounding world]... Moreover, they serve too well the cause of institutional restraint, where Francis declares his interest as fidelity to the life (34). Given the strange note struck by the long passage, we have to remember that we do not know how the Testament got put into words and passed around... Nor could Francis control what was published as his parting words once he had parted. He did take the precaution of telling people not to edit the text (35), which suggests a suspicion. Anyway, there is no proof for the authenticity of the text as it stands, and therefore any good reason for suspecting its parts has the validity of the reason. The third admonition should be stamped with a question mark."[116]

In his *Francis of Assisi and the Franciscan Movement*, Flood leaves open the possibility that the passage actually is not by Francis, but asks himself how to interpret the text in the presupposition that it really originated from Francis: "In his Testament (27–33), Francis speaks about unruly brothers. He has them hauled off to the cardinal protector. If he actually put the passage into his Testament (a strange, protracted outburst from a dying man), it is regrettable he did not first read the third case and the admonition in the set of rules [contained in RegNB 5:5–6;7–8]. For here he, and his brothers, handled the weakness of a brother much better than in the Testament."[117]

[116] 2. Flood, The Testament as Recall, *Haversack* vol. 11, 1 (October 1987) 18–19.

[117] Flood, *Francis of Assisi* 127. Freeman and Sevenhoven propose a different explanation in their Commentary on the Testament: "[Francis] knew the history of a variety of orders, which after a fervent beginning had in no time slipped off to the level of a respectable, insipid and lukewarm average. He saw the signs of this in his own order (sic!). He understood them all too well: the brotherhood had become a convenient opportunity for university students to live a pious and evangelical life and at the same time build up a good career; priests and learned men had come who thought the order offered a more effective way to continue pursuing their own glory as preachers and teachers (2 Cel 194–195)... The pope and the cardi-

After dealing extensively with the brother who was spiritually weak and sinned, I now turn my attention to the brother who is physically weak, the sick brother. With regard to him, Francis writes: "If, [on their missionary journeys], a brother falls ill, no matter where, the other brothers should not leave him behind unless one of the brothers, or more if need be, are assigned to serve him as they would wish to be served themselves" (RegNB 10:1). Whatever the nature or the importance of the mission they may have been on, these brothers have to see the sickness of their brother as a clear sign that the Lord wishes them to give up their mission in order to take care of their brother. What is even

---

nals were favourably disposed towards the order; they were only too ready to support the order by means of privileges, and they thought out loud about appointing brothers as bishops: this was the kind of people the church needed! (2 Cel 148)... But the question, which for [Francis] was literally of vital importance, was what all these developments had to do with his vocation, with the revelation the Lord had given to him. Why did this kind of people have to come to his order?... Why did poverty have to be replaced by presumption and fame?... Yet, this sketch of the situation does not sufficiently explain why he reacted so sharply, so sternly. He exaggerates, so much seems certain. Of course, there are other texts in which he writes sternly about obedience. But he never was so bitter, so absolute, and at the same time so impractical. Why does he exaggerate? Why does he—put in literary terms—use a hyperbole here? He had done that before. His words about the true joy are a striking example... He describes an extreme situation in order to make a point. He knows that, in order to be heard, you sometimes have to break through a thick layer of misunderstandings. And that is what he wants, as a true teacher, a true spiritual guide, who sometimes speaks softly and at other times tells an entertaining story, sometimes like an actor acts out what he means, and at other times—when the pupils are noisy—thumps with his shoe on the desk. What kind of resistance was it he wanted to break through? If we are not mistaken, yet another element plays a role here, apart from the growth of the brotherhood outlined above. Francis was already declared a saint even in his lifetime; he was a living legend. This is exactly why he was not heard anymore... People were out to venerate his habit and his almost-dead body more eagerly than to listen to his message. It was nice for the order to have such a founder, but his remarks had no longer much effect... Francis sees this situation, on the one hand, as a challenge to remain humble and unassuming... On the other hand, he does want his message to be heard. That is why he exaggerates. That is why he, as it were, shouts it out. In the tension... between his brothers" lukewarmness and his desire for an unsoiled order, he chooses a renewed emphasis on his original charism with a forcefulness and a severity which, after so many centuries, come across as oppressive, but which he needs in order to be heard." The Legacy of a Poor Man IV, *FrancDigest*

more striking, is that when it is a case of a sick brother in need, Francis is ready to dispense with the prohibition to accept coins or money which is so basic to the way of life in poverty which the brothers have chosen under divine inspiration in order not to become entangled in the unjust structures of the society of their days. For he writes: "None of the brothers, wherever he may be or wherever he goes, should in any way carry, receive, or have received [by another] either money or coins, whether for clothes or books or payment for any kind of work—indeed, for no reason—unless it is for the evident necessity of the sick brothers" (RegNB 8:3). A little further Francis makes a similar exception in the case of "evident necessity of the lepers" (ibid. 8–10).

Apparently, the Spirit speaks louder and clearer in and through the immediate needs of the sick brothers than through the need, real but not felt so directly or personally, to change the sinful economic system that divides people into rich and poor, powerful and powerless, free and exploited, and leaves so many victims along the road. Or, formulated in a different way, there exists apparently a higher form of obedience than obeying certain basic prescriptions of the rule and the ideals expressed therein as regards a society that is more in accordance with God's plans. This implies that the immediate needs of the sick brothers or the lepers have preference over the law; in fact, needs not only know no law, they even go beyond ideals.[118] For if laws and ideals do not take the manifest

4,2 (December 1994) 78–83. This explanation, however, seems to contradict their own statement at the beginning of their commentary where they write that Francis resigned as minister general because "he came to realize that the order needed a strong and powerful leadership which could punish abuses and take the organization into a vigorous hand. This kind of leadership did not appeal to him. It was not in keeping with his own choice: to follow the humility of Jesus. His leadership had to be of a different nature: out of love for his brothers—whether they lived a good or a bad life—he wanted to live an exemplary life." The Legacy of a Poor Man I, *FrancDigest* 3,1 (June 1993) 3.

[118] "The fact that [the brothers] did use money to alleviate serious sickness reveals their acquaintance with its possibilities... they used it without believing in it, and they used it because people went before rules." Flood 27. "Francis and his brothers refused to handle a means [i.e. money] whereby Assisi negotiated the exclusion [of those living in almshouses]... All the same, they knew well the practical services of money, and if there was no other way to relieve lepers in dire need, then they used money. They put people over politics. In their freedom, they could think money against Assisi." Flood, *Work for Everyone* 38.

needs of people into consideration, they lose touch with reality and become ideological tools in the hands of intolerant and intransigent people ready to force their views on others and to sacrifice even innocent people for the realization of their views. All this is far from Francis' mind for, as we indicated already, he wants to convince people and to draw them to his ideals by his way of life, his deeds. In this context he is more than ready to suffer himself, even to give his own life for his ideals; he is not ready, however, to sacrifice others.

The picture of obedience that emerges from the various passages of the *Regula non bullata* I have discussed extensively within the broader context of Francis' other writings is one of brothers who, in the love of the Spirit who inspires them and binds them together as brothers (cf. RegNB 2:1; Test 14), listen to each other's needs, spiritual and material, and serve one another with love and affection as brothers or, as if this is not yet enough to make the difference with the feudal, monastic system clear, as mother and son. This description of the loving relationship of service and obedience between brothers finds its climax in the image of the brothers washing one another's feet (RegNB 6:4), an image that is then especially applied to the office of the minister for it is the minister who, as his name indicates, embodies in a special way the ideals of humble service within the brotherhood (cf. Adm 4:2–3). Just as Jesus, the Son of God and God's servant, washed the feet of his disciples, so the brothers, led by their ministers, renounce all power that they might have over their other brothers on account of office, knowledge or any other personal quality, and place themselves humbly at their service, washing one another's feet. And indeed, when they do this, when "through the love of the Spirit [the brothers] voluntarily serve and obey one another, [they practice] the true and holy obedience of our Lord Jesus Christ" (RegNB 5:14–15). Thus, in Francis' view, love and obedience belong inseparably together: Lady holy Charity and her sister holy Obedience.

The other text which joins Lady Charity and her sister Obedience is, as I mentioned already, to be found in the Third Admonition where Francis speaks about "loving obedience" (*caritativa obedientia*). According to Desbonnets, this admonition, entirely devoted to obedience, represents a stage in the development of the brotherhood from a small group into a numerous entity where the problems about obedience increased considerably.[119] However, its present text clearly shows the character of a

[119] See Desbonnets 62–67.

reportatio: a text written down by an auditor on the basis of notes taken during a lecture or conference. While it can therefore be admitted that the ideas expressed in the text reflect those that were expressed by Francis, it is at the same time quite certain that the vocabulary used is not that of Francis![120] For the term *praelatus* is used five times in the text where one would expect to find the Franciscan term *minister*; moreover, it is only here that this non-Franciscan term is found. The same can be said about the corresponding term *subditus*, which has quite a different meaning in the RegNb and the Testament, and in the non-Franciscan meaning which it has here, namely of a brother being *subditus* to his brother minister which is a double *contradictio in terminis*, has only once found its way into the Later Rule 10:2.[121]

[120] Desbonnets differs here, rightly I think, from Armstrong-Brady who in a footnote to their translation of the Third Admonition write: "The Latin word *praelatus* is used frequently by Saint Francis in speaking of the friar who is a 'superior.' It should be noted that nowhere is the word 'superior' used to describe a position of responsibility or authority; 'minister' and 'servant' are used in general terms to describe this office." R. Armstrong and I. Brady, *Francis and Clare. The Complete Works*, New York 1982, 28, note 5. Armstrong-Brady's remark may be true of the biographical tradition; it is certainly not true of Francis' writings where *praelatus* occurs only in the Third Admonition which, as already noticed, is a *reportatio*. As in other cases, e.g. brotherhood-order, there exists here a discrepancy in terminology to which Armstrong-Brady and others pay far too little attention, especially since it is very revealing as regards the ideology of the biographies. In this connection, it is interesting to quote here an observation Armstrong made on another occasion: "While the expression *[praelatus]* can readily be found in the biographical tradition, it is curious that it does not appear more frequently in Francis' descriptions of the brother chosen to minister to the fraternity, especially in the *Later Rule* in which at least one curial official, Hugolino, had a role." R. Armstrong, Prophetic Implications of the "Admonitions," *Laurentianum* 26 (1986) 396–464, here 409. Unfortunately, Armstrong does not draw any further conclusion as to the meaning of this curious phenomenon. Could it be that, although under pressure, Francis succeeded in holding on to his original view on the place and role of leaders as ministers and servants of the brotherhood, whereas soon after his death his brothers were already prepared to adapt themselves to the ideas and language of the dominant ecclesiatical culture in which there only exist prelates or superiors and subjects within a religious order?

[121] See my *Francis and Islam*, 52–53; 75–86. While we may be happy that the non-Franciscan, juridical meaning of *subditus* occurs only once in RegB, notwithstanding the curial influence, it remains unfortunate that *subditus* in its Franciscan meaning has completely disappeared from RegB. See further also my commentary on humility under e, and especially note 70..

Further, a large part of the text, with the exception of verses 6–9, could very well have been taken from a treatise on obedience by a monk or canon regular.[122] In this context Regis Armstrong quotes Ignatius Brady, who proposes that "these admonitions (i.e. 3 and 4, where the term *praelatio* is used) were written under the influence of the Cistercian Cardinal Rainerio Cappocci who was present at the Pentecost Chapter of 1219 and spoke at the saint's canonization in 1228."[123] Armstrong then continues: "Indeed, we can read a collection of letters of Innocent III and Honorius III to this monk in which his role as a roving papal emissary responsible for the education of religious is evident. This being the case, it is plausible that the term *praelatus*, which according to Niermayer's *A Medieval Latin French-English Dictionary* can be more commonly found among the Cistercians of this period of history, entered Francis' [sic!] vocabulary in the presence of Capocci. Such an interpretation is quite reasonable when we consider that during the chapters of 1219 and 1221 the roles of the ministers—provincial, custodian, and guardian—were being defined as the fourth, fifth and sixth chapters of the *Earlier Rule* suggest."[124] On this basis, we may therefore conclude that the present Third Admonition is a *reportatio* in which into a most probably Cistercian text, expressing certain commonly accepted ideas about religious, monastic obedience, some typical Franciscan view, contained in vv. 6–9, is inserted. That these verses are inserted indeed, is clear from the fact that v. 10 refers explicitly to the problem mentioned in v.5.

The admonition has a clear structure: it opens with two texts from the gospel quoted in the present tense as if Jesus addresses them to the brothers here and now (1–2). Then follow three particular problems which can arise within a relationship of obedience. Originally referring to the monastic relationship between prelate and subject, they have to be read here within the context of the brotherhood where these problems take on a special colour. With each of the three problems, a particular type of obedience is connected: *true* obedience (3–4); *loving* obedience (5–6); *perfect* obedience (7–9). These three types are not three stages in the development of an obedient attitude, as the problems to which they refer need not happen in this particular sequence, nor does the individ-

[122] See Sevenhoven 229–230.

[123] Jordan 16; 1 Cel 125.

[124] Armstrong 409–410.

ual brother necessarily meet all three problems in his life. They do, however, present an ascending order of seriousness both as regards the nature of the problem involved and the difficulty in solving it correctly. The admonition concludes with a very severe warning for those who, instead of being obedient, "return to the excrement of their own will" (10–11).[125]

The two opening verses indicate that obedience has its foundation in the gospel words of Jesus about the conditions of discipleship. At first glance these words do not seem to be the most appropriate for an introduction to an admonition on obedience. However, looking at them in light of the Second Admonition, they fit very well.[126] The central idea of the Second Admonition is that Adam's sin, his disobedience in eating of the tree of the knowledge of good, is continued when anyone "appropriates to himself his will and thus exalts himself over the good things which the Lord says and does in him" (3). In other words, the original sin is renewed every time someone refuses to accept the lordship of God who is the source of all good and to whom all good belongs, and rather wants himself to be lord. As a consequence of this act of disobedience, "it is necessary that he bear the punishment," i.e. death (5). This means that a human person can only find life if he acknowledges again the Lordship of God by renouncing all that he possesses (1), i.e. if he "loses his body [and] offers himself totally to obedience" (3) to God, after the example of Jesus who "placed his will in the will of his Father" and offered himself, his body, his life "as a sacrifice and oblation on the altar of the cross... for our sins" (2 LetFaith 10–12), for "he did not want to lose the obedience of his most holy Father" (LetOrder 46). Thus he "left us an example that we should follow in his footprints... and be saved through him" (2 LetFaith 13–14), find life for ourselves and others through following his example of obedience, and so undo the consequences of our disobedience.

Obedience then is the basic attitude of the human creature before God, the Creator. Confronted with God, the giver and owner of all good, it is the duty of all humans not to appropriate anything to themselves as if they were lord; rather, they must renounce all their possessions, all that

[125] See Sevenhoven 230.

[126] P. van Leeuwen and S. Verheij, *Woorden van heil van een kleine mens*, Utrecht 1986, 31; 34–35. See also Armstrong 443–444; id. *St. Francis of Assisi. Writings for a Gospel Life* 160–161.

they consider their own, and acknowledge God's lordship by surrendering themselves in obedience to the will of God. It is evident that obedience is intimately connected with poverty. In fact, they mutually define one another. Obedient people who acknowledge God's lordship over their lives are at the same time poor people who do not appropriate anything to themselves, for they know that all they are and have does not belong to them but to God and vice versa. This underscores once again the statement which Francis makes in *The Salutation of the Virtues* that "whoever possesses one [of the virtues] possesses all; and whoever offends one [of them] does not possess any and offends all" (6–7).

The brothers make this basic human attitude, so beautifully made manifest in Jesus' life, concrete and visible by "surrendering themselves totally unto obedience in the hands of their prelates" (3). And this not only at the moment of their profession,[127] but throughout their whole life (Test 28). For, as we have seen, the minister has the special task of guarding the *rectitudo vitae*, the right direction of the life according to the form of the gospel which the Lord has revealed (cf. Test 14). He is responsible for maintaining the divine inspiration. As such, he interprets God's will for the brothers and speaks to them in God's name. But, as we have also seen, this obedience to the minister is not absolute or unconditional, because the minister can wrongly interpret God's will. Instead of upholding the divine inspiration, he can become a hindrance to it. As a result, conflicts can arise. What is a brother to do in such a situation? Or, more in general, what is the relationship between brother and minister in matters of obedience?

Francis considers first an aspect of the normal situation. Even in the monastic situation, a subject did not always have the abbot or prior close by to ask them for advice as to what to do. This was even more so with the brothers at the beginning, when they had no friaries and were mostly wandering about in the world on their mission of peace, sharing the life and work of people (RegNB 14).[128] Much was left to their own initiative. In this situation it was of the utmost importance that they would

[127] Whether the brothers actually made their "profession" in the hands of their minister is not clear. It certainly was a custom among Benedictines and Cistercians. Both the Rules, however, when speaking about a brother being "received into obedience" (RegNB 2:9; RegB 2:11) do not give any indication as to the manner in which it was done. Also in the other writings we do not find any further information.

[128] See my *Francis and Islam* 54–58.

live in an atmosphere of obedience: that is, in whatever they do or say, they must not act or speak on the spur of the moment; rather they must constantly make sure that their words and deeds are not against the will of their minister (4). On their mission journeys, they maintain thus a link of obedience with their minister and through him with the brotherhood and its mission of peace according to the gospel. And the less the brotherhood is organized externally, the more vital and necessary this link with the minister becomes to keep the brotherhood together. Yet—and this is the other side which Francis always stresses because of his experience—however vital and necessary this link with the minister may be, it never takes away the personal responsibility of the brother, as the added proviso indicates: "provided that what he does is good" (4). Beyond making sure that something is not against the will of the minister, the brother must, according to his own Spirit-guided conscience, be convinced that what he is about to do or say, is good. The brother who acts in this way, obedient to his minister and to the Spirit, practices *true* obedience (4).

Now, on their wanderings, landing in new and different situations, or on some other occasion, a brother "may see things that are better and more useful for his soul than those which the prelate may command" (5). Acknowledging the possibility of such a situation, Francis recognizes at the same time its possible disruptive character. For what would happen if he would allow every brother to go his own way whenever it is not a matter of a real opposition as to what is good or not, but of a difference of opinion about what is better? Hence, he pleads with this brother to have a good look at the situation from the perspective of what he calls "*loving* obedience." In light of this Franciscan concept which the *reportatio* introduces here in the text, Francis proposes to him that out of love for the Lord, to whom he has promised obedience and out of love for his neighbours, his brothers (6), he gives up his own insights and does what the minister asks him to do (5). Francis invites him thus to let the well-being of the brothers and the brotherhood prevail over his own personal views. In this way Francis takes the problem out of the legal sphere and places it on the level of the moral values, the virtues, which should characterize the brotherhood. As Francis describes it in the Earlier Rule 5:14–15: it is in the love of the Spirit that the brothers freely and humbly serve and obey one another after the example of Jesus' true and holy obedience.

Finally, Francis considers in verses 7–9 the situation of a brother who cannot and in fact "does not obey" his minister because he "commands something contrary to his conscience" (7). These inserted verses have a strongly autobiographical character. Hence the brother and the prelate are actually referring to Francis and his minister(s) and the problems they had towards the end of Francis' life when, according to the story of True Joy,[129] the ministers and the learned brothers had become "so numerous and of such quality" *(tot et tales)* in their own opinion that they did no longer need "such a simple and illiterate person" *(simplex et idiota)* like Francis (11). Francis feels himself marginalised. His deepest convictions, which are not his but the Lord's, are no longer shared by those brothers as they want to move in a different direction. Therewith, they have drifted away from the right direction of the life according to the form of the gospel. When now in those circumstances the minister does something which is against Francis' conscience, e.g. he is "so bold as to seek a letter from the Roman curia under the guise of preaching" (Test 25), Francis cannot possibly go along with him and obey him, even though he would wish to do so (Test 27). For he would become unfaithful to himself and to what he had promised the Lord to observe. He feels obliged therefore to do what he advised Brother Leo to do: "in whatever way it seems best to you to please the Lord God and to follow his footprints and his poverty, do this with the blessing of God and my obedience" (LetLeo 3).

At the same time, however, Francis will not leave the minister (7). Whatever the conflict may be, Francis will stay with him and so, at all cost, try to avoid the breaking up of the brotherhood. The minister and the other learned brothers may not very much appreciate this attitude; they may even persecute him, throwing him out of the Portiuncula; yet, Francis will try to remain patient (TrueJoy 15) and "love [him] even more because of God" (8). Thus, following his policy of love, of doing good even to his enemy, he hopes to draw him back to the Lord (LetMin 11). In doing so, "choosing to endure persecution rather than be separated from his brothers, [Francis] truly remains in perfect obedience for he lays down his life for his brothers" (9) as Jesus did. The norm for this *perfect* obedience is thus again Jesus' obedience. He gave his followers a

[129] For a good commentary, see A. Jansen, "The Story of the True Joy. An Autobiographical Reading," *FrancDigest* 2,2 (June 1992) 1–27.

new command: "Love one another as I have loved you" (Jn 13:34), and showed them the sign of the greatest love a man can have by laying down his life for his friends (cf. Jn 15:13). It was Jesus' final act of perfect obedience to his Father: he not only renounced all he had, he even lost his life (3), so that "he might not lose the obedience of the most holy Father" (LetOrder 46).

As Francis struggles with these problems, there are brothers who "under the pretext of seeking something better"—one may think here again of the ministers and the learned brothers looking for a greater integration into the church's pastoral policies—"look back and return to the vomit of their own will" (10). On entering the brotherhood, they promised obedience, renouncing their will (RegB 10:2), but they have appropriated it again and no longer wish to place themselves "under the yoke of service and holy obedience" (2 LetFaith 40). Rather than giving all their attention to guarding and preserving the *rectitudo vitae* in obedience to the Spirit, they want to follow their own ideas, to go their own way, even if this leads to division within the brotherhood and to the undoing of so much good which the Lord had worked in and through the brothers and through which they had given birth again to Jesus in their world. Francis is utterly disappointed by their behaviour, as the severe language with which he condemns them clearly indicates. "Murderers they are" (11)! For rather than losing their life, their body, in obedience to the Lord in order thus to save it for themselves and for others, they hold on to it following their own will and so destroy their own life and that of others.[130] That this had to happen to what began so beautifully under God's inspiration was Francis' greatest illusion and pain during the last years of his life.

Yet, he never gave up believing in his ideal of loving obedience, of brothers serving and obeying one another in the love of the Spirit and

[130] Armstrong is right, I think, when he draws our attention here to "the scriptural reference that lies hidden in [verse 11]... 'Everyone who hates his brother,' John writes, 'is a murderer, and you know that no murderer has eternal life remaining in him' (1 John 3:15). The bond of brotherhood... demands expressions of love... that foster, enhance, and deepen that [bond]. To act contrary to those bonds, that is, to act without love, is to snuff out life or to murder. This seems exaggerated except when read in light of the mystery of Christ. 'The way we came to know love,' John continues, 'was that he laid down his life for us: so we ought to lay down our lives for our brothers'" (1 John 3:16) (162).

even giving their lives for one another in perfect obedience after the example of Jesus. In fact, at the end of his *The Salutation of the Virtues* Francis proposes that the brothers extend the model of their obedient relationship within the brotherhood to the outside world: the truly obedient brother is not only obedient to the Spirit and to his brother, he is also "subject and submissive to all persons in the world, and not to persons only, but even to all beasts and wild animals so that they may do whatever they want with him inasmuch as it has been given to them from above by the Lord" (15–18). This may lead the obedient brother to martyrdom. However, hoping and trusting in God and in the power of God's holy virtues over evil, Francis is deeply convinced that, in God's good time, holy obedience will undo Adam's disobedience and will bring back the harmony of paradise: all men and women and all animals living together in peace, serving and obeying one another.

Even more clearly than the other virtues, obedience is thus one of the virtues of paradise through which Francis and his brothers, after the example of the poor, humble and obedient Jesus, are committed to redeem the world, undo all the consequences of sin and evil, and so transform society by reestablishing the peace and harmony of the beginnings in accordance with God's original plan of creation.[131] For God never regretted that in the beginning he "placed us in paradise," paradise from which "through our own fault we have fallen." On the contrary, he "willed to redeem us captives," by the life and death of his Son, Jesus (RegNB 23:1–3). It is this redemptive mission of Jesus in which Francis and his brothers wish to share by living the virtue of true and holy obedience and all the other virtues after the example of Jesus, for through the realisation of these virtues Jesus fulfilled his Father's

[131] Armstrong reached a similar conclusion: "Francis may well have considered these [i.e. the virtues mentioned in Salutation of the Virtues] as the virtues of the Garden when, before the sin, the human person lived without anything of his own and wallowed in the all-loving goodness of the Creator. Now, however, in light of the revelation of God in the Suffering Servant of God, Francis perceived [the virtues as] the ways of undoing the injustice of the sinful human situation and, in the embrace of a Christological minority, realized that they were the only ways of establishing justice and peace according to the divine plan." Prophetic Implications of the "Admonitions" 456. It is not clear to me, however, how Armstrong can reconcile this interpretation with his rejection of the approach of David Flood as found on pp. 425 and 439.

plan of salvation. The virtues are then, as Flood calls them, "the movement's commitments"[132] to the continuation of Jesus' mission of liberating humankind from captivity and placing it back again there where it originally belongs: paradise.

Most Holy Virtues, the Lord Save You All (v. 4)

After greeting the six most relevant virtues by name while they, almost like ladies in a royal procession, stride along in pairs before our eyes, and recommending them to the Lord for his protection and salvation, Francis greets all virtues, named and unnamed together, in the concluding verse of the section on the presentation and salutation of the virtues (verse 4) and prays that all of them may be saved by the Lord. There are two things in the first line of this verse which draw the attention of the reader. First, instead of speaking about holy virtues, as he has done five times in the previous verses, Francis uses here the superlative "most holy"; second, after having enumerated a number of virtues individually, Francis now emphasizes "all" of them, as is especially clear in the Latin text which reads: *Sanctissimae virtutes, omnes vos salvet Dominus*.

The virtues are not only holy, they are most holy. As such this shift is not surprising, for the Lord God, from whom the virtues proceed, is often addressed not just as "holy Father" but as "most holy Father" in Francis' writings, especially in the Office of the Passion. However, the sudden shift to the superlative, which, as Lehmann rightly observes, represents an evident climax,[133] shows Francis' heightened sense of awe and admiration. While busy greeting a number of virtues, addressing them as holy in contrast to the ugliness and sinfulness of this world, Francis becomes ever more profoundly aware of the outstanding beauty and radiance of these and all other virtues in opposition to all the evil around him. In the end he is so overwhelmed in their sight that he cannot but exclaim "most holy virtues," wondering what the world would be when left to itself, without the most holy forces which proceed from God.

[132] See Flood, "The Confusion of Evil: Franciscan Nonviolence," *Haversack* 11,3 (February 1988) 3–5.

[133] Lehmann 231.

It is possible and even quite probable that the use of the superlative "most holy" calls up some further associations in Francis' mind. In his commentary, Jansen suggests that Francis may be thinking here of the "most holy Lord Jesus Christ, the most holy beloved Son" (AntOffPassion 2–3). He finds a possible confirmation for his suggestion in the "unusual expression: 'the Lord from whom they come and proceed,'" which Francis uses later in the same verse when he refers to the origin of the virtues from God.[134] Speaking about the divine origin of the virtues, one would expect Francis to use a more common expression like "the Lord by whom they are created." Why then this unusual expression? Where could Francis have found it? According to Jansen, Francis may have been influenced here by the Creed: "I believe in the Holy Spirit, Lord and Giver of Life, who proceeds from the Father and the Son." This would imply a certain identification, or at least a close relationship, of the virtues with the Holy Spirit, especially since the Holy Spirit is called the *virtus* of the Most High in the story of the Annunciation. And just as Mary was overshadowed by the Holy Spirit, the *virtus* of the Most High, and was to give birth to Jesus (Lk 1:35), so will the hearts of the people "through the grace and the illumination of the Holy Spirit" be filled "with all the holy virtues, so that [through the virtues] they may be made from faithless people into people that are faithful to God" (SalBVM 6) and thus become "mothers of our Lord Jesus Christ who through [their] holy works, [their] holy *operatio*, give birth to him" (2 LetFaith 50–53) in the present world and so confound the evil.[135]

An even more obvious association may be found in the eucharist, which Francis most frequently characterizes with the superlative "most holy": at least 19 times by my count. In the eucharist, "the most holy Body and Blood of our Lord Jesus Christ" (LetCler 1; 1 LetCust 2;

[134] A much similar expression can be found in RegNB 17:17: "et de omnibus ei gratias referamus *a quo bona cuncta procedunt*." In fact, I think that this sentence, which probably has its origin in the Collect of the Fifth Sunday after Easter in the old missal (Esser, *Die Opuscula* 274, note 10), offers an adequate explanation for the "unusual expression" in Salutation of the Virtues. This does not mean, however, that I reject Jansen's suggestion altogether. On the contrary, as it is with Francis often a matter of associations, it may well be that more than one association play a role in Francis' mind with regard to one particular text.

[135] See Jansen 167–168. However, he does not refer here to SalBVM and 2 LetFaith.

LetOrder 12; etc.), the Lord "is always with his faithful, as he himself says: Behold I am with you even to the end of the world" (Adm 1:22). This presence is not a presence in majesty and power. On the contrary, in the eucharist the Lord "daily humbles himself as when he came from the royal throne into the womb of the Virgin; daily he comes to us in humble form" (ibid. 16–17). Thus Francis and his brothers learn in the celebration of the eucharist the truth about Jesus (15)—the truth which many cannot accept because they do not see the most holy Body and Blood of our Lord Jesus Christ according to the Spirit (9)—that Jesus is a poor and humble Jesus who, by giving his body and blood in obedience to the Father for the redemption of humankind, showed the ways of divine wisdom and how these ways are to be followed in radical simplicity.

It is this Jesus, present in the most holy eucharist, in whose footsteps Francis and his brothers want to walk and whose virtues they want to imitate. For over the years, on the basis of their experiences, they have come to know with that typical Franciscan knowledge that they can only realize the ideal of a true brotherhood if they practice those most holy virtues which Jesus faithfully lived unto the end and through which he restored God's original plan of creation. Those most holy virtues, then, are foundational to true brotherhood—a fact that Francis and his brothers were reminded of daily in the most holy eucharist. Celebrating the most holy Body and Blood of the Lord, Francis and his brothers celebrate therefore Jesus' faithful commitment to those most holy virtues and how, through living them unto the end, he was engaged in his ultimately successful struggle against the evil forces and so fulfilled the mission of liberation and redemption the Father had entrusted to him. At the same time, celebrating the most holy Body and Blood of the Lord, Francis and his brothers are invited to renew and strengthen their own commitment to those same most holy virtues, trusting that through their practice of those virtues they will continue Jesus' liberating mission and become ever more intensely involved in Jesus' ongoing struggle to overcome evil.

A second point that draws our attention is the presence of the adjective *omnes*. Like *sanctissimus* and other adjectives denoting a certain universality, *omnes* is rather typical in Francis' writings. According to Lehmann, *omnes* serves here both as a climax and a summary.[136] Just as

[136] Lehmann 236. In what follows, I depend almost literally on Lehmann's study

Francis invokes first many saints individually, and later all of them at the end of the *Regula non bullata* (RegNB 23:6), and just as he honors Mary with many titles and then greets all holy virtues in his The Salutation of Mary, so he does also here. He enumerates by name the six virtues he considers essential to the life of the brotherhood and its mission in the world and then greets all of them together. Thus *omnes* concludes the series of invocations of the individual virtues, while at the same time it includes all the virtues, not only those named but also the unnamed ones. The Lord is then asked to save all these most holy virtues. Though they are constantly being threatened everywhere by the forces of evil, they appear especially now to be in danger within the brotherhood itself due to the increasing influence of the learned brothers who wish to follow the standards of the world rather than to walk the way of the virtues. Francis dares to make his request to the Lord God because all virtues come from God and proceed from God. Therefore, God will really be concerned that the virtues stay alive and active so that they will be able to fulfil their divinely assigned task of being, within the brotherhood and within all humankind, the divine forces for the continuous building up of God's reign in this world.

From Whom You Come and Proceed

This affirmation of the divine origin of all virtues has played an important role in our exegesis. It explains the holiness of the virtues and their redemptive, liberative mission within the world as well as the intimate relationship between all virtues which are sisters of each other and cannot exist one without the other. The affirmation itself is very similar to a text in the Earlier Rule 17:17, where Francis writes: "and let us thank God for everything, [God] from whom all good things proceed" (*a quo cuncta bona procedunt*).[137] In light of this similarity, the affirmation about the divine origin of all the virtues is an invitation to be grateful to God, the giver of all good things. As such, it finds its place among the many statements in which Francis, often with great awe and reverence and with a profound sense of gratitude, joyfully acknowledges and proclaims that God alone is good, all good, the supreme good, the fullness

---

which is the most important and the most comprehensive study in this matter.

[137] For the origin of this expression, see note 134.

of good, and hence the source from which all good things proceed, including the most holy virtues, the forces of God's goodness in the evil world (RegNB 17:17; 23:9–11; LetOrder 61–62; PrHours 11).

Reading these statements and observing how deeply Francis has been touched by the goodness of God, one can understand that, out of a grateful acknowledgement for these gifts, Francis wishes nothing else for himself and his brothers than that they remain united with God, the source of all good. And this all the more so since apart from God, who alone is good, they have "nothing except their vices and sins" (RegNB 17:7) and hence are "miserable and wretched, rotten and foul-smelling, ungrateful and evil" (RegNB 23:8; cf. 2 LetFaith 46). That is why Francis admonishes his brothers: "Therefore let us desire nothing else, let us wish for nothing else, let nothing else please us and cause us delight, except our Creator and Redeemer and Saviour, the one true God, who is the fullness of good, all good, every good, the true and supreme good, who alone is good... Therefore let nothing hinder us, nothing separate us [from God], nothing come in between [us and God]" (RegNB 23:9–10).

Thus united with God, the brothers will also wish to be united with him in the divine plan of creation and redemption and to share his goodness with all humankind, even with the whole world. Thus they will allow the virtues, the forces of God's holiness and goodness, to enter their lives, work in and through their words and works, and so make God's goodness confound whatever evil there exists in this world. As Francis writes in his final admonition to the brothers at the original end of the *Regula non bullata*: "And when we hear someone speak or do evil or blaspheme God, let us speak well and do well and praise God who is blessed forever" (17:19).

Unfortunately, there are brothers who let pride and vainglory come between them and God. They allow themselves to become captives of the wisdom of this world and the prudence of the flesh (RegNB 17:9–10). Instead of humbling themselves and becoming instruments in God's hands, totally at the service of God's plan to share his goodness with humankind, they "pride themselves, rejoice in themselves, and exalt themselves about the good words and works, in fact about any good which God sometimes does or says or works in them and through them" (RegNB 17:5).[138] In doing so, these brothers repeat the sin of the beginning, appropriating to themselves God's goods and acting in their regard

[138] Apparently, this happened rather frequently, so much so that Francis regularly

as if they are lord (cf. Adm 2:3). Thus they deny God's lordship and forget that they have to return to God all the good things which proceeded from God and hence belong to God (RegNB 17:17), in that they share these goods with others and so become instrumental in realising the original plan of God's good creation.

So also with the most holy virtues. There are brothers who forget that the virtues proceed from God and have gratefully to be returned to God with all the good fruits these holy virtues are able to produce in the world through the words and works of the brothers and others. In their forgetfulness, these brothers pride themselves on the words and works God says and does in and through them ,and they regard these as if they are theirs, thereby obscuring and even falsifying the truth of who they, left to themselves, in reality are: "opposed to every good" (Adm 12:2). It is with these brothers in mind that Francis writes: "A servant of God can be recognized as having the Spirit of the Lord in this way: when the Lord does some good through him, his flesh does not exalt itself on this account [as it is inclined to do,] because it is always opposed to every good. Rather, he regards himself in his own eyes as more worthless and esteems himself as lesser than all others" (Adm 12:1–3). If these brothers would listen to this admonition and acknowledge who they themselves are and how the Lord, in spite of all this, wishes to impart the most holy virtues to them so that, through these holy forces, they may transform the world, this acknowledgement would be for them a source of profound joy and gratitude. At the same time it would greatly increase their sense of responsibility and commitment not to put any obstacle to the working of God's most holy virtues. Rather they would wholeheartedly cooperate with them so as to allow them to produce abundant fruit by their victory over evil, and not to return to God empty-handed. It is with the virtues as with the seed, that is, the word of God. Having left the world and wishing nothing else except to follow the will of the Lord, the brothers should "take great care not to be earth along the wayside, or earth that is full of rocks or thorns." Rather they should be good soil; that is, they should be like those "who hear the word with a good and noble heart and understand it and keep it and bear fruit in patience" (RegNB 22:10 and 17).

---

had to admonish his brothers in this most serious matter: Admonitions 2:3; 12:2; 17:1. See R. Armstrong, *St. Francis of Assisi. Writings for a Gospel Life* 168–172.

It is clear then that for Francis virtues are far more than moral attitudes or habits which persons can cultivate and develop by steady exercise and through which they can lead a fulfilling, virtuous life. Rather, in line with the patristic and medieval tradition, Francis sees the virtues as the ways in which God is powerfully present and active in people to realise in and through them the divine plan of creation and redemption as revealed in the person of Jesus Christ.[139] It is this basic insight which, as we have seen in our description of the individual virtues, Francis makes his own and which he through *The Salutation of the Virtues* tries to convey to his brothers: all the most holy virtues come and proceed from the Lord God who gives them to the brothers and to all people so that in the strength of these virtues they will confound evil, redeem the world from its disastrous consequences, and restore paradise.

[139] See A. Jansen, Words of Salvation of Saint Francis. A Commentary on Admonition 27, *FrancDigest* 4,2 (December 1994) 1–24; here 20–21; also v.d. Goorbergh-Zweerman 95.

CHAPTER THREE

The Acquisition and Possession of the Virtues

vv. 5–8

After the first section in which the virtues are introduced and in which the Lord God *(Dominus)* who is their origin and their savior, holds the central place, Francis moves to the second section which centers around the human person *(homo)*, who is to receive the virtues. This move is marked by a shift from a more poetic style to prose, whereby the rhythmic greeting of the virtues changes into a series of doctrinal statements about the conditions for their possession.[1]

TEXT

5.	Nullus homo est penitus in toto mundo qui unam ex vobis possit habere, nisi prius moriatur.	There is no one at all in the entire world who can possess one of you unless he first dies.
6.	Qui unam habet et alias non offendit, omnes habet.	Whoever possesses one and does not offend the others, possesses all.
7.	Et qui unam offendit, nullam habet et omnes offendit.	And whoever offends one, possesses none and offends all.
8.	Et unaquaque confundit vitia et peccata.	And each one confounds vices and sins.

1 See Lehmann 225–226.

DETAILED EXEGESIS

THERE IS NO ONE AT ALL IN THE WHOLE WORLD

The words *nullus*, *penitus* and *totus* reinforce one another. Apparently, for Francis it is not enough to mention that no one *(nullus homo)* can possess one of the virtues unless he first dies. To make sure that every reader understands that no exception whatsoever is possible, he adds: no one *at all (penitus)*.[2] And as if this is still not enough to avoid all misunderstanding, he further adds: *in the entire world (in toto mundo)*. Both these additions serve thus to emphasize in the strongest way possible that when it comes to the acquisition and possession of a virtue, the *only* way for *all* people is that they first pass through a painful process of dying. To die first is an essential condition for possessing a virtue; it is absolutely necessary and does not allow any exception.

Unless He first Dies (v. 5)

To die in order to live is the fundamental paradox of all Christian life, as shown in the death and resurrection of Jesus. The virtuous life of the brothers is no exception to this. They have to die to their vices and sins in order to be able to lead a life of virtue by the grace of God from whom the virtues proceed. According to A. Jansen, this necessity of dying can further be explained by reflecting on a somewhat unusual idea which Francis elaborates in Admonition 27: "Where there is the fear of the Lord to guard the house, there the enemy can have no place to enter" (5). By "the fear of the Lord" Francis does not mean here the fear *for* the Lord, but literally the fear *of* the Lord, i.e., the Lord God dwells as the fearing One in the human heart and with perfect fear, which is nothing but the other side of God's perfect love, guards this heart as God's own house, filling it completely with the divine presence. Hence there is no place for the enemy to enter. God and the enemy radically exclude one another. This implies also that when a person makes a place in his/her heart for anyone or anything else which is not God or not from God, God can no longer dwell there. It is a matter of either/or, for God who is the source of all good either fills the heart completely with

[2] The Latin adverb *penitus* is translated: "Es gibt überhaupt niemanden" (Lehmann 236); "Il n'est absolutement aucun homme" (*François d'Assise. Écrits*, Paris 1981, 271); "There is surely no one" (Armstrong-Brady 152; Armstrong, Hellmann, Short 164).

God's goodness and love or not at all. The human person has therefore to die first to what is not God. More particularly, the person has to die to what constitutes the kernel of sin: the inclination to appropriate to oneself one's own will, that is, to consider oneself as lord and to regard proudly as one's own all the good that God says and does through one's words and works, thereby denying God's lordship (cf. Adm.2). Only if the human person dies to this inclination and acknowledges God as Lord and Giver of every good is there a place for God in his/her heart and hence for one of God's virtues and thus, as will be shown later, for all.[3]

But how did Francis see this more concretely? How did he understand and practise this process of dying to all that is not God, to sin? In this context verse 15 is revealing: "and [the obedient brother] has his body mortified unto obedience of the Spirit and unto obedience of his brother"[4] —a text which has a parallel in the Earlier Rule 17:14: "The Spirit of the Lord wishes the flesh to be mortified and despised, worthless and rejected." From these texts it is clear first of all that by "dying" is not meant a passive undergoing of something that happens to someone, but rather an activity which a brother has to engage in under the guidance of, or in obedience to the Spirit. For, as the texts indicate, it is the wish of the Spirit that the brother mortifies, that is, brings death to the flesh, the body *(mortem facere)*. Further, these texts make it clear that this activity is part of the ongoing struggle between the spirit of the flesh and the Spirit of the Lord.

As such, mortification is not to be limited to a series of acts of mortification, of ascetical practices, often unrelated to real life, which are meant to promote a person's individual moral or religious perfection; rather, it goes far beyond this; it is the necessary consequence of the brothers' commitment to build a new world where people relate differently to each other, "being subject and submissive to all people in the

[3] Jansen 168. For further clarification see from the same author: A. Jansen, "Words of Salvation of Saint Francis. A Commentary on Admonition 27," *FrancDigest* 4,2 (December 1994) 1–24, here 4–6.

[4] See Lehmann: "In v. 15 it is said more clearly how this dying is to be understood, namely as an activity whereby one's own body, that is, the self that pushes itself to the forefront, is kept mortified. Such a person who has died to him- or herself, possesses all virtues, provided s/he does not offend one of them" (236). However, Lehmann does not elaborate here what Francis means more concretely by this mortification of the body, of the self that pushes itself forward.

world" (SalVirt 16). As it is not possible to build this world within the sinful structures of Assisi's system where the external appearance of religion prevails, but the *operatio* is missing (RegNB 17:11–12), the brothers leave Assisi: they die to it and go and "stay among *(inter)* those who are considered worthless and are despised, among the poor and powerless, the sick and the lepers, and the beggars by the wayside" (RegNB 9:2). This is the work of the Spirit of the Lord "who wishes the flesh to be mortified and despised, worthless and rejected" (RegNB 17:14), in that the brothers reject the moral and cultural standards of Assisi and identify with those who, according to those same standards, are worthless and despised, rejected and declared dead. In doing so, they recognise their human dignity as men and women created in God's image and likeness—a dignity often denied them by Assisi—and bring them back to life again within the solidarity of a new brother—and sisterhood.

Enlightening in this context is a passage of Celano where he describes how Francis admonishes his brothers towards the end of his life: "Let us begin, brothers, to serve the Lord God, for up to now we have made little or no progress." And Celano continues: "He [Francis] did not consider that he had reached his goal as yet, and persevering untiringly in his purpose of attaining holy newness of life in the Spirit, he wished always to be as in the beginning. He wanted to go back again to serving lepers, to be held in contempt, as he once had been" (1 Cel 103). This does not mean that Francis wanted to be held in contempt for contempt's sake! Rather, he saw the contempt he did incur in the beginning as a clear sign of his identification with the lepers. Thus it became evident that he had broken away from the world of Assisi and its values, or rather its vices and sins, and had opened himself to the working of the Spirit of the Lord who alone led him among the lepers where he would be held in contempt as the lepers were. And it was there, in their midst, in a new place away from Assisi, that the Spirit was able to empower him so that he could discern a new set of values that were radically opposed to the values of the dominant class in Assisi.

Concretely, then, the dying which is an essential condition for the acquisition and the possession of one, and thus, of all virtues is to leave Assisi, with its value system and its way of looking at and dealing with people, and thus to create the possibility of discerning and adopting a whole new valuesystem, a whole different set of virtues, by identifying with the poor and despised. This dying, this exodus, is not done once and for all, but has to be continued during one's whole life in the choices one makes for the poor and marginalized and against the dominant culture. And although difficult, as all dying is, it is at the same time most worthwhile, for the virtues which one thus acquires enable a person to confound the spirit of the flesh, the spirit of the world, and instead to bring about a new world in the Spirit of the Lord.

Whoever Possesses One, Possesses All(v. 6)

With this somewhat surprising statement, Francis repeats the traditional doctrine as formulated by St. Ambrose and St. Jerome, among others. St. Ambrose writes: "The virtues are connected with one another and concatenated, so that whoever possesses one, seems to have more." And St. Jerome states: "The virtues follow one another and adhere to one another so that whoever has acquired one, possesses all, and whoever has lost one, loses all."[5] In turn, they go, via Cicero, back to the Greek philosophical tradition.[6] This does not mean that Francis directly depends on Ambrose or Jerome or some other Father of the church. They do, however, provide the historical background.[7]

As a result of this traditional affirmation—"whoever possesses one, possesses all"—the distinction between the virtues becomes rather blurred. Consequently, as we have seen before, the individual virtues cannot be clearly defined in isolation. Rather, in the description of each individual virtue, reference often has to be made to the other virtues. This is but natural because the virtues are intimately united with one another and cannot exist one without the other, since they proceed from

5 "Connexae igitur sibi sunt concatenataeque virtutes; ut qui unam habet, plures habere videatur." Ambrosius, *Expositio evangelii secundum Lucam*, Lib. V,63; PL 15,1653. "Virtutes... invicem se sequuntur et sibi haerent. Ita ut qui unam habuerit omnes habeat, et qui una caruerit, cunctis careat." Hieronymus, *Comment. in Isaiam prophetam*, Lib. XVI; PL 24,538. Quoted by Esser, *Die Opuscula*, 429.

6 "A traditional doctrine... because it refers to St. Ambrose, St. Augustine and St. Gregory the Great. It goes even back much further, if it is true that, via Cicero, it is linked with the Greek philosophical tradition." E. Gilson, La Sagesse de Saint François, in *Les Amis de St. François* 6 (1939), no. 22, 7–15; here 8. Quoted by Lehmann 235–236.

7 Or as Lehmann writes: "... thus a look at the texts mentioned by Esser has shown that they indicate the soil on which Francis' SalVirt has grown, but not its immediate model" (235).

one and the same source: the Lord God. As such, as Verhey rightly observes, they are but "various aspects of the one reality, various activities of the one sanctifying force of life *(Lebenskraft)* of the divine Spirit."[8] This implies that, whenever a person possesses a virtue, the Spirit of the Lord God dwells in his or her heart (cf. 2 LetFaith 48)—an indwelling where the Spirit is accompanied by all God's virtues, for God's Spirit is one and undivided and hence cannot exist without all God's virtues being present at the same time.

Whoever Offends One, Offends All (v. 7)

What holds good for the acquisition and possession of the virtues is also valid as far as their loss is concerned. Because the virtues are intimately united in their origin from God, who dwells within the human heart together with all God's virtues or not at all, it is not only true that whoever possesses one virtue, possesses all, but also that whoever offends one, offends all, and thus loses all and is left without a single one. This view finds a clear confirmation in the Scriptures, for James says: "Whoever keeps the whole of the law but offends against it in one point, is guilty of breaking it all" (2:10).[9] A different expression of this view can be found in the above quoted text from Admonition 27: "Where there is the fear of the Lord to guard the house, there the enemy can have no place to enter" (5). As we have seen already, this text implies that God and the enemy radically exclude one another. They are as incompatible as are holiness and sin, virtue and vice. It is a matter of either/or. Hence, when a person "does something good... the devil will find that person occupied" (RegNB 7:10).[10] On the other hand, when a person offends a virtue by doing something evil and thus letting the devil occupy his or her heart, God and hence also God's virtues can no longer dwell there. For, as the Lord's Ladies, the virtues accompany the Lord wherever the Lord goes. Conversely this implies that wherever the virtues are present, there the Lord is present, and wherever the virtues are absent, there the Lord is absent.

8 Verhey 108. Quoted by Lehmann 236.

9 "Quicumque autem totam legem servaverit, offendat autem in uno, factus est reus omnium" (Jac. 2,10).

10 Francis quotes here a saying from St. Jerome, *Epistola* 125 (PL 22,1078).

Summarizing these verses, Reijsbergen writes: "He [Francis] stimulates the people by telling them that they must die first before they can acquire the virtues (v.5). Next, he stimulates them by proposing the virtues as a unity: Whoever possesses one, so he promises, possesses all of them. But he also arouses tension by mentioning the other side: whoever offends one, has lost all of them (vv.6–7)... The central part of *The Salutation of the Virtues* (vv.5–7) has thus something of a challenge. It is almost like a game of chance about which is mentioned only that it demands that people put everything at stake, and that it pays out all or nothing... Giving no commands, but just a few inviting suggestions, Francis makes it clear to them, with a friendly smile, that they must first will and act. [In this way] they feel themselves addressed, appealed to, as free, willing subjects, able to act. They feel that confidence is being placed in them, in their uniqueness and their possibilities. In a similar way, Francis invites people to conversion in his Canticle of Brother Sun... They need not to be told how to go the way to a virtuous life. This would be counterproductive. People need to be stimulated, esteemed, exalted as persons who are aware of the exalted height where God has placed them (Adm 5)."[11]

I agree with the basic thrust of this summary. After Francis has introduced Queen Wisdom and her Lady Virtues in all their beauty, because they proceed from the most holy Lord God who is all beauty, the very contradiction of the ugliness of evil (PrGod 3–4), it is but natural for him to wish that his brothers be attracted by those holy and beautiful virtues and that they be prepared to leave behind whatever is evil in order to acquire and possess them. This is all the more so for the brothers are created in the image of God's beloved Son and called to walk in the footsteps of Him who lived those virtues to the full during his life here on earth: hence Francis' appeal to the brothers and their sense of responsibility. Conscious of their dignity, created as they are in Jesus' image, they should strive to acquire and possess one of those virtues in order thus to become truly like Jesus, God's most holy Son. It will not be easy to heed this appeal, but seeing the holiness and beauty of these virtues, these forces of God, the brothers will hopefully feel sufficiently motivated to live up to their responsibility and to make the choices they have to make in order to pass through the difficult yet necessary process of dying. For thus they will be led out of the captivity in

[11] Reijsbergen 112–113.

which they are held by sin and evil (RegNB 23:3) and freed for the working of God's Spirit.

If they do, a wonderful surprise will be awaiting them: possessing one virtue, they will in fact possess all of them. And so, filled with God's virtues, they will not only be liberated from their vices and sins, but will also become sources of holiness and beauty in this world themselves, as they were always meant to be. For in the beginning, "having made us in [God's] image and likeness, [God] placed us in paradise." But now that "through our own fault we have fallen," it is up to the brothers to cooperate with Jesus in undoing the consequences of the fall and putting an end to sin and evil. To this end the brothers must allow the most holy virtues of God to work in and through their activities for the redemption of this world. Thus they will continue the redemption that Jesus brought "through his cross and blood and death" (RegNB 23:1–2). The brothers carry this treasure in earthen vessels. They have to live up to their high calling in the midst of the many dangers which the dominant culture around them presents: hence Francis' brotherly yet serious warning. In fact, the brothers cannot be careful enough. For if they offend any one of the virtues, they offend all and are left with none. Deprived of God's indwelling, they will be thrown back on themselves, with nothing but their vices and sins. Thus they will no longer be able to fulfill their God-given mission to inaugurate a new world that reflects the original goodness of paradise. Such a new world can only be brought about if the brothers rely not on their own strength but on God's holy virtues. For they, and they only, can empower the brothers to become Jesus' co-operators, his co-redeemers.

And Each One Confounds Vices and Sins (v. 8)

This verse (8) forms the link between the second section, on how the brothers acquire and keep possession of the virtues (5–7), and the third section, which speaks about the working of God's virtues once the brothers have acquired them (9–14). This is evident in that verse 8 is connected with the previous verse by *et* and with the following verses by introducing the verb *confundere*, which appears to be the keyword that is repeated six times in those verses to describe what the virtues work out vis-à-vis the various forms of vices and sins.

As the verb *confundere* is the keyword in the next section, where it is repeated six times to indicate the activity which is essentially the same for each of the six virtues, it seems appropriate to try to determine its more precise meaning. This is not so simple, as each author gives his own translation. Lehmann translates: *zunichte machen* (bring to naught) or *zu Fall bringen* (to bring down). And he concludes: "The singer is conscious of the victory of the virtues. Hence he is able to speak about them with praise."[12] Hardick-Grau use the weaker *zuschanden machen* (to put to shame).[13] The Dutch translation of the writings of Francis has *ontmaskeren* (to unmask). In an added footnote the editors explain this rather unusual translation as follows: "*Confundere* means: to throw into confusion, to destroy, to put to shame. Our translation refers to medieval mystery plays where virtues were often presented as persons by means of a mask."[14] This translation and its explanation sound rather farfetched to me. Moreover, if the virtues do unmask the vices and sins, showing what they really are, they do not leave it at that. They aim at undoing whatever evil the vices and sins have done to the people, to the world. Armstrong-Brady translate "to destroy,"[15] whereas Armstrong in his later publication uses "to confound," the verb that is also used in the recent translation, edited by Armstrong, Hellmann and Short.[16]

[12] Lehmann 226–227.

[13] Hardick-Grau 131.

[14] *De geschriften van Franciscus van Assisi*, Haarlem 1987, 181, note 7. Reijsbergen follows mostly this translation. He has, however, the following observation: "Beside the forceful meaning of treating people or things in such a way that they are beyond recognition and of crushing, the verb *confundere* also carries the meaning of joining, melting and mixing one thing with another." In the last case the verb has an ablative with or without *cum*, and not an accusative as here in the SalVirt. For this reason, I find the conclusion which Reijsbergen draws highly speculative. He writes: "Hence the unmasking could take place as a result of the fact that the virtues join with the vices and sins. Biblically, this thought could be inspired by the way in which the light by coming into the world dispels the darkness (cf. John 1)" (64). Beside being speculative, the combination of dispelling by joining seems rather odd.

[15] Armstrong-Brady 152. The same translation can be found in Martin Steiner, El 'Saludo a las Virtutes' de S. Francisco de Asís, *Selecciones de Franciscanismo* 46 (1987) 135: "The essense of the virtues' action is described by the verb *confundere* which has to be understood in its most strong sense: to destroy, to demolish, to devastate, etc."

[16] Armstrong, *St. Francis of Assisi. Writings for a Gospel Life* 192; Armstrong, Hellmann, Short. *Francis of Assisi: Early Documents. Vol. I: The Saint* 164–165.

Besides these authors who do not explain any further the more specific meaning of the verb *confundere* in the particular context of *The Salutation of the Virtues*, there are two authors, Jansen and Flood, who deal with this matter more extensively. According to Jansen, "the Salutation seems at first glance to be inspired by the idea of the struggle between virtues and vices [which has its origin in Greek philosophy and was very popular in the middle ages, due to the influence of the *Psychomachia* of Aurelius Prudentius Clemens]. There are, however, very great differences as is evident in the use of words. Francis does not use the image of struggle, of fight, with its connotations of winning or losing. This image leads to an ascetical vision of the human person, in which the person is seen as a battle field between two or more equal forces: good and evil, of which one may win now to be followed later by the other. This implies first and foremost a strange view of evil, as if it would be an independent force, equal to the good... We have the impression that Thomas of Celano in his first biography thinks somewhat like this, seen his preference for words like knight, to conquer oneself, to despise oneself, etc. But Francis does not think like this at all. The image of fight and of battle field are completely absent. Instead we find here the word... 'to put to shame, to unmask'... What does this mean that evil is a force that must be unmasked?"

"The verb *confundere* means in Church Latin: to put to shame. It is a verb that frequently occurs in the psalms...[17] Many of these psalms were written when people who were falsely accused sought their last refuge with God in the temple... In this situation, lies and false accusations had put on the mask of truth and enjoyed social prestige. Their victims hoped and prayed that these lies would be pulled off and that the enemies and their false witnesses would have to slink away, full of shame. They hoped that the truth, their truth, would finally come to light and that they would restored in their rightful place. The context is therefore always a context of hope... This meaning of *confundere* is also intended by Paul in his famous passage about God's wisdom and the wisdom of the world (1 Cor 1:18–2:16): "No, it was to shame the wise that

[17] Jansen refers here to psalm 25 (Vulg. 24) 2–3. He could much better have quoted Ps 70 (Vulg 69)3: "Confundantur et revereantur qui quaerunt animam meam," which Francis uses in the Office of the Passion, Psalm VIII,2; and Ps 71 (Vulg 70) 1: "In te, Domine, speravi, non confundar in aeternum," which Francis uses in the same Office, Psalm XII,1.

God chose what is foolish in the eyes of the world, and to shame what is strong that God chose what is weak in the eyes of the world" (1:27). If we look at the similarities of ideas and words, it seems evident that Francis has been directly inspired by Paul. This implies that we must hear the proclamation of the "foolishness of the cross," God's wisdom in the world, resonating as background in the whole of Francis' *The Salutation of the Virtues*. Francis sees thus the tragic "fight" between good and evil not as a struggle, a fight between two equal parties. He is concerned about the power of the truth which ultimately unmasks the evil as a lie, as empty vanity, and thus strips it of its power. He is concerned about the truth of Jesus' cross which unmasks all human wisdom of honour, possessions, prestige, etc., as a lie, as empty vanity."[18]

Though Jansen sticks to the Dutch translation of unmasking the evil, yet he feels it necessary to further qualify its meaning by adding some other verbs. Apparently, he too is of the opinion that the verb "to unmask" does not adequately express the real meaning of *confundere*. Certainly, "to unmask" indicates an aspect of all that takes place during the confrontation between good and evil, virtue and vice. But there is something more to *confundere* than just revealing or exposing the true nature of vice and sin. And it is precisely this something more, which Jansen expresses by adding some qualifying verbs, that takes us more closely to the real meaning. *Confundere* then here means not only to expose evil for what it truly is. It also has the connotation of putting evil to shame so that it cannot but shamefully slink away from the scene. depriving evil of its influence and power, and overcoming evil and undoing its evil consequences.

All this, and here I disagree with Jansen, happens in a real struggle between good and evil, virtue and vice. In this respect Francis does not differ from the medieval tradition which goes back to the New Testament: e.g., the story about Jesus' temptation in the desert.[19] This

[18] Jansen 64–66.

[19] See e.g. Zweerman who writes that "the structure of the *Salutatio virtutum* makes it abundantly clear... how Francis considers the life of the person who tries to risk it with God's power, as a struggle *(als einen Kampf)*.' And a little further he rightly observes that "the motive of the struggle *(Kampfmotiv)* is certainly also connected with the numerous passages in the writings where Francis admonishes the brothers to endure and to persevere" (38 and 43). I am not convinced, however, by the way Zweerman argues on the basis of Christograms which Francis would have

struggle does not imply that we have to do with two equal parties, as Jansen suggests. On the contrary—and the teaching from the New Testament onward is clear on this point—God's power and virtues will always prevail if people open themselves to the working of the Spirit of the Lord. Francis expresses this conviction most clearly by using the indicative *confundit* in the next verses of his *The Salutation of the Virtues* not just once, but six times for each of the six virtues. In other words, Francis does not express a wish; he states a fact. And to leave no doubt whatsoever in the mind of the brothers, he repeats it six times: yes, God's virtue, working in and through the words and works of a person, does indeed overcome evil. Only if people turn away from God and allow themselves "to be deceived by the devil" can the devil can take hold of them. They then become "the devil's children, whose works they perform" (2 LetFaith 66). It is this possibility, tragic for the person concerned as well as for the world, which highlights the responsibility of each human person, and especially of each brother.

Flood considers the term *confundere* from another angle, placing this activity more clearly within the context of the theory which Francis and his brothers, on the basis of their experiences, developed about the way the brothers should behave in their social relations with the people they met on their journey through the world. Flood writes: "When Francis specifies the contribution of each virtue to the synthesis [presented in *The Salutation of the Virtues*], he also lines up the opposition... It is out there, claiming to be the master of events and of the world... It is what we call today structural evil... All of this merely sets the scene for Francis' definition of the action. It arises out of the word *confundere*, confound (and not the aggressive *destroy* of Armstrong's translation)[20] ... The action speaks to the humanity of others and works with them: it seeks out allies in the enemy camp. Franciscan action constantly and

---

woven in the text, that the struggle of the human person unites him or her most intimately with Christ. Of course, Francis believed very strongly that the struggle to lead a life in accordance with God's holy virtues unites a person most intimately with Christ. Because of various reasons indicated already above in the introduction, it remains however very doubtful whether Francis has indeed woven these Christograms in SalVirt. Reijsbergen in his turn points to the importance of the theme of the struggle between God and Satan, heaven and hell, spirit and flesh in the medieval popular faith (147–148).

[20] Armstrong-Brady 152. See above note 15.

persuasively postulates a new and better context for handling life's questions. As soon as the minds of others begin turning to the new approach, the regulations and habits obstructing the human cause begin crumbling away."[21]

In other words, after Francis and his brothers have become convinced on the basis of their analysis of the society that the way followed by Assisi does not really work because it leaves many victims along the roadside, they set out to try and convince the citizens of Assisi of the validity of the brothers' way of life. They do so in the first place by living an alternative society in the hope that the people of Assisi will see that it works and will feel attracted to it. They may then start doubting their own social context, their own social structures, and become confused about the way they lived, and the values that directed their lives. Looking more attentively at the alternative the brothers offer, they may, in a next stage, be able to discern the structural evil present in their social context, disengage their minds from its thought patterns, accept the values and virtues of the brothers' alternative society, and eventually become committed to their realization. This process will lead to a complete redefinition of people and things as Francis and his brothers had achieved earlier upon leaving Assisi. Thus, as Flood observes, "lepers were redefined for many people in and around Assisi and re-entered history because of the brothers' and sisters' active solidarity with them." Also, by their "policy on work, with its quality of humility, [the brothers] waged a patient battle on class distinctions in Assisi."[22] Thus they enabled many to redefine the organising principle of a just society for, through their way of life, they made many understand that a just society cannot be organised according to the principle of a continuous increase of wealth and power which keep people divided, but instead has to be built on the basis of humble service that brings people together. They even succeeded in getting many to agree to a redefinition of society itself as a brotherhood and no longer as a hierarchical structure in which the rich and powerful were lording it over the poor and the weak.[23]

---

[21] D. Flood, The Confusion of Evil: Franciscan Nonviolence, *Haversack* 11, 3 (February 1988) 4.

[22] Flood ibid.; see also Flood, *Francis of Assisi and the Franciscan Movement*, 168–173.

[23] Returning to the question of the meaning of the verb *confundere* in his *Francis of Assisi and the Franciscan Movement*, Flood recalls the story of "a man in Bettona

It is evident that, according to this interpretation, a great respect for others is to be found at the heart of the Franciscan action. Franciscan action is far removed from using power to impose ideas or practices on others or to force them to think in a particular way or to move in a particular direction. Essentially nonviolent, Franciscan action invites people by appealing to the goodness or humanity that lives in each human person but sometimes knows only a dormant existence, in the hope so to awaken this goodness or humanity and to make it a force towards building a new, alternative society.

A good illustration of this nonviolent approach, but in a quite different field can be found in chapter 16 of the *Regula non bullata*, where Francis describes how the brothers are to act when they live among the Saracens. Negatively, the brothers are "not to engage in arguments and disputes" (6). In the historical context of the crusades, this means that they are not to join all those preachers who, as an alternative to the crusades, from a position of imagined superiority and power "attack [the Saracens] not with arms, but with words"[24] and thus want to confound them.[25] For such aggressive and negative apologetics, one-sided as they are, are totally inadequate to establish a real contact with the others. In

---

who, through sales of cloth as well as the practice of usury, amassed himself a tidy sum. He kept his eye on his business, tossed his weight around in Bettona's politics, and celebrated the church's feastdays sumptuously. By his usury he had ruined one farmer, with his money he had bought himself a place of honor in church for mass. One day he glanced at Francis as Francis was passing by—someone had gibed at Francis and got wit in return, along with laughter. The laughter got through to the usurer, for he could not explain it. The more he thought about it, and later listened to Francis more closely, the more the hold of his passion for wealth began slipping. (He was becoming confused, the hold of the wisdom of this world on him was slipping.) One day he reconsidered the plight of the farmer and did right by him. Soon he belonged to the lay wing of the Franciscan movement, much to the solace of the poor in Bettona. Other merchants and usurers in and around Bettona scoffed at such piety, and felt uneasy at the peace in the new Franciscan's household and the new attention given the plight of the lepers. The Franciscan movement could not grow save Bettona's control over its wealth and the marginalization of its poor decrease" (171–172).

[24] Petrus Venerabilis (+1156): "Aggredior inquam vos, non ut nostri sepe faciunt armis sed verbis, non vi sed ratione, non odio sed amore..." PL 189, 673. See my *Francis and Islam*, 71–74; 236–237, notes 39–40.

[25] To confound is the explicit goal of the disputes to which Innocent III commissioned Durandus of Osca and his group of reconciled Waldensians when he

fact, they are a clear form of non-communication. Worse still, they repel people and drive them away rather than invite them and bring them together as Franciscan action is supposed to do. Hence, instead of engaging in arguments and disputes, the brothers are "to be subject to every human creature for God's sake and so to confess that they are Christians" (6). Briefly, the brothers should not act as *maiores* and *domini*, and approach the Saracens or any other people with a feeling of superiority that is very humiliating and divisive, nor should they preach against *(contra)* them; rather they should act as *minores* and *subditi* and, living among *(inter)* them, bring people together through their humble service. In this way, i.e., by their humble, peacemaking action, they should convince the Saracens that they are not crusaders who trust in power and the might of arms, but followers of Jesus who did not come to be served but to serve (RegNB 5:9–12). This would be a first step in the process which should lead next towards inviting the Saracens to join in the brothers' peace mission, and so build an *oikoumene* of peace where the peace greeting which Jesus gave to all his followers (RegNB 14:2; Test 23) is reciprocated by the Muslim wish of peace, *salaam*.[26]

Summing up the discussion about the Franciscan action with regard to the evil, vices and sins in the world, as expressed in The salutation of the Virtues by the verb *confundere*, we may quote here again the text of the Letter to a Minister: "And if [a brother] should sin thereafter a thousand times before your eyes, love him more than me so that you may draw him back to the Lord" (11).[27] But I think can do no better than to quote the last sentence of the original ending of the *Regula non bullata*, where Francis in a last reminder summarizes what the action within the movement is all about. After having exhorted his brothers "to return all

---

approved their *Propositum*. "disputando et exhortendo... debeamus illos (sc. hereticos) confundere et eis verbo dominico, veluti Christi et ecclesiae adversarios, fronte usque ad mortem libera contraire" (PL 215, 1512B) "Disputationes tamen a doctioribus fratribus in fide catholica comprobatis et instructis in lege domini dispensentur, ut adversarii catholicae et apostolicae fidei confundantur" (ibid. 1513A). The language used makes it very clear that something quite different and much stronger is meant than what Francis has in mind when he uses the same verb.

[26] See my *Francis and Islam*, passim.

[27] Francis seems to forget his own advice to a minister when in his Testament he wishes a disobedient brother to be treated very severely. For an explanation of Test 31–33, see my commentary on the virtue of obedience in II C g.

good to the most high and supreme lord God and to acknowledge that every good belongs to God," he ends by saying: "And when we see or hear that someone says or does evil *(malum dicere vel facere)* or blasphemes God, let us speak well and do well *(bene dicamus et bene faciamus)* and praise God, who is blessed forever" (RegNB 17:19).

Francis' inviting, nonviolent approach is very well illustrated in various stories peculiar to the Legend of Perugia,[28] which stress that "after he had resigned from the office of prelate *(sic)*, blessed Francis' highest and most important concern was to teach the brothers, more by actions than by words, what they ought to do and what they ought to avoid" (85). In another place the author makes Francis say: "Since my brothers know what they have to do and to avoid, there remains for me only to teach them by my actions, for that is why I was given to them during my lifetime and after my death" (87). Most interesting in our context, however, is the passage where Francis, in a discussion about the reason why he did not correct certain abuses in the brotherhood, is said to have answered: "My duty as prelate *(sic)* over the brothers is spiritual because I must suppress vices and correct them. But if through my preaching and my example I can neither suppress nor correct them, I do not wish to become an executioner who beats and flogs as the powers of this world do... Until the day of my death, I will not cease to teach my brothers by my example and my action to walk the way the Lord showed me and which I in turn showed them, so that they may have no excuse before the Lord" (76). An example does not impose; it does not force; it continually invites others to follow out of their own free will, drawn by the power of the example which they cannot resist.

This, then, is how Francis dealt with evil within the brotherhood and the world, and how he wished to confound it, not on his own strength, but in virtue of God's Spirit. Allowing God's virtues to work

[28] Even though these stories show a certain bias in that they wish to emphasize the continuing authority of Francis and of all he said and did, for the brotherhood even after he had resigned as general minister, and even though because of this bias questions may be raised as to the historicity of these stories, it remains true that those responsible for their transmission saw Francis' role in dealing with the evil within the brotherhood not in terms of exercising force and compelling others, but rather in terms of being an example, a model, appealing to the inner goodness and the initial enthusiasm of the brothers. It is this kind of Franciscan action which they themselves wish to follow and to recommend to others in order to confound the evil, the abuses that have crept into the order.

in and through him, he hoped that all of his brothers as well as many other people would be attracted by the beauty of these virtues to become allies in realizing God's plans for the world. For Francis believed in the persuasive force of a life in which God's virtues shine forth. And, if some of the brothers or others would refuse the invitation or, even worse, if they would turn against him and persecute him, he would, faithful to his nonviolent approach, not resort to force but "flee into another country to do penance with the blessing of God" (Test 26; RegNB 16:14). Or, if this would not be possible, "they should make themselves vulnerable to their enemies for love of the Lord Jesus Christ" and be happy "to suffer persecution for the sake of justice, for the kingdom of heaven is theirs" (RegNB 16:11–12).

In this respect, too, there exists a fundamental difference between Francis and the official policy of the church regarding heretics, confirmed in chapter 3, *De haereticis*, of the Fourth Lateran Council (1215). There we read that, if the preachers were not successful in confounding the heretics with their arguments and disputes, the latter "were to be handed over for their punishment to the secular powers" who, on taking office, had "to take a public oath that, according to the best of their abilities, they would strive to exterminate *(exterminare)* from the territories under their jurisdiction all heretics who were as such indicated by the church."[29] Unfortunately, however, even Francis' brothers who handed down the stories about Francis' nonviolent approach as an example to be followed by the brothers seem to have accepted this official church policy. For they make Francis say: "I have confidence in the Lord that invisible enemies... will punish them by having them corrected by the men of this world to their great shame and disgrace" (LegPer 76). This is not surprising as, in the course of years, the brothers became more and more involved in the preaching of crusades and in the collection of funds to bring them to a succesful end[30] —a clear sign that

[29] "Damnati vero saecularibus potestatibus praesentibus... relinquantur, animadversione debita puniendi... Moneantur autem et inducantur et si necesse fuerit per censuram ecclesiasticam compellantur saeculares potestates... ut... praestent publice iuramentum, quod de terris suae iurisdictioni subiectis universos haereticos ab ecclesia denotatos bona fide pro viribus exterminare studebunt..." *Conciliorum oecumenicorum decreta*, J. Alberigo et al. (eds), Bologna 1973;, 233.

[30] See C.T. Maier, *Preaching the Crusades: Mendicant Friars and the Cross in the Thirteenth Century*, Cambridge, 1994. In the first chapter, Maier deals also with

they had forgotten Francis' original approach. In light of my analysis, however, such a reply does not fit the voice of Francis, to whom the Lord had revealed "May the Lord give you peace" as a greeting (Test 23) and who therefore did not engage in arguments and disputes but was subject to all people for God's sake (RegNB 16:6).

As to the object of the virtues' confounding action, namely the vices and sins, we will deal with them *in extenso* when commenting on the next verses where the various vices and sins are mentioned individually. Here we may briefly describe what Francis more generally states about vices and sins in his writings. Vices and sins originate from the human heart which, under the influence of the devil, has turned away from the Lord (RegNB 22: 19–20; 15–26). Through these vices and sins people serve the world (2 LetFaith 65), instead of God and God's plan for humankind. In fact, through their vices and sins they continue the original sin through which they lost paradise where God placed them, and continue to lose it even until today (RegNB 23:1–2). For their vices and sins prevent them from cooperating with God's efforts to redeem humankind from its fallen state and to restore paradise. Instead of bringing Jesus to life again through their holy deeds in the strength, the *virtus*, of the Holy Spirit (2 LetFaith 53), they "crucify [Jesus] even now by delighting in vices and sins" (Adm 5:3). Because of the grave harm these vices and sins cause to humankind, it is of vital importance that the holy virtues succeed in confounding them in whatever form they present themselves. Then the holy virtues will be able to empower people to effectively serve God and to cooperate in God's redeeming activity by following in the footsteps of the poor and humble Jesus.

Francis and his attitude toward the fifth crusade. Unfortunately, however, he bases himself here exclusively on the biographies and does not even mention chapter 16 of the *Regula non bullata*, although this is the most important source for our knowledge of Francis and his attitude towards the Muslims. For an extensive commentary on RegNB 16, in its literary and its historical context, see my *Francis and Islam*, Part I, 3–134.

CHAPTER FOUR

The Effects of Each Individual Virtue

vv. 9–14

After Francis has explained how the human person acquires the virtues which proceed from God, he continues in the third section, verses 9-14, of *The Salutation of the Virtues* to describe the effects of these virtues, these divine forces, once a human person has succeeded in acquiring them. As has already been indicated in general terms in verse 8 which forms the link between the second and the third section, each one of the virtues confounds vices and sins. It is now to these vices and sins more in detail that Francis pays special attention in the third section. Francis follows here a fixed scheme as he did in the first section (vv. 1–3). He introduces again each one of the six foundational virtues of the brotherhood, and then mentions immediately the particular vices and sins, the counterforces, which each of these virtues confounds. However, in this section Francis personifies neither the individual virtues nor their counterforces.

Further, each virtue has to deal with more than one counterforce, which, moreover, are not described in a uniform way. There is Satan and all the people who are in the world; there are sins, temptations, fears and desires. In their variety they cover the entire range of evil and its sphere of influence.[1] By naming them all specifically, Francis and his brothers

[1] "Every virtue has more than one opponent. Thus Francis appears to cover the full width of evil's sphere of influence... Francis distinguishes visible and invisible enemies. They can be found inside as well as outside the human person: those from the outside are: the devil/Satan, the people who are in the world; the dark forces inside the human person are referred to as flesh/body. They operate from the inside, that is, from the heart." v.d. Goorbergh-Zweerman 106–107.

show that they have made a profound analysis of the evil forces that are dominant in the society at that time and threaten the brotherhood and its mission to build an alternative society. After he has introduced the virtue of obedience and its counterforces in v.14, Francis abandons the scheme he has followed so far and adds a few more verses on obedience, or rather on the obedient brother, because the practice of this virtue had apparently become an urgent problem within the brotherhood at that moment. Because of its special character this addition, verses 15–18, will be dealt with separately.

TEXT

9.	Sancta sapientia confundit satan et omnes malitias eius.	Holy Wisdom confounds Satan and all his malice.
10.	Pura sancta simplicitas confundit omnem sapientiam huius mundi et sapientiam corporis.	Pure holy Simplicity confounds all the wisdom of this world and the wisdom of the body.
11.	Sancta paupertas confundit omnem[2] cupiditatem et avaritiam et curas huius saeculi.	Holy Poverty confounds all covetousness and avarice and the cares of this age.
12.	Sancta humilitas confundit superbiam et omnes homines qui sunt in mundo similiter et omnia, quae in mundo sunt.	Holy Humility confounds pride and all the people who are in the world and all things that are in the world.

[2] "In verses 9–14 the adjective *omnem* or *omnes* occurs regularly in the second negative part of each verse. An exception in Esser's critical edition is verse 11 where *omnem* fails. Yet, the two big families of manuscripts a and c have an *omnem* before *cupiditatem*. However, since it is absent in the groups d and k, Esser believes that it must have been added later according to the accepted laws of addition and adaptation to the context in the tradition of texts. But would it also not be possible that for some copyists *omnes* occurred too often in the Salutation? In any case, "all the desire of riches" would fit very well in the text and agree with Francis' preference for the adjective "all." Lehmann 237. I follow Lehmann's suggestion.

13. Sancta caritas confundit omnes diabolicas et carnales tentationes et omnes carnales timores.	Holy Charity confounds all the temptations of the devil and the flesh and all carnal fears.
14. Sancta obedientia confundit omnes corporales et carnales voluntates.	Holy Obedience confounds all wishes of the body and the flesh.

Detailed exegesis

Holy Wisdom confounds Satan

It seems somewhat strange that Holy Wisdom is not contrasted with the wisdom of the world and the wisdom of the body, but rather with Satan and all his wicked ways.[3] It seems less strange, however, if we look at the Letter to the Faithful where a similar contrast can be found. Towards the end of that letter Francis addresses those who are "not living in penance... [and] do not observe what they have promised," but "practice vice and sin and... bodily serve the world by the desires of the flesh, the cares and anxieties of this age and the cares of this life." In an attempt to explain how such a situation can arise, Francis writes that these people "are deceived by the devil, whose children they are and whose works they perform. They are blind because they do not see the true light, our Lord Jesus Christ. They do not have the spiritual wisdom because they do not have within them the Son of God who is the true wisdom of the Father" (2 LetFaith 66–67).[4] Francis thus saw the lack of wisdom as a direct consequence of the deceiving and blinding activity of Satan, who keeps trying to get hold of the faithful and even of the

[3] In Adm 27:1 wisdom is opposed to and drives out ignorance. This opposition occurs rather frequently in medieval religious literature, but in all of Francis' writings only in this verse. Does this imply, that in Adm 27 Francis borrows an existing text from the monastic tradition without making it fully his own on this particular point? For if he would have done so, would he not have changed the text of Adm 27:1 and brought it more in line with SalVirt 9 where wisdom is opposed to and confounds Satan, or with 2 LetFaith 66–69, where wisdom is opposed to the deception, the blindness caused by Satan? For the monastic tradition behind Adm 27, see A. Jansen, Words of Salvation of Saint Francis, *FrancDigest* 4,2 (December 1994) 1–24. See also II B d, note 14; II C c, note 32.

[4] See Verhey 109–110.

brothers (RegNB 8:4) and establish his dwelling in their hearts. There he wants there to take over, as it were, the place which rightfully belongs to Christ, and to make the faithful his children whereas, because of their creation and redemption, they are meant to be God's children.

This ongoing struggle between Jesus and Satan as to who will reign in the human heart and guide the faithful in their actions is described in chapter 22 of the *Regula non bullata*. First Francis admonishes his brothers there: "We must hate our body with its vices and sins, for the devil wishes us to live according to the flesh and so to take away from us the love of Jesus Christ" (5). Later Francis returns more extensively to these evil intentions of the devil and explains at the same time how the devil tries to realize his plans. And because the devil uses very subtle pretexts, Francis considers a serious warning necessary here. He writes therefore: "And let us be much on our guard against the malice and subtlety of Satan, who wants people not to raise their mind and heart to God. And roaming about, Satan desires to ensnare the human heart under the guise (*sub specie*) of some reward or help and to choke out the word and the precepts of the Lord from the human memory, wishing to blind the human heart by worldly affairs and cares, and to make a dwelling there... Therefore, all my brothers, let us keep close watch not to lose or turn away our mind and heart from the Lord under the guise (*sub specie*) of some reward or work or help. But in the holy love which God is, I beg all my brothers, both the ministers and the others, to remove all obstacles and put behind all care and anxiety, and in the best way they can to serve, love, honor and adore the Lord God with a clean heart and pure mind, for this is what the Lord desires above all things" (19–20; 25–26).

These passages make it very clear that the struggle between Jesus and Satan was very much alive in Francis' mind. For it concerns the basic struggle between light and darkness, between seeing and blindness, that Francis saw taking place not only in the life of the people, but in the life of the brotherhood as well. And as he described it, it is up to the brothers, especially the learned ones, who had come under the influence of Satan and gone back on their promises to the Lord, to make their choice or rather to renew and to reconfirm the choice they once made to follow the footsteps of the poor and humble Jesus. If they do, Jesus Christ, the Wisdom of the Father, will again take his dwelling in their hearts. He will free them from Satan's deception, to which they had fallen prey, and make them walk in the light and the truth, in the holy Wisdom of the

Spirit. In the strength of this spiritual Wisdom they will then be able not only to resist but to confound Satan, who will no longer have a hold over them and keep them captive. With Satan gone, those brothers will also no longer choke from their memory the word and precepts of the Lord, as they had come to understand them in a new and often radically different way when they joined the brotherhood of the lesser brothers. Remembering the Lord's word and enlightened and strengthened by it, they will not feel attracted any more by Satan's subtle pretexts so as to give up their original choice for the sake of some reward or some work or some help.

Rather, they will keep their minds and hearts turned to God and treasure the word and precepts of the Lord as truly liberating, redeeming and life-giving, especially the Word spoken, loud and clear, in the life, passion and death of the poor and humble Jesus. This Word will lead the brothers into an ever deeper understanding of Holy Wisdom as the wisdom of the Cross, which makes them see themselves and their world in a completely different light and thus brings about a complete reversal of norms and values. Worldly affairs, cares and anxiety for worldly things do not count any more. What really counts is that the brothers have their hearts and minds purified from whatever held them in bondage to Satan, and thus are set free to follow the footsteps of the poor and humble Jesus. With a clean heart and a pure mind *(mundo corde et pura mente)*, they are then to serve and love the Lord, and commit themselves totally, as Jesus did, to the realization of God's plans with humankind—which are not fulfilled through might and power, accumulation of wealth and riches, places of honor and esteem in church or society, as Satan would have us believe, but through humble service, as Jesus showed us so beautifully by his life and ministry, even unto his death on the cross.

From Francis' descriptions, it is evident that, just as in the case of the virtues, he does not excel in clear-cut definitions of who Satan is and what his works are. Several counterforces which later are explicitly mentioned as contrasts to one of the virtues are enumerated here promiscuously, without making any distinction. This indicates that, just like the virtues, all the counterforces are intimately connected with one another and hence cannot be described one apart from the other. As Francis said earlier: "Whoever offends one [of the virtues] possesses none and offends all" (7). And just as the different virtues are but "various activities of the one sanctifying force of life of the divine Spirit," so are the different counterforces various activities of the one deceiving and blinding force of sin and death: Satan.[5] The struggle between virtue and vice is thus a matter of life and death. And the choice of which side they want to be on rests entirely with the brothers themselves. It is not an easy choice, certainly not for the learned brothers who, notwithstanding or because of their learning, have been taken in by the subtle pretexts of Satan. But if they do choose to be wise with the wisdom of Jesus, the wisdom of the Cross, they can be sure that, in virtue of that Holy Wisdom, they will overcome the power of sin and death and, seeing people and things in a new light, they will release new powers and open for themselves and others the way to new life. Indeed, Queen Holy Wisdom will confound Satan "who wishes to take from us the love of Jesus Christ and eternal life" (RegNB 22:5).

All this may sound rather abstract and far removed from daily reality. We ought to remember then that Francis sees Satan's activity very concretely, as is clear from the Earlier Rule 22:19–20; 25–26, quoted above. There Satan provides certain pretexts like reward, work and help, that are clearly intended to choke out from the brothers' hearts the word of the Lord—the word, that is, which the Lord revealed to Francis and which he continues to reveal in the foundational texts of the brotherhood (cf. Test 14; 39). In this way, Satan wants to blind the brothers and to move them away from the life of humble service and sharing which they had promised to live after the example of Jesus, who precisely in his poverty and humility revealed the wisdom of the Father. For us it may not be immediately evident what these pretexts exactly refer to in the historical context of the brotherhood, but the brothers knew it very well. For they had been discussing the subtle ways in which the devil was trying to entice the brothers, as is evident from various admonitions.[6]

Thus the question of looking for a reward is explicitly mentioned in Admonitions 21, where the word "reward" is mentioned three times in as

[5] See Lehmann 237. With reference to Verhey 41–56, 108–109, Lehmann writes: "Here too, Francis specifically enumerates several forms in which evil manifests itself... All of them can be summed up in the concept of self-glorification and self-righteousness of the human person."

[6] I differ here from W. Egger who writes: "There are some passages in chapter 22 that belong to the so-called 'Caveamus-passages' in which certain abuses are denounced. No concrete abuses are mentioned, as the text speaks rather in general

many verses, and 28. Apparently there were brothers who, when speaking to people, boasted about all the good they were doing in the hope of being rewarded by the applause and esteem of the people. Francis severely condemns these brothers because, like Mary, they should have kept all the good things which the Lord revealed to them in their hearts and shown them to the people by their deeds, their *operatio.* We touch here on a word that is very characteristic for Francis. Rather than getting involved in the "culture of the word" which was dominant among the leading people of Assisi and looking for the social esteem connected with it, the brothers should commit themselves to the *operatio* which I described above as the liberating, transforming activity in the power of the Spirit, through which men and women bring Jesus to birth again in this world and give him a new concrete, historical existence in their surroundings (cf. 2 LetFaith 48–53).[7] This *operatio* demanded from the brothers that they be "simple, humble, and pure,... and subject to every human creature for God's sake" (ibid. 45,47). Such a life, however, was not very rewarding in the world of Assisi, which followed quite different standards. The learned brothers-preachers especially found it difficult in such a situation to withstand the honor and praise which church authorities and people were bestowing on them. And, so these brothers argued, what is wrong if our God-given talents are recognized? What is wrong if we are rewarded for the good use we make of these talents? Francis saw the argument for what it really was: a subtle pretext to devote themselves to the office of preaching and to pride themselves about their achievements and the social esteem they brought, even to the point of wanting to appropriate the office of preaching to themselves (RegNB 17:4.6), instead of leading the life of humble service according to the

---

about *saecularia negotia, cura* (20), *impedimentum, cura, sollicitudo* (26)... The text refers to the danger in all its depth and its demonic character and explains it as a conflict between Satan and God." "Verbum in corde - cor ad Deum," Analyse und Interpretation von RegNB XXII, *Laurentianum* 23 (1982) 296–297. I think that, in mentioning two, respectively three, subtle pretexts of Satan, namely reward, help and work (20. 25), Francis points to concrete abuses within the brotherhood which were then being discussed and hence were well known to the brothers. These abuses also provide the historical context which makes it possible to reach a more concrete understanding of what is meant by the worldly affairs and concerns mentioned in the text.

[7] For a more detailed analysis of the various texts dealing with the *operatio*, see above in my treatment of the virtue of simplicity under II C c.

gospel which the Lord had revealed to Francis and the brothers (Test 14.19; RegNB 17:5) By means of his admonition Francis wished to make his learned brothers reflect on where true happiness and joy are to be found. At the same time, referring to a word of the Lord, he severely warned those who continued to let themselves be blinded and deceived, that they have received their reward (cf. Mt 6:2; Adm 21:3; RegNB 17:13).

As to the pretext of work, a concrete example from the historical context might be found in verse 25 of the Testament, where Francis firmly commands all his brothers "through obedience that, wherever they are, they should not be so bold as to seek any letter from the Roman curia... under the pretext of preaching *(sub specie praedicationis)*." With the help of the Legend of Perugia 115, this pretext could be reconstructed as follows: The Fourth Lateran Council (1215) had called for reforms in the church. If this call was to be realized in the everyday practice of the life of the faithful, it was necessary to have good preachers available who were not restricted in their activities by bishops and certainly not by poor parish priests who were often not well educated and were even living in sin (cf. Test 7). Hence, it would be very beneficial to the brothers-preachers in the exercise of their preaching office if they could obtain from the pope a letter of recommendation so that bishops would receive them in their dioceses and grant them permission to preach.[8] Francis flatly rejects this way of arguing in his Testament and "firmly commands all of the brothers through obedience that, wherever they are, they should not dare to ask for any letter from the Roman curia either personally or through an intermediary... under the pretext

[8] Pope Honorius III issued two bulls in which he "beseeched, exhorted and commanded" the bishops that, "when members of the aforesaid brotherhood [of the Lesser Brothers] present themselves bearing these letters, [they should] receive them as catholic and faithful men," and show themselves "sympathetic and kind toward them out of reverence for God and us" *Cum Dilecti*, June 11, 1218 or 1219. There is no explicit mention made of a permission to preach, though the pope does say that these lesser brothers, "after the example of the apostles, sow the seed of God's word and travel around through the regions of this world." As some bishops continued to have their misgivings about the brothers, the pope issued a second bull *Pro Dilectis* as a reminder on May 29, 1220. The second bull too does not speak explicitly about preaching. Hence it seems that Francis in his Testament does not explicitly refer to these two bulls as such but, not at all happy about their existence and that of others, firmly commands his brothers not to ask for any letter from the Roman curia, also not under the pretext of preaching. The complete

of preaching or even for the persecution of their bodies; but wherever they have not been received, let them flee into another country to do penance with the blessing of the Lord" (25–26).

Francis could not have stated his disapproval more emphatically for he forbade them "under obedience." Moreover, as he was doing this when he was on his deathbed, it becomes all the more clear that Francis saw this pretext, used mainly by the learned brothers, as a serious threat to the brotherhood's original ideal of not seeking any position of power but of being subject to all in humble service. This did not lead them to a slavish, servile attitude, for Francis and his brothers held firmly to their convictions, convinced as they were of the validity of their insights, their "knowing" (RegNB 9:7), which was not their own, but was revealed to them by the Lord. In obedience to the Lord, they were then also fully committed to find a way to win the other over to their insights, their ideals.

This is beautifully illustrated in the story of the Legend of Perugia to which I referred above. "One day, certain brothers said to blessed Francis: 'Father, do you not see that the bishops sometimes refuse us permission to preach and thereby oblige us to remain several days doing nothing in a region before we can speak to the people? It would be desirable to obtain a privilege from the lord pope for the brothers for the salvation of souls.' He answered vehemently: 'You, lesser brothers, do not know the will of God and you do not allow me to convert the whole world as God wishes. For I want first to convert the prelates by humility and respect. And when they see our holy life and our respect for them, they themselves will ask you to preach and convert the people. And they will call the people together for you with greater success than the privileges which you want and which will lead you to pride. And when you keep yourselves far removed from all greed and lead the people to respect grant the churches their rights, they will ask you also to hear the confessions of their people. You need not however to be concerned about this, for once they are converted, they will easily find confessors. For myself, I ask this privilege from the lord: to receive no privilege from of any person, except to show respect to all and to convert all through obedience to the holy rule, more by example than by word.'"

---

texts of the two bulls can be found in *Bullarium Franciscanum*, vol. I, Rome 1759, 2 and 5. For an English translation, see Armstrong, Hellmann, Short 558–559.

A story in 2 Celano 147 tells us how Francis practiced this advice himself and got permission to preach, even after having been refused at first. "Once when Francis came to Imola, a city of Romagna, he presented himself to the bishop of the region, asking his permission to preach. The bishop said to him: 'It is enough, brother, that I preach to my people.' Bowing his head, Saint Francis humbly went outside, and after a short time, he came back in. The bishop said to him: 'What do you want, brother? What are you seeking now?' And blessed Francis said: 'Lord, if a father drives his son out of one door, he must come back in by another.' Subdued by this humility, the bishop embraced him with a happy countenance and said: 'You and all your brothers may preach in my diocese in the future with my general permission, for your holy humility has merited this.'"

A historical context for the third pretext of help can be distilled from chapter 8 of the *Regula non bullata*, where in verse 4 Francis moreover explicitly introduced the devil into the brothers' discussion about receiving money. Already in the Earlier Rule 7:7, Francis and his brothers had laid down that "they might receive for their work everything necessary except money." Apparently this was much easier said than done, for in the practice of everyday life many problems arose. And so the brothers had to sit down, look at the arguments brought forward, evaluate them, and finally come up with new provisions, which they then formulated in chapter 8.[9] One of the arguments was almost certainly that, if they were allowed to receive money, they could do so much more good, especially to help the sick brothers and the lepers. Francis and the brothers partly agreed with this argument, as is clear from the exception they made for the sick brothers (3) and the lepers (10) in cases of evident necessity. Indeed, as said earlier, for Francis, people were above laws and rules.[10]

This, however, did not imply that the brothers should return to Assisi's economic practices. On the contrary, Francis and the brothers saw any attempt made in this direction as coming from the devil, who very cleverly used many well-meaning people to try to convince the brothers that there was nothing wrong with Assisi's money system and that the brothers, therefore, need not look at money and coins as if they

[9] See above, under the virtue of poverty, II C d.

[10] See above, under the virtue of obedience, II C g.

were no better than stones (3–4). However enticing Assisi's reasoning might have sounded, especially the argument about all the help they could give if they would accept money, Francis and his brothers knew better. The devil was only using help as a pretext to try and blind them for the real meaning of money and coins. For, from the time they had left Assisi and had started working in the almshouses, they had seen and experienced the evil consequences of money: money blinds and corrupts; money separates and divides; money victimizes people and leaves them poor and powerless by the wayside.

For this reason, Francis and his brothers could not but refuse to handle money as it was the means whereby Assisi negotiated the exclusion of rather than the help for all those living in almshouses. This implied that, if one of the brothers would collect money or coins and join again the money game of Assisi, the other brothers would have to consider him "as a false brother and an apostate, and a thief and a robber, and as one who held the purse, unless he truly repented" (7). For he would have abandoned the brotherhood's ideals of solidarity and sharing; thereby he would deprive the poor, the sick, and the lepers of their rightful share in the goods of God's creation and become like Judas (cf. Jn 12:6). The strong language used here indicates that the whole question of receiving money touched Francis and his brothers very deeply. In fact, it touched the very heart, the very essence of the fundamental choice they had made when they left Assisi and its economic system in order to follow in the footsteps of Jesus. By using such strong language, they hoped to impress upon a brother who had been blinded by the devil an awareness of the seriousness of what he had done and so persuade him to repent and return to the brotherhood. At the same time, they hoped to alert the other brothers so that they would not fall to the devil's pretext of money as a means to help the poor and the sick. If they really want to help the poor and the sick, they should do so not by joining the money game, but by placing themselves at their service as Jesus had done. Through their solidarity with them, they would then be able to build a new society where the poor and the sick would not be excluded because of their lack of money, but welcomed to sit at the table of the Lord and to receive their rightful share of the goods of God's creation.

The insertion of chapter 8 in the *Regula non bullata* shows how conscious the brotherhood was of the danger of being blinded by the subtle pretexts of Satan and so losing sight of the goals they had set for themselves when leaving Assisi. It was a danger to which they were constantly exposed in their unavoidable confrontation with the world of Assisi, and even more so during the last years of Francis' life, with the growing influx and influence of the learned brothers. To overcome this danger, the brothers needed "the true light, Jesus Christ, the true Wisdom of the Father," as Francis wrote in the already often mentioned passage from his Letter to the Faithful (66–67). Enlightened by Holy Wisdom, they would unmask all the subtle pretexts of the devil and so undo his evil influence. Thus liberated from Satan's power and no longer exposed to his blinding actions, their minds and hearts would turn towards God. This would help them to renew and strengthen their original resolve to see people and things no longer from the perspective of Assisi, but from God's perspective of love, of unity and solidarity among all God's creation. This vision, the vision of the truly wise, would guide them to faithfully follow the road on which they had set out after they had heard Jesus' call. Their unwavering commitment to their calling might, in its turn, win over others to join the movement and to let themselves be guided and inspired by Queen Holy Wisdom, who Francis trusts will confound Satan.

And All His Malice (v. 9)

In our reading,[11] Francis uses the adjective *all (omnis)* in the negative part of each of the verses 9–14. We touch here upon one of the adjectives denoting totality and universality that enjoy Francis' preference also in his other writings.[12] At times Francis even adds this adjective when referring to a text of the New Testament. This is very clear when he speaks about the wisdom of the world. Whereas Paul in his First Letter to the Corinthians asks "Hasn't God made foolish the wisdom of this world" (1:20) Francis, re-echoing this text, asserts that "pure holy Simplicity confounds *all* the wisdom of this world" (SalVirt 10). The adjective *all* could have been absent from this text without in any way changing the essence of Francis' assertion. It is clear therefore that, by inserting it, Francis wishes to emphasize more strongly the message he wants to convey.[13] The same holds true for verse 13, where Francis writes about holy

[11] See above note 2.

[12] See especially Lehmann, passim.

Charity confounding *all* carnal fears, while the First Letter of John only states that charity drives out fear (4:18).

The message, then, which Francis wished to underline once more by his frequent use of the adjective *all*, and especially by adding it to quotations of Scripture texts, concerned the radical incompatibility between virtue and vice, between holiness and sin, between God and Satan. He had dealt with this earlier when speaking about the possession and the loss of the virtues (6–7). If a brother possesses one virtue, Francis wrote there, he possesses all of them. For if a brother possesses one virtue, the Spirit of God dwells within him—the Spirit of God who is one and undivided and hence cannot exist without all God's virtues being present at the same time. All this implies that, if a brother possesses one virtue, there is no room whatsoever left for any evil. The possession of each virtue therefore has a total effect, inclusively as well as exclusively, in that it includes all other virtues and excludes all evil, as is clearly expressed also in the text I quoted from Admonition 27: "Where there is the fear of the Lord to guard the house, there the enemy can have no place to enter" (5).[14]

This total effect is first of all the result of the activity of Queen Holy Wisdom, who confounds Satan and all his malice. The Latin *malitias* is translated differently by different authors. Brady has "wicked ways," while Armstrong has "cunning" and Flood "wiles." From my description of Francis' understanding of who Satan is and what he does, and especially also from the fact that Francis in his warning against Satan in the Earlier Rule 22:19 combines *malitia* and *subtilitas*, it can be concluded that *malitias* refers to Satan's malicious activities of blinding and deceiving through which he in a subtle, cunning way tries to entice the brothers towards abandoning their original purpose as a community of lesser brothers and returning to the dominant values and perspectives of Assisi which they had left behind. Satan's way of working is then further made concrete in the following verses, where Francis deals more in detail with the struggle in which the virtues are involved. These verses suggest that Francis has observed how Satan's efforts have been successful in persuading at least some of the brothers to follow the wisdom of the world, to covet more and more things and avariciously hold on to

[13] See Lehmann 234–235.

[14] See above, III B b. Also Lehmann 237.

them, to take pride in themselves and their achievements, and to strive to be over others rather than to be subject and submissive to them. Therefore, Francis reminds them and all the other brothers of the foundational virtues of the brotherhood. He does so in the hope that the brothers will indeed allow these virtues of God to become ever more active forces in their lives. The virtues will help them to see and judge things properly and to be on their guard against all the evil that Satan through his malice has caused and still tries to cause to the brotherhood.

This last idea is especially emphasized in the Earlier Rule 8:1, at the beginning of the chapter on the question of receiving money. Quoting there a command of the Lord from the gospel of Luke: "See and be on your guard against all avarice" (Lk 12:15), the brothers took the liberty to insert the word "malice." Why did they make the insertion of exactly this word? It surely must have been something of special importance to them. I have observed already how Francis and the brothers saw the devil at work in the brotherhood when it came to the understanding of the true reality of money. Right at the beginning of this very important chapter, they wanted therefore to open the eyes of all the brothers to what was really going on. They did not have to deal merely with some well-meaning people who wished the brothers to change their views on money. No, they had to deal with Satan and his malice! That is why they had to see well and to be very much on their guard. For, in his malice, Satan would do anything to blind (4) the brothers to the truth with all kinds of subtle arguments and so open the way for avarice to enter their hearts, accompanied by all the other vices and sins. If Satan succeeded in his endeavors, all that the brotherhood stood for and wanted to achieve on its journey through the world would be radically jeopardized. A strong warning, based on a command of the Lord, was therefore highly appropriate at the beginning of this chapter on the problems of money. The brothers should, first of all, see things in their proper perspective. This they could do only if they were guided by the word and wisdom of God. Thus they would be properly equipped to see through, to unmask, the evil intentions of the devil and to be on their guard against whatever he might try to do to have his evil ways and to entice them away from God's plans for the brotherhood.[15]

[15] For this passage, see also below, under IV B d.

Pure Holy Simplicity Confounds All the Wisdom of this World

As mentioned already, the wisdom of this world and the wisdom of the body turn up somewhat unexpectedly in this verse. One would have thought to find them mentioned rather as forms of a false kind of wisdom in contrast to the virtue of holy wisdom. And, indeed, in my exegesis it hardly appeared possible to describe Holy Wisdom's activity in confounding Satan's subtle, blinding pretexts without referring to the wisdom of this world and the wisdom of the body as they are manifest in the wisdom of Assisi, its written and unwritten laws and customs and its value system. Yet, Francis relates these forms of false wisdom very explicitly to the virtue of simplicity.[16] This shows once more that in his *The Salutation of the Virtues* Francis does not deal with the virtues in a systematic way, but rather takes his own experience within the brotherhood as a starting point. He saw that the learned brothers were easy prey for the enticements of the wisdom of this world and the wisdom of the body, whereas these enticements had no impact on the simple brothers. What exactly does Francis mean by these false forms of wisdom? Of course, they figured already in the description of their opposite virtue of simplicity, but my commentary on this verse gives us an opportunity to go into more detail, although it will be unavoidable that ideas, expres-

[16] Jansen thinks that in verses 9–10 we can hear an echo of James 3:14–15: "If you have a bitter jealousy and if there is ambition in your heart, do not glory nor tell lies in opposition to the truth. For this is not the wisdom that comes down from above: rather it is earthly, animal and devilish." The reasons for his view are that "James too distinguishes between wisdom that comes from above and false wisdom. Further, the false wisdom has three characteristics: earthly, animal and devilish. The same triad is also clearly woven into the verses of the SalVirt: Satan and all his malices, wisdom of this world, wisdom of the body" (a.c. 170). Jansen's arguments do not look very convincing. Of course, the triad is well-known in the Christian tradition. However, the Latin terminology that James and Francis use in the triad's formulation is quite different. James uses the adjectives: *terrena*, *animalis* and *diabolica*, while Francis speaks of *Satan*, *sapientia mundi* and *sapientia corporis*. Moreover, whereas James, in line with the tradition, contrasts the earthly and animal wisdom with the wisdom from above, Francis, as I observed already, contrasts the wisdom of the world *(mundi)* and the wisdom of the body *(corporis)*, rather surprisingly, with the virtue of simplicity. Hence, there exists little or no reason to support Jansen's argument. v.d. Goorbergh-Zweerman too refer to James 3:15 and observe that "the many similarities between the Letter of James and the Salutation are remarkable" (106, note 43).

sions and texts that were used earlier return in the following considerations. It is hoped, however, that they do so in a somewhat new and different perspective.

It is clear that in the expression "wisdom of the world"—a wisdom which contrasts with "holy Simplicity"—the word "world" is used in a negative sense, as it is later when *The Salutation of the Virtues* speaks about humility confounding "all the people who are in the world and all things that are in the world" (12). Like Satan in the previous verse, the world too belongs to enemies who, according to Francis' well-known description in Second Letter to the Faithful, wish to deceive the faithful (69). It is this world which the brothers left when they decided to follow the will of the Lord and to please him (RegNB 22:9). Historically, then, the world meant here is the religious, cultural, socio-economic and political world of Assisi in Francis' day, insofar as there exists, on account of the sinful structures that have grown through the ages, an irreconcilable opposition between this world, with its false ideas and its values or rather nonvalues, and the plans which the Lord had and still has for the world. Because of this opposition, the world as it has developed concretely in the course of history hates those to whom Jesus gave the word of the Lord and who, as a result, broke with the world in their desire to live according to the Lord's word (cf. Jn 17:14; RegNB 22:47). In its hatred, the world, just like Satan, will therefore not rest until it has choked out from the brothers' heart the word which the Lord spoke in calling them to leave the world and has installed itself, together with its vices, there where the Lord is supposed to dwell, accompanied by the holy virtues that proceed from the Lord (cf. RegNB 22:19–24; 27; SalVirt 4). Together with Satan, the world then strives to make its ideas and its values, its "wisdom," occupy the place of Queen Holy Wisdom and her sister, Holy Simplicity, in the human heart.

The expression "wisdom of the world" occurs only once more in the writings of Francis, namely in the oft-quoted RegNb 17:10, where Francis admonishes his brothers: "And let us keep ourselves from the wisdom of this world and the prudence of the flesh." And the reason which Francis gives in the next two verses is that "the spirit of the flesh strives greatly towards having words, but little towards deeds *(operatio)*. And it does not seek the religion and holiness of the spirit within, but it wishes and desires to have a religion and holiness outwardly apparent to people." The wisdom of the world has thus everything to do with the "culture of the word" prevailing among the leading groups in Assisi.[17] It was the mastery of this culture, not his deeds, which made a person wise in the eyes of the world and gave him prominent status within society. He belonged to the elite in the city and, according to the rules of the well-ordered medieval world, deserved the respect of others. It is not surprising that this culture and its accompanying status and privileges exercised a great attraction on the brothers who, as preachers and theologians, were devoted to the word and who often were acclaimed because of their eloquent preaching and teaching. In these circumstances, to resist the pull of this cultural climate and not to go along with the wisdom of the world and the rewards the world had in store for those who complied with its standards[18] required great strength and determination. That these qualities were not always present, and that, as a result, the wisdom of the world made inroads among the brothers, is clearly shown in some of the Admonitions.

In Admonition 6, Francis admonished all brothers, but especially the brothers-preachers: "It is a great shame for us, servants of God, that while the saints actually performed the deeds *(fecerunt opera)*, suffering tribulation and persecution, we wish to receive glory and honor by merely speaking and preaching about them" (3). In Admonition 7, Francis addressed especially the theologians, those who were supposed "to minister spirit and life" to the brothers and to the people, but at times miserably failed to do so because the wisdom of the world, which attaches such great importance to the cultivation of empty words and the promotion of a person's status, had corrupted their original intentions. Instead of ministering spirit and life, they allowed themselves rather "to be killed by the letter" for they "wished to know the words alone, so that they might be esteemed as wiser than others and be able to acquire great riches to give to their relatives and friends" (2).

Notwithstanding these serious admonitions, the culture of the word continued to have its followers among the brothers, so much so that even the Rule and the Testament were not safe from them and their interpretations. With their mastery of the culture of the word, they knew how to talk their way out of the solemn promise they had made of leaving

[17] Zelina Zafarana: "la cultura della parola." La predicazione francescana, in: *Francescanesimo e vita religiosa dei laici nel 200*, Assisi 1981, 203–250, here 205.

[18] As to the rewards which Satan uses as a subtle pretext to separate the brothers from God, see above under B a..

the world and how to justify their becoming part of that very same world again and following its wisdom. It was these brothers that Francis felt obliged to address once more in the final admonition of his Testament as he was naturally deeply worried about their continuing influence and their attempts to move the brotherhood away from its original inspiration. In a very last bid to prevent them from tampering with the rule and his Testament, he commanded them under obedience—stronger language was not available to him—not to make any glosses, which was precisely their specialty and earned them their place of respect in the world. Rather, they should understand the rule and the testament "simply and without gloss, and observe them with holy deeds *(operatio)* until the end" (38–39). They should again bring together words and deeds, which the world in its own wisdom had separated. To this end, they should renounce the culture of the word. They should no longer use their learning and eloquence to find rationalizations to accept the values or rather the nonvalues of the world's wisdom. Instead they should return to the simple understanding and observation of the words that the Lord had revealed to Francis, even if this would lead to suffering and persecution.

In other words, the learned brothers must become simple again. It is then that holy Simplicity will get an opportunity to confound the wisdom of the world. That is, holy Simplicity will motivate the brothers to free themselves from seeking what is valuable in the eyes of the world, from looking for social recognition, from needing clever rationalizations to avoid observing what they have promised the Lord, and from separating words and deeds. So they will be free again for their God-given mission in the world: to order the world not in conformity with the insights of the wisdom of the world, but in accordance with God's wisdom which God, in the inseparable unity of the words and the life of the poor and humble Jesus, revealed and continues to reveal to the little ones but keeps hidden from the wise and learned of this world (cf. Mt 11:25).

And the Wisdom of the Body (v. 10)

The expression "wisdom of the body" is unique and occurs only here in the writings of Francis. In the present context, one might have expected the expression "wisdom of the flesh" (cf. 2 LetFaith 45) or "prudence of the flesh" which we find mentioned together with the "wisdom of the world" in the Earlier Rule 17:10. For it is the flesh that is usually described as the opponent of the Spirit of the Lord in the ongoing struggle of who will reign within the brotherhood (RegNB 17:11–15; cf. Adm 1), and is considered one of "our enemies," together with the world and the devil (2 LetFaith 69). Moreover, in the next verses Francis uses thrice the adjective *carnalis*, "of the flesh" (13–14), once in combination with *corporalis*, "of the body." All the same, Francis prefers here to speak about "body," as he also does in v. 15, where he speaks about the obedient brother who "has his body mortified," although in the Earlier Rule 17:15 he writes that "the Spirit of the Lord wishes the flesh to be mortified." Given this preference, the question must be asked whether the word "body" has any special connotations in the mind of Francis "Body" has various meanings in the writings of Francis. It is clear, however, that in the present context it carries a negative connotation, just as "world" does. And whereas the "world" stood for the totality of all the negative tendencies at work in the world in Francis' day, especially the culture of the word and the search for power, possessions and prestige it involved, so the "body" stands for the totality of negative tendencies and desires present within people who, under the influence of the world, have allowed the word of God to be choked out and, instead, made their own the false ideas and nonvalues of the world. They have internalized the world's way of thinking and learned to act in conformity with the way the world expects them to act in order to increase the world's and their own wealth and glory, even at the expense of others. The wisdom of the world has become their wisdom, the wisdom of the body, blinding their individual minds and enticing them to act in the ways of the world, which are evil. Thus, as Francis says, "they serve the world with their body" in that they let themselves be guided by "the desires of the flesh, the cares and anxieties of this age and the cares of this life" (2 LetFaith 65) and so contribute to maintaining the world in its present sinful state. In other words, the body is that facet of the human personality which makes people disobey the word of the Lord and refuse to serve their fellow humans, because power, possessions and prestige, claiming as their own the good that belongs to God alone, are the nonvalues that motivate them in their actions.[19]

[19] In their commentary on Adm 10, P. van Leeuwen and S. Verhey write: "The word 'body' has here the biblical meaning of the human person who is self-centered,

It is in the pursuit of these nonvalues that people find a certain sense of security. Hence, they will do whatever they can to hold on to their power, to enhance their possessions and prestige and to avoid whatever jeopardizes them. In this light, it is very understandable that they do not want to expose themselves, their bodies, in the humble service of others. For in thus exposing their bodies, they make themselves vulnerable and run the risk, not only of no longer being able to control their own lives, but even of being hurt. The basis for their security and their feeling of safety is being threatened. And fearing to lose their bodies and therewith their lives, they withdraw within the protective walls of their own world, of their possessions and wealth. Thus they try to keep the other far away from them so that they and their bodies cannot be wounded in their service, their love of the other, but rather will be kept safe and sound, untouched by the other.[20] In doing so, however, they do not save their lives, their bodies; rather, their bodies, kept safe and secure in accordance with the teachings of the wisdom of the body, become "the enemy... through which people sin" (Adm 10:2) and thus in the end lose their lives, their bodies.

People would have the power to hold this enemy captive and to wisely guard themselves against it (ibid. 3) if only they would allow the virtue of pure, holy Simplicity to rule their lives, confound the wisdom of the body, and open them to the true wisdom of God. However, often they do not exercise this power and let their body follow its own wisdom, leading them far away from the true wisdom, for "it is sweet to the body to commit sin and bitter to serve God" (2 LetFaith 69). Francis had himself experienced this very profoundly at the beginning of his conversion when "the Lord himself led [him] among the lepers." Until then, under the influence of the wisdom of the world and of the body, Francis had "sweetly" gone along with the sinful way Assisi treated the lepers and found it "bitter" to be among them, let alone serve them. And he had justified his behavior with the help of all the arguments which the world had mustered in the course of time. But while in their midst, he no longer saw people and things no longer in the way the world wished him to see them. Rather, freed from the blindness caused by the wisdom

---

who is directed towards his/her own possessions, his/her own glory. 'Body' can be substituted by: the human person who is caught up within him/herself." *Woorden van heil van een kleine mens*, 73.

[20] See A. Jansen, My Yoke is Sweet, *FrancDigest* 9,1 (March 1999) 28–38, here 33–35.

of the body and guided now by what he would later call Lady pure, holy Simplicity, who unmasks all the rationalizations of human wisdom, he came to see the lepers as the Lord wished him to see them, simply and truthfully: as his brothers and sisters. And Francis concludes his brief description of this episode which radically changed his way of life, saying: "And when I left the lepers that which seemed bitter to me was changed into sweetness of soul and body" (Test 2–3).

This process of conversion was never finished, but had to be started over and over again, even until the end of Francis' life. "Brothers, let us begin to serve the Lord God, for up to now we have made little or no progress," were his famous words (1 Cel 103). And he kept admonishing his brothers: "We must hate our bodies with their vices and sins." Or more positively: "We must place our bodies under the yoke of service and holy obedience" (2 LetFaith 37 and 40; cf. RegNB 22:5). Similarly he wrote in SalVirt 15: "[The obedient brother] keeps his body mortified to obedience to the Spirit and to obedience to his brother, and is subject and submissive to all people." And meditating on the Our Father he wrote that all human beings are called by their God Creator and Saviour "to spend all [their] energies and affections of soul and body in the service of [God's] love and of nothing else and to love [their] neighbors as [themselves]" (ExpOurFather 5). All these admonitions about the way the brothers were to treat their bodies presuppose that they have confounded the wisdom of the body, which does not believe in service or in being subject to others, and that instead they have discovered the true meaning and dignity of the body as God revealed it in Jesus, the true wisdom of the Father.

Francis summarized his discovery of the theological meaning of the body at the beginning of his fifth Admonition: "Consider, O human being, in how excellent a position the Lord God has placed you, because God created you and formed you to the image of God's beloved Son according to the body..." (1). When speaking here about God's creation of the human body in the image of the beloved Son, Francis is not indulging in any kind of abstract theological reflection.[21] Rather, he

[21] See my *Francis and Islam* 119–121. In Adm 5:1, Francis combines the text of the creation story in Genesis with ideas found in the Letter to the Romans 9:28–29 or the Letter to the Colossians 1:15. These NT texts particularly have led to all kinds of abstract theological reflections. Thus Eric Doyle asks if Francis meant to say here "that the incarnation of God's Son—Jesus of Nazareth—was first in the mind of

thinks of the concrete, historical person of Jesus who "was poor and homeless and lived on alms, he and the blessed Virgin and his disciples" (RegNB 9:5). For it was by this earthly Jesus that Francis had been touched. The meaning and dignity of the human body must therefore be sought in all that happened to Jesus and his body during his life here on earth. Jesus gave his body in a life of service, especially to the poor (RegNB 4:6). He even lost his body, dying on the cross in obedience to the will of the Father (cf. 2 LetFaith 10–11) and in order thus to undo the divisions which resulted from human disobedience (cf. Adm 2) and to restore the lost paradise where God originally had placed humankind and where also the poor have their rightful place at the table of the Lord (RegNB 9:8; 23:3; Test 22).

In the Eucharist, Jesus repeats this historical act and so continues to give his body over and over again for the liberation of humankind (cf. Adm 1:10).[22] Meditating on Jesus' life and death, and especially on the Eucharist where Jesus continues to be with us in humble form till the end of time (Adm 1:16–18. 22), Francis discovered the meaning and dignity of the human body in the way Jesus himself had lived it before us in his own body. And he began to see that he could realize the dignity of his body only by following in Jesus' footsteps, by leaving the world of power and possessions and committing himself with his whole person, with body and soul, to the building of God's world. In this way, Francis, like Jesus, "loses his body in obedience" (Adm 3:1–3) to God's plan for the liberation of humankind.

The truth of this view on the meaning and dignity of the human body, created in the image of Jesus, was difficult for the wise and learned brothers to understand, just as it was difficult, if not impossible, to understand the truth about the poor and humble Jesus being the Son of God, and about the Eucharist as the sacrament of God's humility (Adm 1:15–18). They had some very different ideas about what they wanted to achieve in life with their bodies. In particular, they shied away from the hardships, the sacrifices and the persecution which a life of ser-

---

God before Adam?" And he continues: [Francis'] words are clearly a seminal formulation of that view of the reason of the incarnation which is theologically expressed as the unconditional primacy of Christ." See his *St. Francis and the Song of Brotherhood*, London, 1980, 60.

[22] See my Eucharist and Priesthood according to Francis, with special reference to the First Admonition, *FrancDigest* 7,2 (December 1997) 13–27.

vice after the example of the poor and humble Jesus might lead to. As I mentioned earlier, they were ready to ask the Roman curia for letters in order to avoid "the persecution of their bodies" (Test 25). Because of various theological arguments and especially because of the support of the official church authorities, they felt they were acting wisely, even though they had promised the Lord differently when joining the brotherhood. That is why Francis reminds "all his brothers wherever they are" on their mission journey trying to bring peace by "being subject to every human creature for God's sake," and that they "should remember that they have given themselves and have abandoned their bodies to the Lord Jesus Christ. And for his love they must expose themselves to enemies, both visible and invisible, for the Lord says: "Whoever loses his life for my sake, will save it for eternal life" (RegNB 16:6.10–11), or, as he invites his brothers in the Office of the Passion, "to offer up [their] bodies and take up [Jesus'] holy cross and follow his most holy commands even to the end" (7:8).

In other words, remembering or rather taking to heart again (*re-cordentur)* their original calling, the brothers should look at life with the simplicity that was theirs in the beginning (Test 15,19) and live it simply out of love of Jesus, whatever might happen to them, even exposing themselves to their enemies trusting Jesus' words: "Blessed are you when people hate you, and malign you and persecute you and drive you out and abuse you and cast out your name as evil and when they utter every kind of slander against you because of me. Rejoice on that day and be glad, for your reward is great in heaven. and I say to you, my friends, do not be afraid of these things and do not fear those who kill the body and thereafter can do no more... Through your patience you will possess your souls and whoever perseveres to the end will be saved" (RegNB 16:15–21). As this concatenation of gospel texts indicates, Francis and his brothers could not find enough texts to encourage the brothers to have that simple faith and trust in God that would allow them to see people and things from God's perspective of love and so open themselves for the working of the divine virtue of pure holy Simplicity, confounding the wisdom of the body and helping the brothers to see the true meaning and dignity of the body created in the image of Jesus' body and to live accordingly. Then, they will "carry [Jesus] in [their] heart and body... and give birth to him through their holy works" (2 LetFaith 53).

Holy Poverty Confounds All Covetousness and Avarice

The first counterforces that try to obstruct the working of Lady Poverty are covetousness and avarice. They are mentioned as such in Admonitions 27:11. Apparently they form a fixed couple whereby the latter presupposes the first and at the same time seems to take it one step further and to intensify it. For whereas covetousness expresses the strong desire of coveting things, that is of appropriating and possessing things and so becoming rich, avarice is the equally strong or even stronger desire, the greed, of people who, at all costs, want to hold on to and to appropriate even more things once they have become rich. Considering their possessions as exclusively their own, no matter how they have been obtained, avaricious people are in no way prepared to part with them and to share their riches with others; on the contrary, their minds are completely set on increasing their riches ever further, often, so it seems, just for the sake of having them and showing them off, while not at all concerned about the social consequences of their avarice, their greed, and the victims they make.

Whereas covetousness and avarice were always condemned and riches were always frowned upon in the Christian tradition, this was especially so at the time of Francis when preachers, writers and artists targeted the easily made riches of the merchants, the class profiting most from the advance of the money economy. Within the city states, the new centers of power, the merchants formed a new elite whose economic power was no longer based on the possession of land, but of money.[23] Often they made their money through exorbitant profits in times of scarcity of goods, and through lending the money thus earned at high interest rates to people in need. These practices were rightly condemned as a great injustice in which, all too often, the poor were the victims. Because of the negative impact which the merchants had on the society, they began to be depicted as usurers who by the weight of their bag of money are dragged into hell. And whereas before *superbia*, pride, was considered the feudal sin par excellence and mother of all other sins and vices, gradually it started to lose its prominence and its place as the most important sin was taken by *avaritia*, avarice or greed.

However, in his writings, Francis nowhere referred to this change of views. He mentioned both avarice and pride as serious threats to the

[23] Le Goff, *De cultuur van middeleeuws Europa*, Amsterdam 1987, 314–316.

original ideals of the brotherhood, but did not try to determine which one of the two would be the most prominent. Even if he knew about this discussion at all, he would probably not have been very interested in it, as in his eyes it must have been a largely academic problem, whose solution was of very little significance for the brotherhood. The closest he came to what could be taken as an expression of his view in this matter can be found in verse 12 of *The Salutation of the Virtues*. There he follows the traditional view as regards pride—namely , that all that is in this world is pride—and thus seems to give first place to pride.[24] But as *The Salutation of the Virtues* can hardly be seen as a theological treatise about the virtues and their order of prominence, it is necessary to read this statement for what it is: a part of a poetic testament in which Francis makes use of a traditional datum in order to remind his brothers of the original ideals of the brotherhood and to motivate them to be faithful to these ideals against the enticements of the world.

After this short excursus, let us return to avarice and its companion covetousness, which Francis presents as the first counterforces of the virtue of poverty. It is remarkable that, although avarice and covetousness were so characteristic of his age and constituted such a serious threat to the practice of holy poverty, yet in his writings Francis referred to them rather sparingly. He did not even mention them at all in his Letter to the Faithful. However, when Francis did refer to them, it always happened in important texts which dealt with serious problems facing the brotherhood at one time or another. Thus, besides in *The Salutation of the Virtues* and in Admonitions 27:3, covetousness, *cupiditas*, is mentioned once more in Testament21. In this text Francis enjoined his brothers to learn an honest trade, that is, a trade which contributes to the building up of good relations with others within society,[25] and asked them to do so "not from a desire *(cupiditatem)* of receiving wages for their work, but as an example [of honest work at the service of others] and in order to avoid idleness [for as the Apostle says: Whoever does not wish to work shall not eat]."[26] As this request is expressed in the Testament, where Francis at the end of his life reminded his brothers once more of the original ideals of the brotherhood and urged them for the last time to remain faithful to them, it is clear that he considered cov-

[24] See my commentary on the counterforces of humility, below under IV B h..

[25] D. Flood, The Politics of "Quo Elongati," *Laurentianum* 29 (1988) 370–385, here 372; reprinted in *FrancDigest* 3,1 (June 1993) 39–55.

etousness a serious problem for the future development of his brotherhood. Clearly, some of the brothers had begun to take on work in order to obtain wages. In this way they showed that they were no longer satisfied with their role of lesser brothers who worked with their hands to earn their own livelihood and to be of service to people (Test 20), and so to build a new type of social relationship among the people. Instead, they wanted to return to the money economy of Assisi and all the evil consequences such an economy entailed, especially in that it divided people, whereas Francis wanted the brothers to be committed, heart and soul, to bringing people together as brothers and sisters mutually serving one another in peace according to God's original plan of creation.

Avarice is mentioned three times more in Francis' writings: first, at the beginning of chapter 8 of the Earlier Rule, the chapter which Francis and his brothers inserted when problems arose about receiving money.[27] We encounter here thus the same problem Francis addressed in his Testament (20–21), albeit at an earlier stage in the history of the brotherhood. After Francis and the brothers had analyzed the situation at that moment and unmasked Satan's blinding activity therein (3–4), they renewed their earlier decision not to receive money (RegNB 7:7) and added a more elaborated text on not receiving money in the present chapter 8. They prefaced this new chapter with a text of the gospel. Thus they wanted to support and confirm their decision, presenting it as a command of Jesus, addressed to them there and then, as it is formulated in the present tense: "The Lord commands *(praecipit)* in the Gospel" (1). For in Jesus' name they had decided to leave everything. In his name therefore they also wanted to determine how they would more concretely fill in their program of life.[28] They found the appropriate word for their new situation in a text of the gospel of Luke into which, as we saw, they inserted the word: "malice." Thus the text reads: "See, be on your guard against all malice and avarice" (RegNB 8:1; cf. Luke 12:15).

To this text the brothers added another text from Luke's gospel, in which they made yet another change, omitting certain words and adding

[26] This text of St. Paul in his Second Letter to the Thessalonians 3:10 is quoted by Francis in RegNB 7:4, where he, as the title of the chapter indicates, speaks about "the manner of serving and working."

[27] See above under IV B a and b.

[28] See D. Flood, Franciscans and Money, *Haversack* 4,2 (December 1980), 12–21, here 13; also his *Francis of Assisi*, 24–25.

the words, "the anxieties of this age." The adapted text links together the anxieties of this age and the cares of this life, which Francis also mentioned together in Second Letter to the Faithful 66. I will return to this text later when I deal with the third counterforce, the cares of this age. For the moment it suffices to say that, just as in *The Salutation of the Virtues*, so in the Earlier Rule 8:1 avarice and the cares of this life are mentioned together as counterforces of the virtue of poverty. By placing both of them at the very beginning of the chapter in words of the Lord's warning to the brothers then and there to be on their guard against them, Francis showed most clearly that he considered both of them as some of the evil forces that were most threatening to the brotherhood and the way it was to function within the society of those days. For Francis wanted the brothers to free themselves from the prevailing economic system and, through a liberating poverty not of appropriating the goods of creation to themselves but of sharing them with others, to establish an alternative society—ideals which were the exact opposite of the avarice and the cares of the age so typical of the behavior of the dominant classes. The threatening character of both these counterforces is further underlined by the fact that Francis links both of them explicitly to Satan and his blinding activity.

This link with Satan is repeated in RegNB 22:7, the second place where avarice can be found in Francis' writings. Freely quoting Mk 7:21–22, Francis mentioned avarice there in a long list of sins and vices which proceed from our heart. They illustrate how miserable and inclined towards evil we human beings are, an inclination which the devil gladly uses to take away from us the love of Jesus Christ and therewith our eternal happiness (ibid. 5–6).

The third place where avarice is mentioned occurs in combination with the cares and anxiety of this age is in the Later Rule 10:7. In this text, almost at the end of the Rule, Francis gave a final admonition as to how the brothers should behave. He spoke thereby in the first-person singular form while at the same time appealing to the authority of Jesus Christ. In this way he voiced in strong and unmistakable terms his serious personal concern for the future of the brotherhood: "I admonish and exhort the brothers in the Lord Jesus Christ that they be on their guard against all pride, vainglory, envy, avarice, care and anxiety of this age, detraction and murmuring. And those who are illiterate, should not be eager to learn. Instead let them pursue what they must desire above all things: to have the Spirit of the Lord and his holy working *(operatio)*." Both avarice and the care of this age figure thus prominently among those sins which are considered to hinder seriously the working of the Holy Spirit and so to prevent the brothers from observing the rule through their holy deeds *(operatio)* until the end (Test 39).

Naturally, the brothers should not allow this to happen. Rather, as Francis reminded them, they should open themselves to the working of the Holy Spirit and his holy virtues. If they do so, the virtues will definitely confound their counterforces. But, as Admonition 27 rightly observes, poverty will not leave any place for covetousness and avarice within the brotherhood only if it is accepted and practiced with joy. It was again his own experience that prompted Francis to make this observation. He had seen how some of his brothers gradually became less and less happy with the poverty they had promised the Lord, and how covetousness and avarice were especially able to make new inroads among them, often in very subtle ways. For if people are no longer happy with the choices they have made, they start looking for something else. They become easy prey for all kinds of appealing arguments that offer them a way out of their predicament without losing face.

Several of these arguments I have described already when explaining Satan's subtlety.[29] The only way for these arguments to lose much, if not all of their weight, would be for the brothers to embrace poverty again with joy. Then they would be placed again in the right position to see the fallacy of all these arguments. Poverty would cease to be a cruel and shameful burden that was becoming more and more intolerable. Instead poverty would become again a virtue, a divine redeeming force which, poured out by the Spirit (SalMary 6), inspires the brothers to commit themselves joyfully to the redemption, the liberation of humankind from covetousness and avarice, and hence to the restoration of paradise.[30]

[29] See above under IV B a.

[30] Very enlightening in this context is the way the anonymous author of the *Sacrum Commercium* describes very imaginatively how Avarice proceeded in trying to win the brothers over to her camp. And this all the more so if SC has been written in 1227, one year after Francis' death, as some authors believe. In order to achieve her plans, Avarice presented herself to the brothers as Discretion (43). Thus, from the very beginning, she placed herself in sharp contrast to the founders of the brotherhood for they were considered to be "indiscreet, unmerciful, cruel" (38) and hence no longer worthy of respect. Avarice, on the other hand, showing herself

And the Cares of this Age (v. 11)

I have already mentioned the cares of this age, the third counter-force of poverty, when dealing with texts where Francis and his brothers referred to them in connection with avarice. From the three counter-forces, the cares of this age *(huius saeculi)* or of this life *(huius vitae)* occur the most frequently in Francis' writings. Whenever they are mentioned together with covetousness and/or avarice, it is possible to see them as their inevitable companion. For it is clear that covetous and avaricious people are constantly worrying not only about how not to lose their possessions and wealth, but how to increase them. On the other hand, however, the cares of this life, often in combination with the anxieties of this age, are regularly referred to without any mention of covetousness and avarice. This seems to indicate that the cares of this age are a coun-

---

full of mercy and kindness, discreetly counseled the brothers not to be strict and unbending as the founders had been. Rather, they should be affable to the kings, princes and the other great of this world, and cultivate their friendship and company. For when they would come to meet the brothers, many who would see them and observe their way of life, would be "the more easily turned to God by their example" (43). When this approach failed to have the desired effect, Avarice changed her tactics and decided to disguise herself as Providence. She addressed the brothers "in humble words: Why do you stand here all day idle, providing nothing for yourselves for the future? What harm will it do you to have the necessaries of life, so long as you avoid having superfluous things? You would be able to work out your own salvation and that of others with greater peace and quiet, if everything you really need were immediately at hand. While you have time, provide for yourselves and for those who will come after you... It would be good for you to remain always as you are, but that is not possible since God daily adds to your company. Would not God be pleased if you had at hand what you could give to the needy, being mindful of the poor, since he said: It is more blessed to give than to receive? Why do you not receive the goods that are offered to you and thereby avoid depriving the givers of their eternal reward? There is now no reason why you should be afraid of companionship with riches, since you consider them as nothing. Vice is not in the things, but in the heart, for God sees all the things he made and they are very good... O how many who have riches make but ill use of them; if you had these things, you would convert them to good use, for your purpose is holy, your desire is holy! You do not desire to make your parents wealthy, for they are rich enough; but if you had the things that are necessary, you could live a more becoming and more orderly life" (45). See D. Flood, *Poverty's Condition. A Reading of the Sacrum Commercium, Haversack* Occasional Paper 2, Chicago 1990, 31.

terforce in their own right with a meaning of their own. Such references can be found in RegNB 9:14; 22:26 and especially in Second Letter to the Faithful 65 and Letter to the Rulers of the Peoples 4 and 8.

A characteristic of some of these passages is their eschatological context. Thus in the Earlier Rule 9:14, Francis wants his brothers to recall a word from the Lord who warns them: "Take heed that your hearts do not become heavy... through the cares of this life and that day does not come upon you suddenly; for like a snare it will come upon all who dwell on the face of the earth" (Lk 21:34–35). In the Letter to the Rulers, Francis admonishes "all podestàs and consuls, judges and rulers, everywhere on earth, and all others who may receive this letter,.. [to] pause and see that the day of death is approaching." He begs them, therefore, "with all possible respect, not to forget the Lord or to turn away from his commandments because of the cares and anxieties of this age, for all those who forget the Lord... will be forgotten by him. And, when the day of death comes, all that they thought to have, will be taken from them." Therefore, Francis firmly advises them "to put aside all care and anxiety and to receive the most holy Body and Blood of our Lord Jesus Christ in holy remembrance of Him" (1–4; 6). At the end of Second Letter to the Faithful, Francis directs a similar admonition to "all those who are not living in penance and do not receive the Body and Blood of our Lord Jesus Christ,... [but] bodily serve the world by the desires of the flesh, the cares and anxieties of this age and the cares of this life" (63–65). For "they are deceived by the devil... [and] do not have spiritual wisdom" (66–67). This will be revealed at the moment of death, for—and Francis changes here from the neutral "they" to the more direct and more personal "you" —"See, you blind ones... You have nothing in this age or in the age to come. You think that you possess the vanities of the world for a long time, but you are deceived, since the day and the hour will come of which you do not think, do not know and are not aware" (69–71).

These texts show Francis' deep concern for the eternal happiness and salvation of his brothers as well as of all the faithful and their political and other leaders: a concern whose seriousness he underlined by his accumulation of expressions. He warns them not just about the worthlessness of the cares of this age, but about the worthlessness of "the cares and anxieties of this age and the cares of this life." For, as he kept emphasizing, they simply are not worth all the worries they cause people, because the goods of this world and age, whatever they are—house, money, social status—will all perish when "that day" comes. Though they may seem to provide a strong and solid basis for a person's life and happiness, they are in reality but vanities, "no more than the dust which we crush with our feet" (RegNB 8:6). It is, therefore, not a sign of wisdom at all, however much the people of this age may think themselves to be very wise and clever, but rather a sign of blindness when people put all their trust in these goods as if they will bring true and lasting happiness while in the mean time forgetting the things that are really worthwhile, that will not perish, but last forever: the things not of this age, but of the age to come, of God. True wisdom, then, is for the brothers "to put aside all care and anxiety and, as best as they can, to serve, love, honor and adore the Lord God with a clean heart and a pure mind" (RegNB 22:26; cf. 2 LetFaith 19). And it is the virtue of joyful, redeeming poverty, confounding the cares of this age, which will empower them to do this. Trusting in the Lord, they will be free from all their worries about worldly goods. Thus they will be free to commit themselves to the loving service of the Lord. Therein they will find a new source of happiness: the freedom to share the goods the Lord gives them with others as the Lord meant them to be and so to inaugurate God's age, God's kingdom already now.

This is very much the idea behind the admonition Francis gives in the Letter to the Faithful: "And let us give alms... For people lose everything they leave behind in this age; but they carry with them the rewards of charity and the alms which they gave" (2 LetFaith 31; cf. RegNB 9:9). Again Francis warns people that they should not put their trust in the things of this age, because in trying to hold on to them, they are bound to lose them. Rather, giving alms, they should share the things they possess with others. Then they will undo the sinful situation which they created by their accumulation of possessions (2 LetFaith 30) and start the new age, God's age, which they will carry forward with them until they arrive before the Lord to receive their reward (ibid. 31). For in giving alms, they give to the poor what was their birthright from the very beginning, a right which Jesus regained for them (RegNB 9:8), thus restoring the situation as it was in the beginning when God placed humankind in paradise (RegNB 23:1). And it is this paradise which is a foreshadowing of the paradise to come.

Further, it is interesting to see how Francis, both in the Letter to the

Faithful and in the Letter to the Rulers, links the reception of the Eucharist and the putting aside of the cares and anxieties of this age. As I mentioned earlier when speaking about the First Admonition in my treatment of the virtue of humility,[31] Francis emphasized that those who are "heavy of heart" with the cares of this age do not recognize the truth about Jesus Christ and the Eucharist (14–15), for they can see only with the eyes of the flesh and not with the eyes of the Spirit. Hence they do not see how Jesus in his humanity, that is, in his poverty and humility, is the Son of God. Nor can they see how this Jesus is "the way, the truth and the life" (1) and how he invites them to follow him and to build a new society, to inaugurate a new age, based not on wealth and possessions, but on poverty and humility, on sharing and service. In other words, only if they put aside the cares of this age and allow the virtues of poverty and humility to determine their perspective, will they be able to see the truth revealed by the poor and humble Jesus, as he once lived among us and as he continues to be with us in the Eucharist until the end of the age (22). Then they will recognize him as who he truthfully is—the sacrament, that is, the sign and the realization of God's new age, of God's kingdom—and receive the Eucharist as a continuous challenge to make God's new age become a visible, historical reality in and through their deeds. If they, however, fail to do so, if they remain "serving the world bodily by the cares and anxieties of this age" (2 LetFaith 65), and "do not share the Spirit of the Lord, [yet] presume to receive the Lord, [they will] eat and drink judgment to themselves" (Adm 1:13; cf. 1 Cor 11:29). One can hardly find a more clear way to express the seriousness of the threat which the cares of this age present to the true life and happiness of every human person, whether they are rulers or ordinary faithful.

Convinced as he was of the grave danger people faced because of their cares for the things of this age and their forgetfulness of the things of God, Francis added to the above-mentioned passage in Second Letter to the Faithful 65–71 yet another severe warning, this time in the form of an example (72–85)—the only example of its kind we have in Francis' writings.[32] As example it is meant to shock people, to move

[31] See above under II C e.

[32] For what follows, see G.P. Freeman, "The Sick Man Who Does Not Repent. A Commentary on Francis' Second Letter to the Faithful," verses 72–85, *FrancDigest* 9,1 (March 1999) 1–10.

them and so to lead them to a change of heart, a conversion. In its present form the example might well have been part of a sermon. Interrupted by short explanations for the benefit of the listener, the example tells the story of a rich man who, when death is approaching, lets the opportunity pass by to put his affairs in order with God. Rather than surrender himself to God, he places himself and all his possessions, out of a mistaken loyalty, in the hands of his relatives and friends. Because of this, he cannot return to their rightful owners the goods which he has obtained through fraud and deception. Yet this restitution is a necessary condition to obtain forgiveness and set things right with God. The final result is that he faces a terrible end, "losing out on all fronts: his soul goes to hell, his body to the worms and his capital to the dogs."[33]

Francis agrees here with the way his contemporaries looked at the accumulation of wealth and possessions by the rich classes. In their desire for ever greater riches, they did not shun fraud and deception. They were always ready to cheat people in order to make an easy profit for themselves either by asking interest on loans, which was forbidden, or by raising prices, especially when goods were scarce. Thus caught up in the cares of this age, they lost sight of the real meaning of the goods of the earth, which God destined to be enjoyed not just by a happy few but by all in solidarity with each other. They were blinded by the fallacy of riches (*fallacia divitiarum*, RegNB 22:16; cf. Mt 13:22), so much so that they were no longer able properly to define their priorities. Even in the face of death, they were concerned more with finding a safe place for their possessions than with saving themselves and putting things in order with God. Thus "not making amends when [they] could have done so," they exposed themselves to the danger that "the devil would snatch up [their] soul out of [their] body with so much anguish and tribulation that no one can know it unless he has experienced it" (82).

In a typical medieval way, Francis enjoined people thus not to allow themselves to be carried away by the cares of this age, but to be attentive to what was really important and could not be taken away from them (cf. 83). He reminded them of the serious consequences of the choices they made in their lives: they themselves were responsible for those choices, and they had better take this responsibility seriously as

[33] Freeman 9.

their eternal happiness depended on them. If they would do so, enlightened by "spiritual wisdom" (67), they would ever better understand "that only a few things are important and that possessions do not belong to them. Possessions do carry the danger within themselves of becoming an obsession, of hoarding and of closing the circle and thus excluding others. Only close relatives count. It is better to share the goods one has with people who fall by the wayside. That is much better for those people as well as for oneself. Some discover this truth only on their deathbed. But all who want to live attentively and in solidarity, better start to do so immediately."[34] In this way, they will not only prepare the way for their eternal happiness in God's kingdom, but also make God's kingdom, God's age, a visible reality in this present day and age. However, such an immediate start will require that people have been touched by the virtue of poverty. For as Francis reminds his brothers in *The Salutation of the Virtues*, it is poverty which confounds the cares of this age and so empowers the brothers and others to live attentively and in solidarity, their hearts and minds focused on the things of God and of God's age.

Holy Humility Confounds Pride

Whereas, outside *The Salutation of the Virtues*, the virtue of humility is mentioned 15 times in the writings of Francis, its first counterforce, pride, occurs only twice, namely in the Earlier Rule 17:9 and the Later Rule 10:7, both times together with vainglory. Given the fact that medieval society attached great weight to this sin, one might have expected more frequent use, even though in Francis' time, pride had lost its first place among the sins to avarice, the sin of the merchant elite in the city states. However, just as in the case of avarice, when the word "pride" is used, it happens in texts that are important for the life of the brotherhood. Thus its mention in the Earlier Rule 17:9–15 occurs in what was originally the last chapter of the *Regula non bullata.* Francis and his brothers gave there a final summing up of what the struggle between the spirit of the flesh and the Spirit of the Lord. is all about. This occasion provided them with a good opportunity to warn the brothers once more to be on their guard first of all against pride, fol-

[34] Freeman 9–10.

lowed by vainglory, the wisdom of the world and the prudence of the flesh (9–10).

Their first warning against pride was made in a sentence beginning with "Therefore, all brothers" *(Omnes ergo fratres).* In other words, Francis established a clear link with the previous paragraph. This indicates that, by mentioning pride and the other sins, he intended to sum up what he had said before. Pride, then, happens when the brothers, "those who preach, pray, work, whether cleric or lay," do not humble themselves but "instead glory or rejoice in themselves or exalt themselves because of the good words and works, or indeed of any good that God sometimes does or says or works in them and through them" (5–6; cf. Adm 2:3; 12:2). In other words, while in reality God is the One from whom all good things come and to whom therefore all good things belong and have to be returned (17; SalVirt 4), the brothers who were proud did not acknowledge this. Rather, they behaved as if they themselves were the source of the good they said or did. Thus they appropriated to themselves what belongs to God (cf. Adm 2:3) and considered themselves its owners or lords, no longer recognizing God's universal Lordship over the goods of creation. In this way, they showed an obvious lack of the most elementary self-knowledge. For, as Francis observed, if they knew themselves, they would humbly acknowledge that "nothing belongs to us except our vices and sins." (7; 22:5; 2 LetFaith 37).

However, this self-knowledge was difficult and for many almost impossible to obtain because of the spirit of the age. The classes of the elite were quite proud of their achievements and successes, their newly found wealth and riches. And the learned brothers were very much tempted to join them. For what was really wrong if they made good use of their talents and felt proud about what they had achieved for the well-being of church and society? Moreover, by their preaching they were able to reach many more people than if they were just serving in a leper—or almshouse. And those people were often the more influential ones as well! Temptation enough.[35] All the more reason for Francis to keep warning his brothers everywhere not to endanger the mission of the brotherhood but to be on the good side in the struggle between the

[35] For the various temptations through which Satan in subtle ways "desires to ensnare the human heart under the pretext of some reward or work or help" (RegNB 22:19 and 25), see above under IV B a.

spirit of the flesh and the Spirit of the Lord: the Spirit of the Lord who strives after humility (15).

When trying to describe the meaning of pride, it appeared impossible to do so without referring to the sin of appropriation and to the desire of people to be owners or lords who no longer acknowledge God's Lordship, but very much go their own way. This shows that, in Francis' appreciation, pride, avarice and disobedience are all but aspects of the one original sin, the sin at the beginning, which continues in people's sinful activities, through which they continue to lose paradise (RegNB 23:2). More than that, through their sinful activities they run even counter to God's efforts to restore paradise, for "by delighting in vices and sins, [they] crucify [Jesus] even now" (Adm 5:3) and thus obstruct his work of redemption. Once again it appears that, just as in the case of the virtues, so also the vices and sins cannot be explained one without the other. It is yet another illustration of the observation Francis made in *The Salutation of the Virtues* 7: "And whoever offends one [virtue], possesses none and offends all."

Pride also stands in first place in the Later Rule 10:7–12, towards the end of the *Regula bullata*, when Francis gave a last admonition to his brothers about how they should live their calling as lesser brothers. I have already mentioned[36] that in this passage Francis used the first-person singular form and appealed directly to the authority of the Lord Jesus Christ, thus underlining the serious character of his admonition to his brothers. In this admonition he warned them to guard first of all against all pride and instead to have humility, one of the fruits of the working of the Spirit of the Lord. Again, it is evident that, by putting pride first before vainglory, envy, avarice, the cares and anxiety of this age, detraction and murmuring, Francis recognized pride as a most serious danger to the life and mission of the brotherhood.

In the Later Rule 10, however, the context is different from the one in the Earlier Rule 17. Whereas Francis in the latter text admonished the brothers a last time about the ongoing struggle between the spirit of the flesh and the Spirit of the Lord, in the Later Rule 10 he was more directly concerned about the relationship between the brothers and their ministers, whereby he placed special emphasis on the ministers' task to visit, admonish and correct the brothers. In the exercise of this task, "the

[36] See above under IV B e.

ministers should receive [the brothers] with love and kindness and be so familiar with them that they can speak and deal with [their ministers] as lords or masters with their slaves. for this is the way it should be, that the ministers be the servants of all the brothers" (5–6). This evangelical injunction on the ministers (cf. Mt 20:25–26; cf. RegNB 5:10–12; Adm 4:1) is then followed immediately by the admonition that the brothers guard first of all against all pride. It seems therefore highly probable that pride received its first place before all the other vices and sins also because of the injunction to the ministers about their duty to serve the brothers, which immediately preceded it and which apparently was especially needed because of pride creeping in among the ministers.

This probability is further strengthened by the fact that, very soon after the ministers were introduced into the brotherhood as a form of evangelical leadership at the chapter of 1217, a good many of them showed a tendency to "appropriate to themselves the ministry of the brothers" (RegNB 17:4). And whereas they were supposed to "glory as much in their office [of leadership] as they would when they were assigned the office of washing the feet of the brothers," yet in reality they "were more upset about the office [of leadership] being taken away from them than about their removal from the office of washing feet" (Adm 4:2–3). Rather than to serve their brothers and so to live up to their name, these ministers, placed "over others" (*super alios* Adm 4:1), forgot this essential characteristic of evangelical leadership. Instead, they were focused on enjoying the authority, honor, respect, social status and many privileges which the office of leader brought along with it within the hierarchical structures of medieval society Theirs was a return to the dominant culture and its practices which, from the very beginning, had been considered unevangelical by Francis and his brothers, at least as far as their brotherhood was concerned (RegNB 5:10–12).

Apparently this negative qualification, even though it was supported by words of the Lord, had not been able to impress these ministers to change their outlook and their lifestyle For they were not prepared to accept and to live the complete reversal of the existing social relationship between lord and servant, superior and subject, as proposed by Francis in conformity with the "form of the holy gospel" which the Lord had revealed to him (Test 14). To be kind and understanding, to become themselves the servant of the servants might be a beautiful ideal recommended by the gospel, but it was not going to work in reality. Therefore, these ministers preferred to stick to the well-tested patterns of a more strict, authoritarian leadership which had proven its efficiency in the past. They were then sure to achieve something, something they could boast about. Moreover, although they would not say so, the old style of leadership was much less demanding and much more rewarding in human terms. It is very likely that the ministers' readiness to be served rather than to serve, to act as master and lord rather than as a subject, to deal with their brothers in a punishing way rather than to receive them with love and kindness, to strive after their own glory rather than to promote the spiritual well-being of their brothers, were all on Francis' mind when, immediately after reminding the ministers how it should be in their relationship with their brothers who seek their help, he warned the brothers against all pride and implored them instead to practice humility, which is the fruit of the Spirit and confounds all pride.

Summing up, it is clear that Francis described pride in relation to both creation and salvation. Pride makes brothers act as lords, as if they own the goods that belong to God, who created them all, thus continuing the original sin of appropriation, they continue to exclude themselves from paradise. And whereas God offered them in Jesus a possibility to regain paradise, it is pride again which prevents them from accepting this offer. For due to their pride they refuse to become like servants, after the example of Jesus, who precisely through his service unto the end redeemed the world and restored paradise. Pride then causes the brothers to forget both their place within the universe of God's creation and their calling to become followers of Jesus and collaborators in his work of redemption and salvation. Instead they keep returning to the standards of this age which they had left behind when joining the brotherhood. Following the ideas prevailing in the culture of their days, they develop a false image of themselves, forgetting who they are really meant to be in God's eyes. This loss of memory which has such fatal consequences can be healed only if, reflecting on God's plan of creation and salvation, the brothers are ready to acknowledge God's lordship and, profoundly aware of their own place as people created and saved by God, wish nothing else but to "serve him with great humility" (CantSun 14). Then paradise will be restored and therewith the proper relationship between all God's creatures as God wanted it to be in the beginning. As Francis writes in the Letter to the Faithful: "We must never desire to be over others *(super alios)*; rather we must be servants and subjects to every human creature for the sake of God" (2 LetFaith 47; RegNB 16:6): God who is our creator, redeemer and savior (RegNB 16:7; 23:3–4; 8–9),[37] who placed us in paradise and wants us to be happy there by humbly loving and serving God and one another.

And All the People Who are in the World and All the Things that are in the World (v. 12)

Francis here interrupts the scheme that he follows in the other verses of this third section. With the exception of verse 9 where wisdom confounds Satan, in all the other verses the virtues confound one or more vices or sins. Here, however, after first confounding pride, humility next confounds "all the people who are in the world and all the things that are in the world." In this way Francis wanted to draw attention to the fact that it is pride which motivates all the people in the world in their thoughts and actions regarding what they consider to be of value, and hence becomes a characteristic of all the things that are to be found in the world. In other words, he wanted to warn his brothers of the all-pervasive character of pride in the world in which they were living, the world of the communes, which were proud of their achievements and determined to continue along the same lines for their ever greater glory.[38]

In issuing this warning, Francis agreed with the tradition, based on one of the most quoted texts from the First Letter of John, and applied it to his own world. According to this tradition, "all that is in the world is the concupiscence of the flesh, and the concupiscence of the eyes, and the pride of life" (16).[39] Limiting himself to pride, he extended its

[37] See my *Francis and Islam*, 105–106.

[38] See Jansen 173.

[39] See Jansen 173. Following van Asseldonk and others, he concludes that, in these verses, Francis opts for the Johannine terminology. It may be fashionable to do so at the moment, yet by introducing the term "Johannine" these authors create, in my view, a false impression as if Francis knew of the distinctions we make at present between the various traditions that come together in the New Testament. Quoting the New Testament, Francis mentioned only once the name of one of the authors, namely the apostle James in RegNB 20:3. In all other cases, it was always "the Lord says" or even "the Lord says in the Gospel" without ever mentioning the name of the evangelist, when he quoted a text from the Gospel, or "the apostle says," when he quoted from one of the epistles, without even indicating

influence from "all the things that are in the world" to include also "all the people who are in the world." In doing so, he created some problems for later copiers of the text who, when reading about all the people in the world thought immediately of the text in Jesus' farewell discourse where Jesus prayed for his followers who "are in the world." In this prayer Jesus did not ask the Father "to remove them from the world, but to protect them from the evil one," so that they may "not belong to the world any more than [Jesus] belongs to the world" (Jo 17:7.15–16). It is clear that the world is bad indeed, for it is under the influence of the evil one. Hence it hated Jesus and his followers. Yet, they had to live in this world without being of the world. Those to be confounded by humility therefore are not just all who are in the world, but only those who do not distance themselves from the world and hence continue to belong to the world. For this reason, a whole group of copiers changed the text. They omitted "who are in the world" and substituted "of this world" *(huius mundi)*.[40]

Although the text from Jesus' farewell discourse was very well known to Francis for he quoted extensively from it in the Earlier Rule 22:42–55; Second Letter to the Faithful 57–60, apparently it did not enter his mind here. By "all the people who are in the world" he understands clearly all those who are of this world and hence allow themselves to be influenced by the evil one and follow the wisdom of the world (9–10). As already noted earlier in our commentary on the wisdom of the world as the counterforce of the virtue of simplicity, the world that Francis meant in *The Salutation of the Virtues* had a very negative meaning. Next to the flesh and the devil, it is one of the enemies who are set on blinding and deceiving the people (2 LetFaith 69). In the expression "wisdom of the world" Francis designated especially the religious and cultural world of his days where the culture of the word prevailed with its clever rationalizations (RegNB 17:10–12), while the *sancta operatio*, the holy

---

whether it was Peter, Paul or John. It is clear then that Francis did not use a Marcan, Johannine, Petrine or Pauline terminology; he used a scriptural terminology. It was in the Scriptures that he heard God's word spoken to him whether it was through the Lord himself or through an apostle.

[40] See Esser, *Die Opuscula*, 425–426. The reason why these copiers change the text is clear. Yet, instead of using the Vulgate's expression *de mundo*, they write *huius mundi.*

deeds performed in all simplicity (Test 38–39), was absent.[41] Here, however, Francis sees the world more specifically as the domain where pride is the dominant force reigning over people. The world, therefore, is the place where God's lordship is no longer acknowledged,[42] but where people who are in a position to do so appropriate to themselves the good that God works in and through them and pride themselves upon it as if they are its lords and masters. And naturally, with such proud people, all the things that are in their world center on possessions and power. They are constantly involved in a struggle for more possessions and greater power, which flatter their pride. However, this involvement blinds them to such an extent that they hardly see the evil consequences of their actions. Everything has to give way to their ambition. That this all too often happens at the expense of the poor and weak ones, who are being victimized by them, is evident. They are even prepared to go to war or, for that matter, to organize a crusade, whenever their lordship, their power, is threatened.

The brothers met this world and its pride wherever they went. They were surrounded by it and, being human, were bound to feel its all-pervasive force and to be attracted by it. They were not to give in, however, but to stand firm in their faith in their God-given mission: to confound this world and to transform it through the virtue of humility. Whereas all the people caught up in the world firmly believed in and were wholeheartedly committed to increasing their possessions and their wealth, getting ever higher on the social ladder, becoming ever more lords and masters and being proud of themselves and their achievements, and whereas all the things in this world, war and violence not excluded, were geared to accomplish this ascent towards ever greater self-exaltation and self-aggrandizement, the brothers were to follow Jesus in the descent of his incarnation. In this descent Jesus humbled himself, becoming a servant, a washer of feet, in a loving act of solidarity, so that through his humility the lowly might be exalted.[43]

To fulfill this mission within a hostile world which did not attach much value to humility, except for servants and the like, in order to keep

[41] See above under IV B c.

[42] See Verhey: "...people who live in the 'world' and hence outside the lordship of God" (122).

[43] For this and what follows, see the commentary on the virtue of humility, under II C e.

them down in their lowly state, the brothers were to find encouragement and strength in the Eucharist: for it is there that Jesus daily renews his descent, coming down from the Father and appearing among us in humble form (Adm 1:17–18). It is thus that Jesus revealed and continues to reveal the truth about his life and his redemptive mission (ibid.15), and hence also about the life and mission of his followers. It is this truth which will give Jesus' followers the proper self-knowledge about their place in God's plan of creation and salvation. It will inspire them to become ever more involved, with their whole person, in their mission to redeem the world through their humility after the example of Jesus. For through their humility, as the organizing principle of a new world of fellowship and solidarity as symbolized in the Eucharist, they will overcome the divisions which pride causes and restore the harmonious relations between people themselves and between people and things as they were in the beginning.

Humility and its counterforce, pride, are thus not to be limited to the individual sphere. As the double reference to the world and the double use of the adjective *omnis* in the text itself clearly indicate, humility and pride have, according to Francis, a profound effect on the whole of the world, on all its people and all its things. Whether the world will be as God meant it to be—a world where God's Lordship is being acknowledged and all people love and serve one another as brothers and sisters, son and daughters of the One Father in heaven: one family, a people, united to one another through humble, loving service (RegNB 5:10)—or a world where people with a false sense of pride and a corresponding lack of self-knowledge usurp the lordship over God's creation and, like the rulers of the peoples, start exercising power and dominion over others, excluding, victimizing, and so dividing people—depends on whether humility or pride is present.

Holy Charity Confounds All the Temptations of the Devil and the Flesh

Having dealt with the world in the previous verse, Francis turns now to the other two enemies, namely the devil and the flesh. Through their temptations they form a threat which can be overcome by the virtue of charity. In my commentary on verse 9, I have already written about the temptations of the devil. From the very beginning (Adm 2:4) the devil's temptations are geared towards blinding and deceiving people and making the evil look sweet to them. In this manner the devil keeps tempting people not to obey the sometimes difficult demands of God's will but to act against them and to do evil (2 LetFaith 66–69). As the devil is intent only on deceiving people, he is obviously not at all interested in the truth. He rather hides his real intentions and uses all kinds of pretexts to achieve his intentions, especially such pretexts as will hit people where they are most vulnerable. The pretexts the devil used especially with regard to the brothers were reward, work and help (RegNB 22:25).

In using these pretexts the devil played on the mind of those brothers, mainly the learned ones, who because of their dissatisfaction with the simple, poor and humble way of life had returned or were on the point of returning to the ways of Assisi. They were ready to abandon the vision of God, people and world which they had developed within the brotherhood, guided by the light of Queen Wisdom and to accept again the wisdom of the world. Thus they became very easy prey for the devil's deceiving tactics. Naturally, he would not let this excellent opportunity to win them over pass by. Wherever possible, he would do his utmost to convince those brothers that there was nothing wrong if the good and efficient use of their talents would bring them a reward from the church authorities and the people. Nor was there anything wrong if they would ask the Roman curia for privileges so that they could exercise their work of preaching anywhere in the church without any hindrance. Nor would it be against their way of life to receive money if this would enable them to more effectively help more people.[44]

The final goal of all Satan's temptations, whether "hidden or manifest, sudden or persistent" (ExpOurFather 9), remained, however, "to take away from [the brothers] the love of Jesus Christ and eternal life and to lose himself with everyone in hell" (RegNB 22:5). Once he got these brothers to look again at people and things with the eyes of the world and no longer with the eyes of God, they no longer would have their hearts and minds raised to God and the word and precepts of the Lord would be choked out from their memory (RegNB 22:19–20). No longer guided by the word and precepts of the Lord, they would no longer be directed toward doing God's will; rather from then on their minds and hearts would be set on following evil ways. This would inevitably lead to their separation from the love of God. As a result, the

[44] For all this more in detail, see above under IV B b.

love that God is and which God has revealed in Jesus would cease to be the driving force of their lives. Hence, these brothers would not only no longer love and serve God, they also would no longer share in Jesus' redeeming, liberating love. Instead of being God's children who, created in the image of God, continue God's creative and redemptive activity in the world, they rather become children of the devil whose works they do, destroying the world as God had planned it. Instead of bringing back paradise, God's place for humankind, they keep losing it and remain outside in a world where Satan gets every opportunity to deceive and tempt them, making it bitter for them to serve God, but sweet to follow the false wisdom of the world (cf. 2 LetFaith 66–69; cf. RegNB 21:8; 23:1).

This situation will prevail among the brothers till they allow Queen Wisdom to open their eyes again and to unmask the temptations of the devil. In the light of true wisdom, they will then discern that their lasting happiness lies in having their minds and hearts raised to God and in loving and serving God with a clean heart and a pure mind (RegNB 22:26)—a heart and mind cleansed and purified from all the evil feelings and thoughts through which Satan may wish to keep them occupied, leaving no place for God and God's love (Adm 27:5; RegNB 7:10). Wisdom and love thus go very much together[45] in overcoming Satan and his temptations and turning people to God. The result is that, whereas Queen Wisdom empowers the brothers to see and appreciate people and things from God's perspective, revealed in Jesus, and so to discern what is truly important in their lives, Lady Charity empowers them to live this vision by bringing God's creative and redeeming love present in them and in their world, especially also in their relationship with their enemies.[46] We should, however, keep in mind that, while this neat distinction may satisfy our need for clarity and systematization, in reality the activities of the virtues cannot be so neatly distinguished one from another. The unity of the virtues means also that in the activity of one virtue, all others concur.

Besides the temptations of the devil, Francis mentions the tempta-

[45] They are explicitly mentioned together as a pair in Adm. 27:1. They also follow each other as names of God in PrGod 4. In both cases, however, in contrast to SalVirt, charity is mentioned before wisdom. This proves once again that Francis is not interested in giving a systematic treatise on the virtues.

[46] See for this the more extensive commentary on the virtues of wisdom and charity in II C b and f.

tions of the flesh as opponents of the virtue of charity. It is here for the first time that the flesh, as the last one of the three enemies of humankind, is explicitly mentioned in *The Salutation of the Virtues*, albeit in the form of an adjective. However, this first mention appears immediately to trigger a repetition in the introduction of "carnal fears" and "all carnal wishes." And whereas, on the basis of the place the flesh has in Francis' other writings, one might have expected this enemy to enter earlier on the scene, its repeated mentioning within the space of two verses emphasizes its importance also within the context of *The Salutation of the Virtues*.

Francis considered the flesh specifically as the enemy of the Spirit. In fact, the opposition between flesh and Spirit formed an important theme in his writings, where it occurs more than fifteen times.[47] Herewith Francis stood in the line of Christian tradition, as found especially in the teaching of Paul. In his Letter to the Galatians, he wrote: "Walk in the Spirit, and do not follow the desires of the flesh. For the flesh desires against the Spirit, and the Spirit against the flesh; they are opposed to each other" (5:16–17). Next, Paul places the works of the flesh over against the works of the Spirit: "The works of the flesh are manifest: fornication, impurity, sexual licentiousness, idolatry, sorcery, enmities, contentions, jealousy, anger, quarrels, disagreements, factions, envy, homicides, drunkenness, orgies and similar things. I warn you as I warned you before: those who do such things, will not inherit the kingdom of God. However, the fruits of the Spirit are love, joy, peace, patience, kindness, goodness, trustfulness, gentleness, faith, modesty, continence, chastity. Against these there is no law. Those who belong to Christ, have crucified their flesh with its vices and desires" (5:19–24).[48]

This text of Paul was known to Francis as it was read on the Fourteenth Sunday after Pentecost. Francis, however, followed very much his own interpretation of the opposition between flesh and Spirit. He came to this interpretation in the light of the problems he and his brothers were facing in their struggle to be faithful to the Spirit both with regard to the ideals which they had discerned, and were to continue discerning, under divine inspiration, and with regard to the practice of the

[47] See O. van Asseldonk, Verso un cuore puro con la pura, semplice e vera pace dell spirito (RegNB 17,15), *Laurentianum* 33 (1992) 481–531, here 486.

[48] I follow here the text of the Vulgate which is slightly different from the original Greek text as used in modern translations.

virtues with which the Spirit empowered them to pursue these ideals in the world of their days. In fact, this struggle to be faithful to what Francis called "the right direction of their life" *(rectitudo vitae)* profoundly affected the brotherhood. This happened especially after the ministers were introduced to provide leadership for an ever growing group. As leaders they seemed particularly vulnerable to the temptations of the flesh, so much so that Francis felt obliged to ask "all the brothers, who are subject to the ministers and servants, to consider the actions of the ministers and servants reasonably and diligently. And if they should see that anyone of them is living according to the flesh and not according to the Spirit, as the right direction of our life requires, if he does not amend his way, they should inform the minister and servant of the whole fraternity at the chapter of Pentecost" (RegNB 5:3–4). This request to examine the acts of the ministers as to whether they faithfully translate the inspiration of the Spirit in the historical reality of their world through their practice of the virtues is immediately followed by a similar request with regard to the actions of the brothers wherever they are. No brother then is exempt from this struggle, no one is free from the temptations of the flesh. Therefore, "if among the brothers anywhere there should be some brother who wishes to live according to the flesh and not according to the Spirit, the brothers with whom he is living should admonish, instruct, and correct him humbly and diligently" (5).[49]

What did Francis mean by flesh and what were, according to him, the temptations of the flesh? In Admonitions 12:2, Francis stated very simply that "the flesh is always opposed to every good *(semper contraria omni bono)*. No good, no virtue is, therefore, excluded from having to deal with the evil force of the flesh. It is an all-pervasive power that seeks to influence all the spheres of life and to prevent whatever good from being realized. As such, Francis would fully subscribe to Paul's list of the works of the flesh in his Letter to the Galatians, and might even have added a few more. Yet, if we look at Francis' writings, it becomes clear that Francis restricted himself considerably when speaking about the activities of the flesh. This happened already in the same Admonitions 12, where Francis told his brothers that a brother, "a servant of God may be recognized as having the Spirit of the Lord if the flesh does not exalt itself when the Lord works some good through him"

[49] See my Ministry to the Friars in the Writings of Francis and the Early Biographers, *FIA Contact*, 6, no.4 (November 1985) 2–9.

(1–2). The main activity, or at least one of the main activities, of the flesh is thus, according to Francis, human self-exaltation.

This is very much confirmed by a reading of the passage in the Earlier Rule 17:5–16, where Francis describes the ongoing struggle between the spirit of the flesh and the Spirit of the Lord.[50] There too the self-exaltation figures prominently. At the same time, it is diagnosed as a fundamental lack of self-knowledge for, as Francis reminds his brothers, "we should firmly know *(sciamus)* that nothing belongs to us except our vices and sins" (7). Hence, it is most obvious that they should not promote the flesh in acts of self-aggrandizement, but mortify it in acts of humble service, identifying with those who have fallen along the wayside;[51] rather than to be proud of their achievements, they should learn to see that the flesh of itself "is of no use" (Adm 1:6); it is of itself worthless, to be despised and rejected. In short, rather than to exalt themselves, all the brothers should rather "humble themselves before God" (5). This is indeed what the Spirit of the Lord invites the brothers to do, for, in contrast to the spirit of the flesh which promotes human self-exaltation, the Spirit of the Lord "strives for humility" (15). It is the practice of this humility which, as Francis indicates in the next verse, is a part of the Spirit's way to achieve within us what the Spirit "desires above all": namely, the presence of "the divine fear and the divine wisdom and the divine love of the Father, and of the Son and of the Holy Spirit" (16).

In this context the temptations of the flesh are thus very much directed towards making the brothers forget who they really are before God, the giver of all good, and giving them a false self-knowledge. Falling for these temptations, some brothers act as lords; they no longer humbly recognize the Lordship of God, nor do they establish this Lordship everywhere in their world, as they are supposed to, by their humble service. As such, the temptations of the flesh seem to be opposed to the virtue of humility rather than to the virtue of love. Logically, this might be correct. The ending of the passage, however, opens a broader perspective. Indeed, the Spirit of the Lord strives after humility, but above all the Spirit strives towards the indwelling of the Blessed Trinity in the hearts of the brothers. And it is precisely this indwelling which, in the last analysis, is destroyed if some of them give

[50] For all this more in extenso, see above under IV B g.

[51] See above, III B c.

in to the temptations of the flesh toward self-exaltation. For, through the sin of self-exaltation and hence of not recognizing God's Lordship, they continue the original sin with all its disastrous consequences so much so that God can no longer dwell in them. This means that the Father cannot any further protect their heart and guard it against evil influences. The wisdom of the world can then enter and take the place of the divine wisdom; that is, the wisdom that seeks external glory and delights in success can take the place of the wisdom of the cross, the wisdom of humble service, which made the brothers walk in the footsteps of Jesus, following his example of love (cf. Jn 13:12–15). Thus, in the end, the temptations of the flesh succeed in opening the way for the spirit of the flesh to have the better of the Spirit of the Lord and to banish the divine love of the Holy Spirit from the hearts of those brothers. But the reverse is also true. The virtues of wisdom and love which proceed from God can and will confound these temptations of the flesh, provided the brothers allow these virtues to become the guiding forces of their lives. They will then empower the brothers to commit themselves, as lesser brothers, to being subject to every human creature for God's sake and so prepare their hearts for the indwelling of God who will guard the truly wise and loving against all vices and sins, which are the sole property of the flesh (cf. 2 LetFaith 47–48; Adm 27:5). The love which God is will prevail and confound temptations and sin.

Besides these temptations of the flesh against humility and toward self-exaltation, the Earlier Rule 17:11–12 speaks about another kind of temptation of the flesh. "The spirit of the flesh," so Francis writes, "desires and is most eager to have words... and [also] to have a religion and holiness outwardly apparent to people." As such, it is opposed to the Spirit of the Lord, who desires the brothers to commit themselves to the *operatio* and to a religion and holiness which, through the *operatio* in the strength of the Spirit, transforms the world from a world of sin into a world where Jesus is at home. As we have seen earlier, Francis rejected here the culture of the word which prevailed among the elite in the city of Assisi and to which the preachers felt especially attracted. From the severeness of the warning of the Lord with which Francis addressed them (13), it is clear that he considered these temptations as a very real and a very serious threat to the brotherhood. These temptations, obviously, led to a situation where some of the brothers identified themselves again with the strivings and the successes of Assisi. They became more and more integrated again into the dominant culture of the word and its rationalizations, and so got ever further estranged from the simple understanding and realization of the original ideals of the brotherhood. These temptations of the flesh must, therefore, in first instance be understood as being directed against the virtue of simplicity. They are a threat to the brothers who wish to persevere, "simply and *sine glossa*," in their holy *operatio* (Test 39).

However, these temptations of the flesh constitute at the same time a threat to the virtue of love. For if the *operatio* fails, religion and holiness are only apparent. The real loving relationship with God is absent and so is the people's cooperation with God's creative and redemptive love in transforming the world through their deeds. Hence, both simplicity and love are to join together to confound these temptations of the flesh which are inherent in the culture of Assisi and which entice the brothers towards "having words" only, without any commitment to loving deeds. These virtues will be successful only if the brothers open themselves to the power of the Spirit working in and through them. Then the brothers will be free to love simply and unconditionally, unhampered by these temptations of the flesh, and, "through love," to give birth again to Jesus in and through their holy *operatio*. In other words, they will give Jesus a new historical existence (2 LetFaith 53); they will build a world where Jesus can be at home and where his redemptive love can become a reality through their transforming deeds in the power of the Spirit. Thus they will restore paradise where God dwells among the people he loves and where people live their religion or holiness in the praxis of their everyday lives, simply and purely loving and serving each other, especially the poor and marginalized.

The way in which I have described the temptations of the devil and of the flesh on the basis of a careful analysis of the text of Francis' writings indicates that Francis did not in the first place relate them to sexual matters. Herewith, Francis went contrary to the way these temptations, starting with Paul, have often been understood in the Christian tradition. For Francis, this was undoubtedly connected with the fact that according to him the sin in paradise was the sin of appropriation, the sin of wanting to be lord, of refusing to recognize God's Lordship. In his view, the struggle between the spirit of the flesh and the Spirit of the Lord within the brotherhood therefore centered very much on undoing the many ways in which original sin tried to get back into the brotherhood and deviate it from its original goals. In other words, Francis' view on the nature of original sin made him pay less attention to sexual matters than might have been expected on the basis of the more traditional understanding of original sin. This seems to be confirmed by the fact that the virtue of chastity is completely absent from *The Salutation of the Virtues*. Apparently, chastity was not uppermost in Francis' mind when, confronted with all kinds of different threats, he wished to remind his brothers to be faithful to their mission in the world and to the practice of the virtues necessary to achieve this mission.

This preference in his vision does not mean, however, that Francis would be blind to the reality of the world in which he and his brothers were living and in which they often came in contact with women on account of their work. All the same, in the beginning Francis and his brothers did not feel the necessity to say anything in the rule about these contacts. The question became more important only after "clerics entered the order in large numbers and brothers undertook the pastoral ministry."[52] It is then that they found it necessary to sound a warning to "all the brothers, wherever they are or go," but more in particular to the priests who "should speak honorably with [women] when giving them [the sacrament of] penance or some spiritual advice" (RegNB 12:1 and 3). This warning is repeated in the Later Rule 11 where Francis "firmly commands all the brothers not to have any associations or meetings with women which could arouse suspicion" (11:1). Although Francis considers this matter important enough to return to it in both rules, it appears clear from the other writings that temptations against the virtue of chastity are not Francis' primary concern here in *The Salutation of the Virtues*.

And All Carnal Fears (v. 13)

In Francis' statement that love confounds all carnal fears echoes the tradition that love and fear are mutually exclusive. This tradition goes back to the First Letter of John. There it is written that "there is no fear in love; but perfect love drives out fear, because fear is linked with punishment. Anyone who fears is not perfect in love. We love God, therefore, because God has loved us first" (4:18). Whereas Francis in Admonitions 27 simply repeated this teaching where he wrote that

[52] Flood, *The Birth of a Movement*, 35.

"where love is, there is no fear" (1), here, in *The Salutation of the Virtues*, he made several additions indicative of the fact that he followed his own interpretation. First, he added the adjective *omnes* (all), and in line herewith put "fear" in the plural form. Thereby he emphasized the total, radical incompatibility between virtue and vice, between love and fear. They cannot possibly exist together.[53] Next he specified the nature of the fears by adding the adjective *carnales* (carnal, of the flesh). Francis thus had a particular kind of fear in mind, namely those fears that originate from the flesh. And as Francis wrote *The Salutation of the Virtues* as a reminder at a particular moment in the history of the young brotherhood, he referred not to fears that would be theoretically possible, but to very concrete existential fears that the brothers experienced within the context of the ongoing struggle in the brotherhood between the spirit of the flesh and the Spirit of the Lord. What were these fears?

It seems that they can be reduced to one basic fear that repeats itself in many different forms according to the situation of the brothers and the problems they face in that particular situation, namely the fear, on the part of the learned brothers and of others, as well, that the choice they made when joining the brotherhood was not really and truly made under divine inspiration, but rather a terrible mistake? Were they really following a divine calling or had they, in their youthful enthusiasm, allowed themselves to be deceived by Francis and to be led astray? Was it really God's will that they leave Assisi and commit themselves to building a new world, based not on power, possessions, and prestige but on the humble service of the poor, the lepers and other marginalized, sharing all God-given goods with them? Or would it not have been more in conformity with God's plans if they would have stayed within Assisi's structures and devoted themselves wholeheartedly to the improvement of its situation through their pastoral ministry and their preaching? Was it really worthwhile to suffer so many hardships and misunderstandings in the world and to expose themselves even to persecution and death in the pursuit of their vision, or would it not be better to keep themselves safe and sound and to insert themselves in the official mission of the church, sanctioned by pope and council? Was it really God's will for the brother-priests that they "for love of love" be content to assist at the celebration of the other priest (cf. LetOrder 31) and not avail themselves of

[53] See for more details, above under IV B b.

the privilege granted by the Pope to celebrate the Holy Eucharist privately, or would they, in abstaining from the celebration of the Eucharist, not cause great harm to themselves and to the church so that they should rather be keen to accept the Pope's privilege?

And what about the foundational virtues of the brotherhood? Did they indicate the true way the brothers should follow in life or was their realization simply asking too much from them? Of course, these virtues were recommended by the Gospel, but did they have to be interpreted so radically? Did the brothers, for example, have to love their enemies, speaking well and doing well to them whenever they would speak and do evil and blaspheme God (RegNB 17:19), or could they invoke the principle of legitimate self-defense as popes and councils had done and were doing still with regard to the Saracens?[54] Did they have to efface themselves so completely in humble service to the poor and the marginalized as to forego the use of their own God-given talents, or should they rather use these talents as best as they could in whatever function given them by the legitimate civil or ecclesiastical authorities, and be truly joyful if they would be acknowledged as excellent bishops, renowned theologians or famous preachers (cf. TrueJoy 4–6)?

These are but a few of the many questions that caused fears and doubts in the hearts and minds of the brothers. They can be distilled from the Rule and other writings of Francis where, in trying to answer them, he reaffirmed the original ideals and/or gave guidelines how to live these ideals in the ever changing situations. Yet, however much Francis insisted that those ideals were not his, but the Lord's who had revealed those ideals to the brothers and, in various gospel texts, contin-

[54] See my *Francis and Islam*, 39–41, where I describe how James of Vitry, bishop of Acre and known to Francis and his brothers, deals with gospel texts that conscientious people in the church quoted to object against the use of violence against the enemies of the church. See also p. 206, note 35, where I relate the reply which Peter Manducator, a famous canonist, at the time of the second crusade gave to a patriarch of Jerusalem who asked whether "it is lawful for Christians to fight against the pagans and kill them, for the Lord says in the law: You shall not kill, and in the gospel: Anyone who takes the sword, shall perish by the sword." Quoting texts from the Scriptures and the Fathers as they are found in the *Decretum Gratiani*, Peter concludes that it is lawful to repel the pagans from the holy places, even by killing them. And in doing so not for his own sake but for Christ's, a crusader "serves the Lord, especially when he acts on the orders of the lord pope, whom Jesus has left us as his vicar on earth."

ued to challenge them to faithfully live up to their consequences, the fears and doubts kept coming back due to the powerful influence of the culture which surrounded the brothers. Underneath all this there lay a deep sense of insecurity. The brothers were tossed between the Spirit of the Lord, inspiring them to follow the footsteps of the poor and humble Jesus, and the spirit of the flesh as it became manifest in the strivings of the people of Assisi as well as in certain official policies of the church. And with this sense of insecurity troubling and upsetting their minds came the fears of the flesh: of failure, of having made the wrong choice; and of the sufferings and hardships the future might have in store for them if they persevered in following this way of life. It was those fears that made the brothers very vulnerable to the temptations of the flesh. In fact, those fears were at the origin of the temptations. For only in a climate of fear could these temptations have any impact. Without such fears, the temptations could hardly arise.

It was therefore a matter of great urgency for the life and well-being of the brotherhood to confound and destroy these fears. For they threatened to paralyze the brotherhood in its thrust towards a new society or world; these fears even threatened to move the brotherhood back into the world which they had left earlier because they could not agree with its way of thinking and doing, its values and its practices. And as Francis interpreted these fears lastly as the result of a lack of love, which made the brothers give in to spirit of the flesh and its temptations, he reminded them in *The Salutation of the Virtues* that they should not allow those fears to hinder and eventually to destroy the virtue of love. Rather, they should give free rein to the Spirit, God's Spirit of love, to confound all carnal temptations and fears and to renew, to re-create the brotherhood, returning it to its original ideals and to the original enthusiasm with which they had set out to transform the world and to restore paradise, not fearing the cost, but ready to give everything out of love.

Holy Obedience Confounds All Wishes of the Body

When his passion and death were nearing, Jesus "placed his will in the will of his Father, saying: Father, your will be done; not as I will, but as you will" (2 LetFaith 10). And as it was the will of his Father that he should lay down his life, "Jesus gave his life that he might not lose the obedience of the most holy Father" (LetOrder 46). Thus by his obedience, by not appropriating to himself his own will, Jesus counteracted the disobedience of Adam, who, in spite of God's warning, appropriated his own will to himself and claimed himself to be lord and master over the good which was not his but which God said and worked in him (Adm 2:3). This disobedience of the beginning continues, because there are only few who are prepared to follow Jesus' obedience and "to place [their] body under the yoke of service and holy obedience" (2 LetFaith 40). Even though "the yoke of Jesus is sweet and his burden light" (ibid. 15), they prefer to follow the wishes, the will of their body *(corporales voluntates)*.

Earlier, when speaking about the wisdom of the body (SalVirt 10), I described the wishes of those who let themselves be guided by this wisdom. Their main wish, the wish of their body, is to place itself at the service of the world with its false ideas and its non-values (2 LetFaith 65). This implies that they want to accumulate as many possessions as possible because the wisdom of the body makes them believe that the more possessions they have, the greater their security will be. Thus, following the will of their body, they deny God's will with regard to their bodies which God revealed in all that happened to Jesus who lost his body for the life of the world. As a result, they do not live up to the dignity in which God has created their bodies. Instead of following Jesus' way of obedience and service, listening to what God invites them to do in and through the persons and situations they meet, their minds and hearts are fully preoccupied with the cares and anxieties of their life, how to keep their power, possessions and prestige and even to enhance them. For in their view and the view of their surrounding world, whether people will be able to keep their bodies safe and sound depends on their possessions, power, and prestige. Hence, so the wisdom of the body and the whole culture around keeps telling them, no one in his or her right mind certainly wants to be so foolish as to run the risk of losing his or her body! And so they go on frantically surrounding themselves with their possessions, building a wall behind which they feel safe and secure, well protected against all dangers.[55]

It is clear then that, as far as the brothers are concerned, these wishes of the body are radically opposed to and incompatible with the demands of the gospel which the brothers have promised the Lord. This

[55] See above under IV B d.

implies that, when the brothers give in to these wishes, they will be so preoccupied with the cares of this life that they choke out the word of God from their hearts and minds. The brothers are then no longer able to hear God's word, to listen to it and to let their lives be inspired by it. They turn more and more away from the way of Jesus, from walking in Jesus' footsteps as they promised. The holy, loving and redeeming obedience to God's will gives way to evil, dividing and destructive obedience to the will of their bodies. Mainly concerned about promoting their own interests in an attempt to secure their own safety, they appropriate to themselves even the good that God worked in and through them, rather than returning it to God by placing their bodies at the loving and obedient service of others of the brotherhood, and of the world as God had wanted it from the beginning.

As Francis sees this happening, especially after his return from the Middle East, he places great emphasis on the importance of the virtue of obedience, right up to the last admonitions and warnings of his Testament. To walk this way of obedience to the Father's will may be very difficult; it may be very bitter (Test 3; 2 LetFaith 69). That is why many people, and even many brothers, in their shortsightedness or even their blindness (ibid.) shrink from going that way. It is with them in mind that Francis keeps insisting, on the basis of his own experience, that they are wrong. They should look at Jesus and no longer be afraid but rather feel encouraged by his example. And when they do take heart and start following Jesus' way of holy obedience, they will experience an incomparable sweetness. But many are afraid of taking the initial step, of exposing their bodies and placing them "under the yoke of service and holy obedience" (2 LetFaith 40). Yet, it is only if the brothers take up "the yoke of obedience" that they can and will experience its sweetness, its joy.[56]

The way of obedience that the brothers should walk after the example of Jesus is thus a liberating way, indeed. But then again, to know what this way really involves, they have to go it. They should therefore not let themselves be put off by the wisdom of the body, of those who are satisfied with things as they are and, feeling comfortable with the situation, do not want to put it at risk so as not to run the danger of los-

[56] Cf. G.P.Freeman, The Word of the Father. A commentary on Francis' Second Letter to the Faithful, verses 2–15, *FrancDigest* 9,1 (March 1999) 26–27; A. Jansen, My Yoke is Sweet, *FrancDigest* 9,1 (March 1999) 38.

ing their possessions, their power, their prestige, their bodies. For thus they remain captives of their own bodies and its wishes, and the sweetness and joy of liberation remain hidden to them. They will be revealed only if, trusting Jesus' word, they decide to accept the way of holy obedience. Holy obedience will then confound the will of the body and open for them the road to liberation. They will be liberated *from* their own narrow, self-centered world, and at the same time be liberated *for* a new world of different social relationships where people willingly (*voluntarie*, RegNB 5:14) abandon the will of their body and, through love of the Spirit, love and serve one another, listening to and being concerned about one another and one another's needs.

And All Wishes of the Flesh (v. 14)

Besides the will of the body, Francis also mentions of the wishes or will of the flesh *(carnales voluntates)*. As in the case of the temptations and the fears of the flesh, here too Francis refers to the will of the flesh as opposed to the will of the Spirit. It seems even that he wishes to put a special emphasis on this opposition of the flesh and the Spirit since he seems to feel that the adjective *corporales* is not fully adequate and needs to be complemented by *carnales.* Further, by adding *carnales* he underlines that the temptations, fears and wishes all have the same source and are therefore very much linked together. I observed already that the fears of the flesh create an atmosphere of insecurity and uncertainty in which temptations can become successful. If they are, the temptations of the flesh will lead a person to make up his/her mind and to wish what the flesh tries to entice him/her to choose and to do. In line with the description of the temptations of the flesh given above, the will of the flesh can be described as the will toward self-exaltation or self-glorification, as if their achievements are theirs and theirs only, which is radically opposed to the Spirit of the Lord who "strives for humility" (RegNB 17:15); or as the will to have words without works, to have only the outward appearance of religion and holiness (ibid. 11–12) which is radically opposed to the Spirit of the Lord who wills that the faithful, through their holy *operatio*, give birth again to Jesus in their own world.[57]

[57] See above under IV B i.

In spite of this opposition to the Spirit of the Lord, people, brothers not excluded, are quite ingenious in finding all kinds of reasons to justify following the will of the flesh. In certain instances they may even point to the fact that the church authorities fully approve of their activities or have even invited them to take on certain tasks for the benefit of the church. They are therefore quite certain that they are acting under obedience! Francis could not disagree more strongly. In fact, he forbids them under obedience to become too closely involved in certain pastoral policies and to forget the mission to which they are called (cf. Test 25–26). The obedience Francis has in mind is the holy, loving obedience of Jesus who placed his will in the will of his Father. Francis would love for his brothers to get an ever deeper insight in the beauty and the significance of this obedience. For it is this obedience which is liberating and truly life-giving. If he would only be able to share this insight with his brothers and to convince them of its truth, the will of the flesh would have no chance to lead them astray, under whatever disguise it might present itself. Rather, holy obedience would then unmask the will, the wishes of the flesh, and expose them for what they really are: misleaders, deceiving and blinding people, including some of the brothers. And, their eyes opened, the brothers would gladly place their will in the will of the Father and do whatever the Father wants them to do: namely, to share in Jesus' redemptive mission to the world, so that they may have life in abundance.

After the will of the body and of the flesh have been confounded, that is, after the obstacles to the virtue of holy obedience have been removed, holy obedience is free to exercise its positive influence on the brothers and to mold the brother who no longer resists the will of the Father into an obedient brother after the example of Jesus. It is this obedient brother whose picture Francis paints in the next verses (15–18). Francis gives a picture of what a virtue can achieve when it is allowed to implement its liberating, lifegiving function only with regard to the virtue of obedience. The reason why he selects obedience for this special treatment and adds these few verses to the original poem will be examined in the next chapter.

❧ CHAPTER FIVE

The Obedient Brother

vv. 15–18

In dealing with some introductory questions[1] in the first chapter, I noted already that in *The Salutation of the Virtues* more place is given to obedience than to all of the other virtues, including poverty. Moreover, Francis' preoccupation with obedience seems to be such that he breaks through the well-balanced structure of *The Salutation of the Virtues*. For verses 15–18 do not follow the same pattern as the previous verses. Also, they have, rather unexpectedly, a different subject than the holy obedience of verse 14, namely, the obedient brother, for *obedientia* does not have a body *(corpus suum)* or a brother *(fratris sui)*, nor can *obedientia* be the subject of the predicates *subditus et suppositus*. This led me to the conclusion that Francis apparently feels free to move beyond the original structure of *The Salutation of the Virtues* as a song of praise, a didactic poem, or a poetic testament, and that in these verses we therefore have to deal with an addition to the original text. This addition had become necessary because of the many problems that had arisen among the brothers with regard to the ideal of obedience as envisaged in the Earlier Rule 5:14–15. It became even more urgent still when the expressions: *subditi omnibus, qui in eadem domo sunt*; and *subditi omni humanae creaturae propter Deum* (RegNB 7:2 and 16:6), which referred to an essential characteristic of the way of life of Francis and his first brothers, completely disappeared from the Later Rule which was approved in 1223. Moreover, it seems that problems arose around the going among the Muslims. Rather than going "as sheep among the wolves" (RegNB 16:1),

[1] See especially I B 7 and I E 2.

the brothers preferred, with papal approval, to work among the Christians. All this is for me reason enough to think that, at least, these last verses were added to Salvirt after 1223 or even later.

TEXT

15.	et [frater obediens] habet mortificatum corpus suum ad obedientiam spiritus et ad obedientiam fratris sui	and [the obedient brother] has his body mortified to obedience of the Spirit and to obedience of his brother;
16.	et est subditus et suppositus omnibus hominibus, qui sunt in mundo,	and he is subject and submissive to all people who are in the world,
17.	et non tantum solis hominibus, sed etiam omnibus bestiis et feris	and not to people only but even to all beasts and wild animals
18.	ut possint facere de eo, quicquid voluerint, quantum fuerit eis datum desuper a Domino.	so that they may do with him whatever they want, insofar as it has been given them from above by the Lord.

GENERAL OBSERVATIONS

Parallel Texts

It is quite clear that these verses express ideas which can, verbally or materially, that is, as far as their content is concerned, be found also in other writings of Francis, such as the Earlier Rule, Second Letter to the Faithful and the Testament. As these ideas will be examined in detail in the special exegesis of each verse or part of it, it will suffice here just to list them together with their parallels in the other writings.

15: habet mortificatum corpus suum	RegNB 17:14: Spiritus autem Domini vult mortificatam... esse carnem
ad obedientiam Spiritus	RegNB 17:15: Et [Spiritus Domini] studet

	ad humilitatem et patientiam et puram simplicitatem et veram pacem spiritus RegNB 2:1: si quis divina inspiratione volens accipere hanc vitam; RegNB 16:2: quicumque fratrum divina inspiratione voluerint ire inter saracenos; cf. RegB 12:1
ad obedientiam fratris sui	RegNB 5:14: obediant invicem RegNB 9:10: secure manifestet unus alteri necessitatem suam; cf. RegB 6:8.
16. et est subditus... omnibus hominibus	RegNB 7:2: sint subditi omnibus qui in eadem domo sunt RegNB 16:6: sint subditi omni humanae creaturae propter Deum 2LetFaith 47: magis debemus esse... subditi omni humanae craturae propter Deum Test 19: eramus subditi omnibus
17. etiam omnibus bestiis et feris	RegNB 16:1: sicut oves in medio luporum OffPas 6:2.5: circumdederunt me canes multi... aperuerunt super me os suum, sicut leo rapiens et rugiens

Structure

These various ideas about obedience, which lie scattered all over Francis' writings, are here, at the end of *The Salutation of the Virtues*, integrated in a clear structure which gradually moves towards a climax. For, as Lehmann rightly observes,[2] in these last verses the radical and all-encompassing character of obedience receives an ever stronger emphasis through the use of various stylistic means. First, there is the use of synonyms and/or reinforcing expressions: *subditus* is supplemented by *suppositus*; *omnibus hominibus* is reinforced by *qui sunt in mundo*, and *et feris* is added to *omnibus bestiis*. These additions indicate that Francis felt he could not be clear enough if he wanted to get his ideas about obedience across to his brothers. It is also interesting to see how Francis frequently uses the conjunction "and." It is as if he found that the statement or characteristic he had just mentioned was not adequate to express what he wanted to impress upon his brothers as regards obedience and that,

[2] For this whole paragraph, see Lehmann 238.

therefore, he needed to complement it by adding yet another statement or characteristic.

Through this accumulation whereby the later statement or characteristic explained or further expanded the previous one, Francis was able to present us in the end with a fuller and clearer picture of the virtue of obedience in all its radicality. For, indeed, the gradual build-up leads to quite an unexpected result, an explosion, to use Lehmann's expression: the followers of holy obedience should not only be subject to all people who are in the world, but to all animals and wild beasts as well! Finally, through the double use of the adjective "all" Francis insists that there are no exceptions to obedience. The brothers, therefore, cannot make a selection as to whom they will obey or not. Wherever they are in the world, they ought to be subject to all: friend and enemy, Christian and Muslim.

DETAILED EXEGESIS

And [the obedient brother] has his body mortified[3]

When a brother has opened himself to the working of holy obedience, and in her strength has confounded the wishes of the body and of the flesh, it is of vital importance that he does not fall back and give in again to the wishes of the body. Rather, he should hold his body mortified and remain dead to all its wishes, for no one can acquire or

[3] Armstrong-Brady insert [and the person who possesses her] only at the beginning of v.16. It is not clear why they do so, nor why they speak of "person" rather than "brother" (152). Armstrong, Hellmann, Short translate: "Holy Obedience confounds every corporal and carnal wish, binds its mortified body to obedience of the Spirit and obedience to one's brother, so that it is subject and submissive to everyone in the world, not only to people but to every beast and wild animal as well that they may do whatever they want with it insofar as it has been given to them from above by the Lord" (165). I find this translation incorrect in several places. First, holy Obedience possesses "its own body," which it binds to obedience. This seems rather odd, to say the least. Second, the possessive pronoun *sui* in *fratris sui* is not translated. In the structure of the sentence which the translators propose, it would have to refer to holy obedience in the same way as the pronoun *suum* in *corpus suum* is made to refer to holy obedience and consequently is translated as: "its (i.e. obedience's) body." However, as it does not make sense that obedience has a "brother," they prefer not to translate it. Third, the conjunction *et* is translated by "so that." Fourth, the neuter *corpus* is made the subject of the sentence where it has two masculine adjectives: *subditus* and *suppositus*.

keep possession of a virtue unless he first dies (5).[4] This mortification is definitely not a wish of the body, because the body wishes above all not to endanger or harm itself but to preserve itself. On the contrary, it is the wish of the Spirit of the Lord who wishes *(vult)* the flesh to be mortified (RegNB 17:14). Further, this mortification is not limited to a series of acts of mortification. It goes far beyond this. It is part of the struggle which goes on between the spirit of the flesh, which wants to preserve and to promote the present world and its value system, and the Spirit of the Lord, who wants to recreate the present world and make it more conform to God's original design. Hence, mortification, of which Francis speaks here, has everything to do with leaving the sinful structures of Assisi, abandoning the wisdom of the world and the body, and not heeding the wishes of the body.

This is not done once and for all in one single act of conversion. On the contrary, as the brothers remain surrounded by Assisi and exposed to its temptations of possessions and power, the brothers will have to enter into a continuous process of letting go, of dying to whatever Assisi wants to offer them. However, this negative, destructive process of dying is not the end. As *The Salutation of the Virtues* declares explicitly, a brother keeps his body mortified unto something very positive, namely unto obedience of the Spirit and unto obedience of his brother. Of course, the positive character of this move is not immediately evident, precisely because of the process of dying that one has to go through. But once a brother has entered this process and has died to the world of Assisi, he will experience a new and beautiful life which emerges in the new space, the new world, which opens itself up for him by his being obedient to the Spirit and to his brother. Even though no longer welcome in Assisi because of the choices he has made, he will find the joy of a new brotherhood in his commitment to and his solidarity with "those who [by the people of Assisi] are considered worthless and [hence] are despised, among the poor and powerless, the sick and the lepers, and the beggars by the wayside" (RegNB 9:2)

To Obedience of the Spirit

Throughout the struggle between virtue and vice, depicted in verses 9–14, this struggle was seen as a concretisation of the struggle

[4] For this and what follows, see also III B b.

between the Spirit of the Lord and the spirit of the flesh with its allies, the devil and the world. That the latter were indeed the antipode which had to be confounded is most evident in the explicit mention of Satan, the world and the flesh throughout these verses, either as noun or as adjective. The Spirit, however, is for the first time mentioned only here, in v.15, although his presence is all the time presupposed.[5] For it is through the grace and light of the Spirit that the virtues are poured out into the hearts of the faithful and can become active there, changing people from their faithless state and making them faithful to God (cf. SalBVM 6). In the struggle between virtue and vice, it is therefore ultimately a matter of whom people open their heart to after they have mortified their bodies. Humans have this freedom of choice: they can listen to the Spirit of the Lord and submit themselves to the will of God which the Spirit reveals to them, or give in to Satan's temptations and follow his wishes. If they choose the latter, they regrettably forget the wondrous state in which they have been placed and the high calling to which they have been called because of their creation and redemption. Unfortunately, this happens all too frequently, so much so that, as Francis complained, the other creatures often serve and obey their Creator better than humans, who delight in vices and sins (cf. Adm 5:2–3) and so become the children of the devil whose works they do (2 LetFaith 66).

It is clear then that the struggle between virtue and vice—a struggle which covers all the aspects of human life and lasts an entire lifetime—can be interpreted as a struggle between being obedient to the Spirit of the Lord or to the threefold enemy. Yet, when Francis speaks

[5] With Lehmann 238, Asseldonk 508, and Jansen 174–175, I agree that Francis speaks here about the Spirit of God. A different view is held by Steiner, who thinks that with the expression "obedience to the spirit" Francis refers to "the situation of the human person under the new law. [This person is] faithful to the new dynamism inserted in our being by the fact that we are reborn and converted in 'the spirit' according to the terminology of St Paul, used here by Francis" (139). Steiner is followed by Lavilla Martin, who writes that "spirit" must be interpreted as "the spirit of the human person regenerated by love through which the person tends towards what is good, in opposition to "the flesh" which moves a person towards what is evil. The spirit is the superior part of the human person which is distinguished from the inferior part: the body or the flesh, according to the terminology of St Paul" (491). For reasons, indicated in the text, I find their interpretation not very likely.

here of obedience to the Spirit, he does not seem to have first and foremost in his mind this all-encompassing obedience which is an essential element of all human life in its dependence on God's creating and saving activity. Rather he refers to a more restricted, special form of obedience, as also other parallel texts suggest, namely the obedience to the Spirit who, in the lives of the brothers, strives for humility, patience, and pure simplicity which will lead them to the true peace of the Spirit (RegNB 17:15). This is confirmed at the beginning of the same rule where Francis mentions that it is the divine Spirit who makes the brothers desire to accept a life according to the gospel (RegNB 2:1; cf. Test 14), that is, a life as lesser brothers (RegNB 6:3) which Francis later, in his Testament, will briefly characterize by saying: "And we were simple and subject to all" (19). Francis stresses this form of obedience to the Spirit once more when he advises those brothers of his who by divine inspiration wish to go among the Saracens. Under the influence of the church's official policy of war against the Saracens who have to be conquered and to be made subject to the Christian powers, those brothers might be tempted to forget their original calling as lesser brothers. Hence Francis finds it necessary to insist that, also in their situation, the Spirit of the Lord wishes that they live among the Saracens, "being subject to every human creature for the sake of God" (RegNB 16:3.5–6).[6]

In light of these texts from Francis' writings, it is quite safe to conclude that by the expression "obedience of the Spirit" Francis means the obedience which is poured out by the Spirit of the Lord in the hearts of the brothers and makes them observe all that the Spirit inspires them to do, namely to live according to the form of the gospel, that is, to live as lesser brothers who, in all simplicity, not looking for any excuses in difficult circumstances, are ready to serve and obey one another and to be subject to all people, even to all animals and wild beasts. All that follows in *The Salutation of the Virtues* seems thus to be a further elaboration of the obedience of the Spirit, leading to a certain climax. This elaboration, in its turn, seems to confirm our analysis of what Francis intends by the obedience of the Spirit.

And to obedience of his brother (v. 15)

We have here one of those "and" statements which, as I mentioned

[6] See my *Francis and Islam*, passim.

earlier, Francis added because he felt that his previous statement might not be adequate to convey his intentions or his anxiety as regards the obedience of the brothers. For there might be some among them who understood the expression "obedience of the Spirit" in such a way that it had little or nothing to do with the concrete, daily life of the brotherhood and might even justify them in their abandoning of the original ideals of the brotherhood. Thus, for example, they might argue that the Spirit had called them to the office of preaching and that, therefore, they could not give it up to return to the humble service of their brothers (cf. RegNB 17:4–5). It is then, as a reaction to such situations, that Francis makes an additional "and" statement to remind those brothers explicitly about the essential relationship between the obedience of the Spirit and the obedience of one's brother which they seem to have lost sight of.

The obedience of the Spirit cannot be lived and practiced except in the obedience of one's brother. The needs, both spiritual and material, of one's brother are the privileged place where a brother is to hear the call of the Spirit, inviting him to willingly serve and obey his brother through the love of the Spirit (RegNB 5:14). As I observed earlier, we touch here upon a new understanding of obedience, which moves out of the feudal, hierarchical structure that, till then, had prevailed not only in the society but also in the church and the monasteries. I worked this out in great detail when I studied the meaning of the virtue of obedience and, in this context, analyzed all the important texts on obedience in Francis' writings. I may be allowed here to refer to this earlier part of my study.[7]

And He is Subject and Submissive to All the People who are in the World (v. 16)

The obedient brother practices his obedience of the Spirit not only in that he serves and obeys his brother. He extends this obedience to all people who are in the world, being subject and submissive to them. For by obeying to the Spirit, a brother enters into the struggle between the Spirit of the Lord and the spirit of the flesh. In that struggle he chooses to be on the side of the Spirit and to commit himself to participate in the strivings of that same Spirit towards establishing true peace through humility (RegNB 17:15). The strivings of the Spirit, however, are not

[7] See my commentary on the virtue of obedience in II C g.

limited to the brotherhood. They go well beyond it and are directed to all people who are in the world, for the Father's creating and saving activity in and through the Son and the Holy Spirit concerns the whole of humankind (RegNB 23:1–4.11). The obedience of the Spirit implies therefore that a brother is ready to go out to all people, to bring them true peace by being subject and submissive to them.[8]

In other explicit or implicit references to 1 Pe 2:13 (cf. RegNB 7:1; 16:6; 2 LetFaith 47; Test 19), Francis limits his advice to "being subject *(subditi)*." Here, however, he reinforces the adjective *subditus* by adding yet another one: *suppositus*.[9] As is clear from what I have repeatedly said so far, it was the situation within the brotherhood that moved Francis to this extra emphasis. The brothers, or at least some of the more prominent ones, were giving in to the desire to be "above others *(super alios)*" (2 LetFaith 47). Or they were looking for influential posts, which they had agreed not to strive after (cf. RegNB 7:1–2). Or they disagreed with Francis' approach to the Muslims as it was not in line with the official church policy of the crusades, sanctioned by the pope and council (cf. RegNB 16:3–6). Apparently, they had forgotten what the real obedience to the Spirit's calling demanded from them, and hence needed a forceful reminder to open their eyes that were blinded by the enemy (2 LetFaith 69). Thus Francis added a second adjective in the hope that it would help them to awaken and to see clearly again that in the life of the brothers, obedience to the Spirit and humility are inseparably linked. Obedience and humility cannot do one without the other. They even overlap one another.

This link is not something strange. It confirms the essential interdependence between the virtues which have a common origin and cannot exist one without the other. Moreover, the same happened in the life of Jesus in whose footsteps the brothers should walk. He humbled himself in the incarnation; he went even so far as to give his life in utter humiliation on the cross in order that "he might not lose the obedience of the most holy Father" (cf. Adm 1; LetOrder 27 and 46). Just as Jesus lived his obedience concretely and historically in his humility, so the brothers should do in the world of their days after Jesus' example. It is also clear

[8] See for an extensive analysis of the meaning of "being subject," a fundamental aspect of Franciscan spirituality, my commentary on the virtue of humility in II C e.

[9] See Lavilla Martin 491–492.

that the obedient brothers, by being subject and submissive to all people in the world, do not intend to uphold the feudal, hierarchical structures of lords and subjects, masters and slaves dominant at that time. On the contrary, through their humility the brothers are "to confound all the people who are in the world and all things that are in the world," as Francis explicitly states in verse 12, and to invite the people to leave behind their world with its prevailing system of power and possessions that only leads to division and violence, and to build a new world where true peace reigns because people, in obedience to the Spirit, willingly serve and obey each other after the example of Jesus!

"Being subject" is thus one of the words which received an entirely different meaning within the Franciscan knowing. It no longer refers to the "being subject" that is forced on servants who must be subject to their masters, whether they like it or not. The "being subject" of the brothers is not imposed on them; rather, it is freely chosen by them, as a way to break through the inequality and oppression that characterize the world of their days, and to lay, together with all people of good will, the foundations for a society of equality and respect through mutual submission and service.[10]

The emphasis on being subject and submissive to *all* people who are in the world is not a merely rhetorical exaggeration, as L. Lehmann correctly observes.[11] Francis indeed means *all* people, including Muslims and others. For Francis composed his *The Salutation of the Virtues* after his visit to the Sultan which took place in 1219. On the basis of his many enriching experiences during this visit, Francis advised his brothers who wanted to go among the Saracens "not to engage in arguments or disputes, but to be subject to every human creature for God's sake and [so] to confess that they are Christians" (RegNB 16:6). For, again, this was the only possible way to bring them the greeting of peace which Jesus had revealed to him and which he therefore was to bring to all people (RegNB 14:2; Test 23) and precisely to those against whom the church

[10] "This choice [of being subject] has a clear aim. It wants to be at the service of reconciliation. The first sin of disobedience led to the break between God and people and between people among themselves. Obedience brings about the reconciliation between God and people and between people among themselves. By their concrete choice of service the lesser brothers wanted to establish a society of reconciliation." Jansen 176.

[11] See for this and what follows: Lehmann 239.

was waging war with all the means that were at its disposal. This peaceful attitude of submission was further underlined by the gospel text with which Francis and his brothers started their advice: "The Lord says: 'Behold, I am sending you as sheep in the midst of wolves'" (RegNB 16:1). For Francis had discovered that, if you go "like sheep," without power and arms but in a spirit of submission and service, you will discover that those who are depicted as "wolves," even by the highest church authorities, are no wolves at all, and that it is very much possible to live in peace with them, and to bring the eschatological vision of the kingdom of God, as described by Isaiah, near at hand: "The wolf lives with the lamb" (11:6).[12]

And Not to People Only but even to All Beasts and Wild Animals

It is here that the accumulation of "and" statements reaches its unheard-of climax: the obedient brother should be subject and submissive to all beasts and wild animals. Francis indeed expresses himself in a most unusual and rather radical way, which has no parallel in earlier or contemporary writings.[13] Using a kind of hyperbole, Francis obviously wants to shake those among his brothers who like to withdraw behind the well-protected walls of the normal, accepted religious and ecclesiastical structures when the going gets rough, when their preaching ministry meets with obstacles or when persecution threatens (Test 25). Rather than having to hear over and over again all this talk about obedience and "being subject," about following their calling as lesser brothers and not asking for privileges, they prefer to go on with their ministry in the church, even if, so they argue, this requires certain dispensations in the rule for the good of the church. And the lord pope Honorius confirmed their argument, for in his bull *Vineae Domini* (1225) he wrote: "no sacrifice [not even when it is required by the rule] is ever more pleasing to God than seeking to gain souls."[14] In this situation the usual

[12] For an extensive commentary on RegNB 16, see my *Francis and Islam*, 43–134.

[13] See Lavilla Martin 492–493, where he mentions the *Psychomachia* of Aurelius Prudentius and *De conflictu vitiorum et virtutum* of Ambrosius Autbertus (✠784). Both these works are usually quoted as possible sources of inspiration for SalVirt, but do not contain a statement similar to Francis'.

[14] See *Bullarium Franciscanum*, vol. I, ed. J.H. Sbaraglia, Rome 1759, 24. For an English translation, see Armstrong, Hellmann, Short 563–564.

forms of advice do not carry much weight. They have become worn out and are simply no longer heard, overpowered as they are by the word of the pope. If Francis is once more to catch the attention of those brothers, he has to have recourse to a completely new and surprising formulation, in the hope thus to open their eyes and their hearts and to stimulate them to look in a different way at their priorities, re-examine their values and virtues, and eventually redirect their way of life towards the original ideals.[15]

It is but natural that this unexpected hyperbole drew also the attention of various commentators. What was its background? What was the message Francis wished to convey to his brothers in this strange text? E. v.d. Goorbergh and Th. Zweerman think that through this text Francis wanted to remind his brothers of Jesus' radical obedience. Thus they write: "As the Obedient One, being subject and submissive, Jesus exposed himself to the threats of all the powers in the world. From the beginning of his public life, Jesus had to resist Satan and his threefold temptation in the midst of wild animals. The drastic submission to 'all beasts and wild animals' (17) receives probably its most eloquent explanation if we connect it with psalm 22, the psalm of suffering, which Francis quotes in psalm VI of his office of Christ. This is the psalm which calls to mind the hour of Jesus' death: "For many dogs have surrounded; a pack of evildoers has closed in on me. They have looked and stared upon me; they have divided my garments among them and for my tunic they have cast lots. They have pierced my hands and my feet; they have numbered all my bones. They have opened their mouth against me like a lion raging and roaring" (OffPass VI, 2–5). Precisely the radical character of this obedience refers to Jesus as the obedient One par excellence. "[This reference] tells much about Francis' understanding of the imitation of Christ." The two authors see their view confirmed because "the last words of *The Salutation of the Virtues*: insofar as it has been given them from above by the Lord (18) evoke once more the image of Jesus. For, during his trial before Pilate, Jesus answers Pilate's question, saying:

[15] As R. Reijsbergen observes, "[Through the use of this hyperbole] it is possible to break through the barriers of establsihed, traditional and conservative views as well as to shift the limits of what is considered normal, realistic and desirable. In this way an atmosphere of freedom can be created in which people can come to a re-evaluation of values and virtues... and, as a next step, can rearrange their way of life" (112).

You would have no power over me if it had not been given you from above (Jn 19:11)."[16]

The image of the obedient, suffering Jesus may indeed have been in Francis' mind, certainly in the last verse with its implicit reference to Jesus' trial before Pilate. Yet, with Lehmann,[17] I am inclined to believe that here too, in mentioning beasts and wild animals, Francis' choice of words was first and foremost influenced by what he wrote in chapter 16 of his Earlier Rule after his experience among the Muslims, rather than by psalm VI of the Office of the Passion, as E. v.d. Goorbergh and Th. Zweerman suggest. Indeed, the whole context of verse 17 and especially the insistence on obedience to the Spirit and on being subject to all people in verses 15–16 point in the direction of the Earlier Rule16, which explicitly mentions divine inspiration or the obedience to the Spirit (3) and also advises the brothers to be subject to every human creature (6). Moreover, and this is the most convincing argument, chapter 16 opens with Jesus' words addressed to his followers in the missionary discourse of Matthew's gospel: "Behold, I am sending you as sheep in the midst of wolves" (1).

Together with many others, Lehmann interprets Francis' quotation of these words of Jesus as a clear expression of his desire that the brothers be ready to accept martyrdom, as he once was when he went to visit the sultan. For Francis, and so for Lehmann, this readiness was "indispensably" a fundamental attitude in the life of the lesser brothers.[18] The emphasis on martyrdom finds ample support indeed in the biographies of Francis by Celano and Bonaventure. Given the fact that the Muslims were generally considered to be "wolves," Celano and Bonaventure could see Francis' desire to go to the Sultan only as foolishness on his part. Such foolishness could be justified in their eyes only if it were transformed into a "holy foolishness," that is, if they interpreted Francis' desire in terms of his desire to become a martyr in order thus to reach the most perfect imitation of Christ, who suffered and died out of love for him.[19]

16 v.d. Goorbergh-Zweerman 116–117.

17 See Lehmann 239–240.

18 See Lehmann 239–240. Other defenders of this view are: Esser, Rotzetter, Bühlmann. See my *Francis and Islam*, 115–117.

19 Cf. 1 Cel 57; Bonaventura LM, IX, 7.

However, this interpretation of what was in Francis' mind when he used this surprising expression can hardly be reconciled with the advice to his brothers that, obedient to "divine inspiration," they should "not engage in arguments and disputes [with the Muslims], but be subject to every human creature for God's sake" (RegNB 16:3 and 6). This advice defines for all the brothers, whether cleric or lay, the first and most important form of how to live "spiritually" (5) among the Muslims. It indicates in a clear and unmistakable way that Francis wanted his brothers first and foremost to go on a peace mission to the Muslims. To live among them peacefully in the Spirit of the Lord and thus to show that they are followers of Jesus was Francis' main intent (5–6). If he had wanted his brothers to strive after martyrdom, he never would have advised them to avoid antagonizing the Muslims and engaging in controversies with them, for antagonizing them was the surest way to achieve martyrdom, as the martyrs in Morocco had shown.[20] Nor would he have advised his brothers to be subject to the Muslims, as this was the surest way to avoid getting entangled in problems with the Muslims and thus to avoid martyrdom or, at least, to minimize its risk, as Francis himself had experienced during his stay among the Muslims and his visit to the sultan. Moreover, in the Earlier Rule 16:14, Francis quotes explicitly the Lord's word in the gospel of Matthew: "If they persecute you in one town, flee to another" (10:23). A further resonance of this text can clearly be heard in the Testament where Francis, at the end of his life, advises

[20] For Francis' disapproval of their approach, see Jordan 7–8. As regards this passage, L. Pelegrini writes: "Let us not forget a certain insistence of the sources on the thirst for martyrdom on the part of Francis: an attitude which seems to be contradicted by the witness of Jordan of Giano. He presents us Francis who indignantly rejected the *legenda* of the Franciscan martyrs of Morocco... One gets the impression, if one must believe Jordan, that Francis had clearly warned the brothers of the drama or rather the tragedy they were to encounter, precisely because of their thirst for martyrdom which led them to risk their lives. Hence there follows that whole series of precautions which characterize the formulation of the mission, as given in chapter 16 of the *Regula non bullata*" (Verbali delle sedute, *Espansione del Francescanesimo tra Occidente e oriente nel Secolo XIII, Società Internazionale di Studi Francescani 6*, Assisi, 1979, 23. However, Francis' advice as to how the brothers should exercise their mission, was not taken up in the *Regula bullata.* It simply did not fit within the context of the predominant culture of the crusades that Christians should be subject to Muslims. For this, see my *Francis and Islam*, 74–87; 114–117.

his brothers: "wherever they have not been received, let them flee into another country to do penance with the blessing of God" (Test 26). It now seems highly unlikely that Francis would give such advice to his brothers and thus deprive them from the possibility of becoming martyrs, while he personally would go out of his way to obtain martyrdom for himself as the highest possible form of following Jesus.

In this light I believe that, as indicated already, Francis' rather unusual advice to his brothers to be subject to all beasts and wild animals has to be interpreted in the context of his own personal discovery during his stay among the Saracens. In their midst he discovered that, if the brothers, following the word of the Lord, go "like sheep among the wolves," they will discover that the so-called "wolves" are no wolves at all. On the contrary, when approached in a spirit of non-violence and of respectful service, the "wolves" appear to shed all their ferocity, if any, and, instead, to be ready to build peaceful, friendly relations with others. Thus the atmosphere is being created in which it will be possible to restore paradise with its original harmony between all God's creatures,[21] as described in Isaiah's eschatological vision of the wolf who lives in peace together with the lamb (cf. Is 11:6). The restoration of paradise in which the "all-powerful, most holy, most high and supreme God" placed us humans, and to which God wants us to return by redeeming us from our present captivity through the life and death of Jesus (cf. RegNB 23:1–3), and inviting us to follow in Jesus' footsteps on the way to redemption and reconciliation, rather than the desire for martyrdom, forms thus the background against which we have to read this unusual verse.

[21] The many stories about Francis and animals are often seen as illustrations of how, through his non-acquisitive way of life in obedience to God's original intentions with creation, Francis had been able to restore paradise and its harmonious relationship between humans and animals. See: S. Verheij, De oorspronkelijke onschuld. Franciscus spreekt met de vogels en de andere dieren, *FL* 61 (1978) 16–30; R.D. Sorrell, Tradition and innovation in Saint Francis of Assisi's sermon to the birds, *Franciscan Studies* 43 (1983) 396–407; id. *St Francis of Assisi and Nature. Tradition and Innovation in Western Christian Attitudes toward the Environment*, Oxford 1988; W. Short, Hagiographical method in reading Franciscan sources: stories of Francis and creatures in Thomas of Celano's "Vita Prima" (21:58–61), *Laurentianum* 29 (1988) 462–495; H. Sevenhoven, Oorspronkelijk en ontroerend. Franciscus' omgang met de dieren, *FL* 75 (1992) 193–201. For a recent article on the presence of this theme in early Christianity, see François Bovon, The Child and the Beast: Fighting Violence in Ancient Christianity, *Harvard Theological Review* 92 (1999) 369–392.

This does not mean that Francis would not have been aware of the difficulties and dangers, the suffering and persecution[22] with which the efforts to restore paradise can be and often are fraught. He very well was! But these sufferings and persecution, eventually crowned by martyrdom, were not the reason why the brothers should be subject and submissive, even to all beasts and wild animals. They were rather a possible or, as experience had taught Francis and his brothers, a most likely consequence of the ideals for which they had chosen to live. However, they should not allow themselves to be deterred from pursuing their ideals on account of such possible consequences. Rather, they should encourage each other to face them patiently, not losing sight of their ideal: to restore paradise.[23]

Read within the context of the restoration of paradise, verse 17 gives us a summary of the overall purpose Francis had in mind with *The Salutation of the Virtues*. For all the holy virtues which proceed from the most holy God, the source of all good, are meant to be received by us and to act within us as God's forces that will confound whatever evil exists in us and in our present world. Thus they are to lead us and our world back to the original state of goodness or holiness in which we and the world were created by God: paradise! That Francis at the end of *The Salutation of the Virtues* confirms this overall purpose of the virtues in this somewhat hyperbolic way, linking it more specifically to the being subject to all humans and even to all beasts, has everything to do with the fact that this fundamental attitude in the life of the lesser brothers had come under considerable pressure at that particular stage in the development of the brotherhood. For this reason, as I mentioned earlier, Francis felt obliged to add these verses to the original text of the *The Salutation of the Virtues* so as to really shake his brothers. He wanted to awaken them again to the enthusiasm of the beginning and to urge them to continue their mission of peace to all people, but especially to the Muslims.

Francis had personally gone to the Muslims in obedience to the Spirit, and he had lived among them, being subject to them for God's sake. But this last advice to his brothers had completely disappeared

[22] It is remarkable how often the words *persequor, persecutus, persecutio*, occur in the writings of Francis: Adm 3:8–9; 6:2; 9:1; RegNB 16:12–15; 22:15; RegB 10:9–11; Test 6 and 25.

[23] See further my commentary under V C f.

from the mission chapter in the Later Rule 12. Moreover, those brothers who, together with curial officials had been responsible for the final redaction of the *Regula bullata* in 1223, had reduced chapter 16 of the Earlier Rule to just two verses of a largely juridical nature. Thus they had degraded chapter 16 to a kind of appendix that no longer had any connection with the previous chapters. It looks as if those brothers did not dare omit the mission chapter completely; yet, at the same time, they failed to show a proper appreciation for the text of the Earlier Rule 16, probably because it seemed rather strange and maybe even foolish in their eyes, and they did not know what to do with it.[24]

Problems did not exist only at the level of ideas. Differences also arose in practice. In 1225, by virtue of his bull *Vineae Domini custodes*, pope Honorius III sent a number of brothers who were clerics and priests to the "kingdom of Miramolim," the present Morocco. They did not go primarily to live in the Spirit of the Lord among the Saracens by being subject to them. The bull does not say a word about this! On the contrary, they were to preach to the Christians, who lived in the midst of the Muslims, and to administer the sacraments to them. Insofar as the Lord would give them time and opportunity, the brothers would have to try to convert the Muslims just as they also had to lift up the fallen and support the weak. It is evident that the Muslims had, to a large extent, if not completely, disappeared from the brothers' sight.[25] A new type of Franciscan missionary made his entry onto the stage of history to replace the missionary whom Francis had in mind, when he wrote the Earlier Rule 16 about the brothers who, by divine inspiration, want to go among the Saracens "like sheep in the midst of wolves" (1). Whereas Francis' focus was first and foremost directed toward a peaceful presence of brothers, whether cleric or lay, in the midst of the Saracens to whom they were subject for God's sake (6), now all the attention was given to the pastoral activity of clerics and priests among the Christians, to whom they preached and administered the sacraments.[26]

[24] See my *Francis and Islam*, 86–87.

[25] *Bullarium Franciscanum*, vol. I, 24. Armstrong, Hellmann, Short 563–564. See also my *Francis and Islam*, 103–104.

[26] "... by singling out roles that only an ordained brother could perform, Honorius is subtly redefining [the mission of the brothers] in a more clerical direction... We see that acceptance of a pastoral mission on behalf of the church is beginning to determine the Franciscan way of life." Armstrong, Hellmann, Short 563. From my observations made here, it will be clear that I disagree with the statement of these

In fact, as is clear from the bull *Ex parte vestra*, issued on March 17, 1226, half a year before Francis' death, the brothers who had been sent by pope Honorius III were afraid to live among the Muslims. Hence they sought to escape a possible persecution in the future with the help and support of the Roman curia.[27] Francis strongly objected to their action, as is evident from the statement in his Testament where he "commands all the brothers through obedience that, wherever they are, they do not dare to ask any letter of privilege at the Roman curia, either personally or through an intermediary under the pretext of preaching or as protection against the persecution of their bodies" (25). Thus he used his Testament to make a last effort to put an end to these practices which over the years had been creeping into the brotherhood and which he considered detrimental to its life and mission.

If it is indeed true, as I think it is, that Francis had the above practices also in mind when composing the last verses of *The Salutation of the Virtues*, these verses, too, have to be interpreted within this missionary context and have to be seen as an attempt on Francis' part to have the brothers return to the vision of their mission among the Saracens as expressed in the Earlier Rule 16. The brothers should not limit their work to Christians only. They should rather go and live among the Muslims, and be subject to them, even if the official authorities were labeling them as "wolves." They should certainly not have recourse to papal bulls to escape eventual troubles and hardships, but remain dedicated to their mission of peace, whatever the consequences might be for them. For to go among them not protected by papal bulls, but ready to be subject to them and to serve them is the only way to join Jesus in his redeeming mission and to break down the divisions and enmities between people, even between Christians and Muslims. People will be reconciled with each other and the harmonious relationship between all

---

authors where they write: "With this bull *Vineae Domini*], the Papacy gave its full support to the missionary initiative among Muslims, so dear to Francis's heart" (ibid.).

[27] *Bullarium Franciscanum*, vol. I, 26. See my *Francis and Islam*, 128–129, where I make special mention of the fact that the brothers in Morocco directly approached the pope and his curia, rather than consult Francis or discuss the matter at the chapter. The church's pastoral policy took precedence over their way of life as lesser brothers. Unfortunately, the text of this bull is not taken up in the new English translation of Armstrong, Hellmann, Short.

creatures that existed in paradise will be restored in all its beauty. Unfortunately, Francis' attempt to encourage his brothers and to strengthen them in their resolve to be faithful to their ideals as lesser brothers were not very successful with those clerics and priests who went to Morocco. And they were not the only ones, judging from Francis' reactions in his Testament.

That They May Do with Them Whatever They Want, Insofar as it has been Given Them from Above by the Lord (v. 18)

Right from the beginning, Francis and his brothers met with strong opposition from several quarters, even from their own family and relatives, on their mission of service and peace. In this context the stories which tell us about how the brothers fared first in Assisi and afterwards in other places after they had been sent into the world (AP 17b–c; 18b–c; 20a–24b) are interesting. There we read, among other things, that the man who treated the brothers well was an exception (AP 23a). In the midst of all these troubles, Francis kept encouraging his brothers not to be afraid but to trust in the Lord (AP 18b). He did the same when at the chapter of 1221, the brothers returned with stories of hardships and difficulties from their travels across the Alps into Germany and across the sea into Syria. Impressed by these stories, Francis then adds a long series of gospel texts, especially chosen from the perspective of encouragement, to the mission chapter in the Earlier Rule 16. The series of 11 verses opens with the words: "The Lord says." It is not just Francis who is saying what follows. No, it is the Lord himself who speaks these words here and now to the brothers. It is the Lord himself then who starts by assuring "all the brothers wherever they are" (10) that "whoever loses his life for the Lord's sake, will save it for eternal life" (11). Whatever their enemies may do to them, whatever suffering or persecution they may inflict upon them, the brothers should know that their life is in safe hands. They should therefore rejoice and be glad (16). They certainly should not fear those who kill the body and thereafter can do no more (18), but should patiently persevere unto the end. For, so the series ends, "whoever perseveres to the end will be saved" (21).[28]

[28] For a more detailed analysis of the text and its composition, see my *Francis and Islam*, 126–128.

Francis similarly encouraged his brothers in *The Salutation of the Virtues*. Introducing the foundational virtues of the brotherhood and expanding on their effectiveness in confounding the evil, he reminded them of the high ideal for which they had left the world of Assisi: to build an alternative society of peace. The way to this ideal was not an easy one. It demanded the total dedication of the brothers, surrounded as they were by a world that followed its own wisdom or standards and that kept tempting them to return to its wealth and comfort, its honor and recognition. They felt these temptations all the more strongly when they were being misunderstood, opposed, ridiculed, or even persecuted. It was then that the question arose whether it was all worth the trouble. Did it really make sense to invest so much in their being subject and submissive to all humans and animals? For what difference did their efforts really make? People in the world continued to live and act along the same lines as they did before, and were honored and appreciated for their achievements. Why not join them and save oneself a lot of hardship and trouble?

Confronted with these questions here, at the end of *The Salutation of the Virtues*, Francis did not have recourse again to a series of words of the Lord, as he did in the Earlier Rule 16. Rather, as he had done also in the psalms of the Office of the Passion which he himself had composed,[29] Francis placed before his brothers' eyes how he Jesus himself

[29] Armstrong, Hellmann, Short mention that the third psalm of Francis' Office of the Passion, assigned for the Prime during the Sacred Triduum and on weekdays throughout the year, recalls Jesus' appearance before Pilate, for "the people of the Middle Ages commonly held that the setting of the prime was the hour when Christ was brought before Pilate" (143, note a). Just like the other Psalms, so also the third one contains "the words of Christ. Nowhere is there any indication that it is Francis who speaks. He does not use a language of his own, but only quotations from the psalms and words from the New Testament which Jesus himself used in hsi conversations with his Father. All the psalms of the Office of the Passion are essentially the prayer of Jesus... the suffering and beloved Son [who] in his deepest suffering is closest to his Father, also then when he is abandoned by all people and even by his friends. Hope and trust in his most holy Father carry him through his ordeal." E. v.d. Goorbergh, The Office of the Passion of our Lord, *FrancDigest* 8,1 (June 1998) 48–60, here 53–54. "In such situations [of anger, despair and depression] Francis took time to meditate and to pray in order to understand how Jesus could keep crying to his most holy, his most high Father (PsFr 3:3); how he, with death before his eyes, could keep asking his Father for help; how he could keep calling God his Father, even when death took away his last breath. Francis

acted at his trial before Pilate, during those last dark hours of his life. Pilate threatened Jesus for, so he said, he had the power to release Jesus and the power to crucify him. Not at all impressed by this threat, Jesus replied: "You, [Pilate], would have no power over me if it had not been given you from above" (Jn 19:11). Jesus knew himself ultimately to be in God's good hands. Whatever Pilate decided, his was not the last word. The last word was God's. And Francis and his brothers knew what God's last word was. Pilate condemned Jesus to die on the cross. This seemed to be the end of Jesus. But how could God abandon this faithful servant who had put all his trust in God? Being a God of life, God raised Jesus from the dead to new life. Whatever sufferings and hardships Jesus had to endure, whatever shameful death Jesus had to undergo, his way of the cross proved in the end to be the way to life, for Jesus and for all humankind.

The brothers, therefore, should "look to the Good Shepherd who suffered the passion of the cross" (Adm 6:1) in order to open the way to salvation, to true life. And they should encourage each other "to follow him in tribulation and persecution, in insult and hunger, in infirmity and temptation, and in everything else" (2), so that they too might find life for themselves and for others, then and there and forever after. However, this brotherly encouragement was not being served if they were to continue speaking about the insults and persecutions they had suffered and which others were likely to suffer on their mission of peace in the future. Rather, when coming together, they should keep telling each other stories about the good they had been able to accomplish and about the life they had been able to share by following Jesus' way. And they should not give up reciting the poem about God's holy virtues and how they had been able, in the strength of these virtues, to confound the evil and to inaugurate a new world. Thus, through their mutual encouragement, they might overcome any form of defeatism that could have crept into the brotherhood and, instead, find true joy and happiness in following Jesus in a life informed by the holy virtues, even if this

---

wanted to learn from Jesus to live in such a way that his many sufferings vould not embitter or harden him but rather strengthen his relationship with the ineffable One... In praying the fifteen psalms [of his Office of the Passion] Francis learned to bring Jesus, his Teacher, closer, to understand him better and to follow him more faithfully." H. de Vos, Your beloved Son, Lord and Teacher, *FrancDigest* 8,1 (June 1998) 38–47.

would involve insults and persecutions. They would count these as nothing compared with what they have found: God's kingdom, a world built according to God's design. And in their joy and happiness about the treasure they have found, maybe after a long struggle, full of insults and persecutions, they would then experience the profound truth of Jesus' word: "Blessed are those who suffer persecution for the sake of justice, for the kingdom is heaven is theirs" (Mt 5:10: cf. RegNB 16:12).

Evoking the memory of Jesus during his trial before Pilate at the end of *The Salutation of the Virtues*, Francis wanted his brothers to keep this image always before them on their journey through the world as a last assurance that, just as in the case of Jesus, so also in their case the power of God would gain victory over the power of the world, the power of evil, even if all odds were against them. This victory was not to be a purely eschatological one at the end of time. On the contrary, however strong the resistance of the world might be—a world that wanted to hold on to its old ways of power and might, of wealth and possessions—God's power was capable of confounding the evil, as the present tense of the verb *confundit* clearly indicates. God's power, therefore, is not only manifested in raising Jesus from the dead and so denying evil its final victory. It also becomes manifest in that God's holy virtues confound the evil in the present world. It is the present world, therefore, where the brothers are first and foremost called to exercise their God-given mission to confound the evil now. This is evident also from Francis' quotation of the Lord's word that, in case of opposition or persecution, rather than becoming martyrs and entering the final glory, the brothers are to flee to another city or country there to do penance, fighting and confounding evil,[30] with the blessing of God (Mt 10:23 = RegNB 16:14; Test 26).

Against this background it is clear what God wants the beasts and wild animals to do with the brothers who are subject and submissive to them. They are not to make them into martyrs whom God then crowns with eternal glory. Rather, in answer to the respectful and loving, nonviolent approach of the brothers, the beasts and wild animals are to overcome whatever ferocity exists in them, due to the situation into which they are forced, and to live with the brothers and with all people

[30] See François Bovon: "I read metanoia which means 'repentance' and 'conversion' to mean also and primarily a new way of acting and of constructing reality" (377).

in peace, as is beautifully illustrated in the story of Francis and the wolf of Gubbio.[31] Trusting therefore in God's power—a power that, paradoxically, manifests itself in weakness, in poverty and humility, in loving service and obedience—the brothers should never give up, however strong and powerful the evil might appear, however much the evil might seem to threaten them, their life, through beasts and wild animals. Through their respect for and their loving service even to beasts and wild animals, they should continue to appeal to their original, God-given goodness, and invite them to affirm this goodness once again by reciprocating the brothers' respect and love.

The more the brothers are convinced of the efficaciousness of their humble and obedient life of service because their weakness becomes the vehicle of God's power, and the more they are able to convince others of this life-giving truth through their infectious behavior as lesser brothers subject and submissive to all, the closer they will come to the realization of their ideal: the restoration of paradise,[32] where God placed

[31] Fioretti 21. Differently from the people of Gubbio, Francis approaches the wolf without arms. He breaks with the way the people see the wolf. For Francis, the wolf is not synonymous with war and death. He addresses him even as brother. He does not conform himself to the system of war, *das Kriegssystem* of the people of Gubbio. Rather, he exchanges it for the religious system of relationship, *das "religiöse Verwandtschaftssystem,"* as it was valid in paradise. The wolf reacts immediately in a favourable way: he becomes gentle like a lamb. Once he has achieved this, Francis has, as a next step, to try and change the attitude of the people. They have to acknowledge that they have made the wolf into a wild, ferocious animal by refusing him food and making him go hungry. And it is this sin of theirs which leads to their death, not the wolf! They have therefore to turn away from this sin. If they do so, they need no longer fear neither wolf nor death. Unanimously, they decide then to see to the wolf's food. and so to create the neccessary conditions to live together in peace. Sin no longer spoils their relationship with the wolf. Paradise is restored. See G.P. Freeman, Der Wolf, Franziskus und Gubbio. Eine synchrone Lesung von Fioretti 21, *WissWeish* 48 (1985) 122–150, where also further literature can be found.

[32] "Already the prophets dreamed about a messianic time when lamb and wolf, cow and bear would feed together and the infant would play over the cobra's hole (cf. Is 11:6–10). The promise of such a time is, as Francis shows, not only something to be hoped for in the future, not simply a utopia, but a real possibility the more

humans and animals together in peace and where God wants all without exception to sit at the table of the Lord and to share in the goods that God has made for the enjoyment and happiness of all.

---

people return to the original innocence and relate to the creation not as lords but as brothers and sisters. Here, a different way of being in the world manifests itself in which it is no longer a matter of being above people and things, but of being with them, as with brothers and sisters at home." L. Lehmann, Franziskus und die utopische Bewegung heute, *FranzSt* 67 (1985) 99.

Conclusion

Francis wished to walk in the footsteps of the poor and humble Jesus who came to lead humankind back to the place where God had placed it in the beginning (RegNB 23:1–3). In doing so, Francis wished to join this Jesus in his redeeming, liberating mission to restore paradise. And he wished his brothers to do the same, not on their own strength—for left to themselves they would miserably fail—but in the strength of God's holy virtues. Empowered by these holy virtues, they would be able to confound the evil in this world, wherever and in whatever form it existed, and to present humankind with an alternative in contrast to the existing world and its sinful structures.[1]

Francis gradually developed this vision and what it concretely meant within the historical context of his days. When the Lord led him among the lepers, for whom life was anything but a paradise on earth, he decided to leave the world of Assisi behind and to live and work among the poor and the lepers. Together with them he was to build a new world, a world of true peace, where they would no longer be excluded. He shared this vision with the brothers whom the Lord gave to him, and together they deepened it in a continuous interaction with the world around them. Whenever they were confronted with new problems and situations, they analysed them carefully, well aware that they were constantly

[1] For a brief history of the contrast community in the Old and New Testament and its relevance today, see T. Malipurathu, Contrast Community: Its Meaning and Relevance for Our Times, *Vidyajyoti. Journal of Theological Reflection* 62 (1998) 606–623.

involved in a struggle between the spirit of the flesh and the Spirit of the Lord. And on the basis of this analysis, they continually tried to formulate their vision anew according to what they discerned to be the inspiration of the Lord at that moment.

Becoming ever more clear in their minds was their vision and its aim: to establish a brotherhood in which the brothers would obey and serve one another unto true peace. They also obtained a better insight into what they had to do to make it a reality. As Assisi's way led to division among people and to the exclusion of the poor and the lepers, it was evident that they had to abandon the value system Assisi had used to justify its striving after an ever greater increase of its wealth, even at the cost of many victims. In a dialectical process, taking Assisi's value system as the existing thesis, Francis and his brothers developed their own antithesis. Often using traditional terms, they were intent on freeing these terms from the oppressive and exploitative content which they had within Assisi's order of things, and on filling them with a new, liberating and empowering meaning after the example of Jesus.

Committed to their vision and its realisation, Francis and his brothers experienced great joy in the midst of all the misunderstanding and even persecution which they suffered at the hands of the people of Assisi, their own relatives not excluded. All the greater and more intense was Francis' pain when, later on, some of his brothers wanted to go a different way. Francis could not approve of the new direction in which they wanted to move because, in his eyes, they deviated from what the Lord had inspired him and his first brothers to do. Deeply disappointed though he was, Francis nevertheless kept appealing to these brothers, inviting them not to give up the original ideal and to keep faithfully to the way of life they had promised to the Lord. In this context, he composed *The Salutation of the Virtues* as a reminder for his brothers. In this poetical testament he let pass before their eyes, as if in a procession, the six virtues which, guided by Queen Holy Wisdom, were the very foundation of his brotherhood as an alternative society and thus formed the heart of its ethic: simplicity, poverty, humility, charity and obedience.

At the same time, on account of his daily reflection on God's doings in the life, death and resurrection of Jesus, he was able to express in the The salutation his deepest conviction, that God's holy virtues were indeed powerful enough to confound the evil in the world and thus to restore paradise. In times of difficulty, when they had to face hardships because of the choices they had made, and fears and doubts might cloud their minds, the brothers should therefore never give up. Rather, they should put all their trust in God and wholeheartedly commit themselves to their vision of a new world, regardless of the cost. They should allow God's holy virtues to operate in and through them. So, by their way of life, they should invite all people in the whole world to free themselves from the captivity in which they are held by the forces of evil, and lead them back on the way to paradise.

Francis was not the first one to believe in this universal vision, encompassing all people and even all beasts and wild animals, and to commit himself to its realisation, nor was he to be the last one. Throughout the ages, this vision has inspired countless women and men to become involved in the struggle between good and evil in the certainty that, all appearances to the contrary, evil would not have the last word. On the contrary, the forces of goodness, of love and of life, were to be stronger than the forces of sin, of hatred and of death. However, the struggle of these women and men was not always welcomed by the dominant powers, as they saw this struggle as a threat to their own established interests. Yet, they persevered against all odds, often paying with their own lives. And although the influence of their efforts as a countercultural movement cannot be measured, we believe that the world would have been worse off if they had not persevered but would have accommodated themselves to the wishes and demands of the dominant culture. For then they would never have been able, as they have been until now, to encourage people to believe in the possibility of goodness and love to confound the evil and to transform the world into a world where all people can live together as sisters and brothers in peace and harmony; nor would they have been able to inspire people to commit themselves to this transformation with their whole being.

Today, too, this vision of an alternative society, of a new world for all, remains of vital importance at a time of increased globalization. It is said that the time of the great traditional narratives, including the Christian narrative, has come to an end, and that the time of globalism as a master narrative has arrived.[2] Due to the speed with which informa-

[2] For this and what follows, I am greatly indebted to W. Cavanaugh, The World in a Wafer; A Geography of the Eucharist as Resistance to Globalization, *Modern Theology* 15 (1999) 181–196. See also: U. Duchrow, God or Mammon: Economies in Conflict, *Mission Studies* 13 (1996) 32–67.

tion and people can travel across space, the spatial barriers that existed in the past have been overcome and the dimensions of the world have shrunk. All the people on earth, so we are led to believe, have become contemporaries, sharing the same time and space within the "global village." Thus all the world's people are able to grow closer together and put an end to past ethnic, tribal, and religious-cultural divisions which have led to much bloodshed over the centuries. Global peace has now become a possibility thanks to the global monoculture that is increasingly penetrating local cultures, which kept people apart. We are not told, however, that the global monoculture which is being advertised as a sign of progress and of a new beneficent catholicity which transcends spatial barriers, creates a new fragmentation. For when the local traditions of people lose out to the propaganda of the global monoculture, the historical continuity of people with their own past endangered.

Yet, this continuity is necessary to forge the identity of individuals and peoples. For who are they if they do not remember their past? It is difficult, however, to maintain the link with their past, with their roots, when they are constantly enticed to dispose, not simply of goods, but of relationships and particular attachments and to follow the whims of quickly changing fashions that are developed to keep consumption and the new economy growing. Thus the late capitalist subjects become "schizophrenic," fragmented; they do not experience continuity but only a series of unrelated present moments in time. Left without a coherent narrative sequence in which past, present and future are unified, they are cast adrift in a sea of disjointed experiences. They lose their ability to construct their identity and are deprived of their self-organizing, self-governing, and self-provisioning capacities. In view of these negative aspects of globalism, it is not surprising that in several places a reaction has set in. People are again looking for a coherent narrative, for a vision that allows them in a meaningful way to unify past, present and future. This explains the reawakened interest of people, both individually and collectively, in their own national or local cultures as well as in their traditional religions which are often inextricably bound up with their cultures.

The transcendence of spatial barriers leads not only to fragmented subjects, but also unleashes an economic war of all against all. Because they are able to make an accurate and up-to-the-minute map of labor markets and exchange rates worldwide, transnational corporations have a far greater mobility. They become detached from any particular localities in that they can easily move operations to any space where wages and other standards are lower and the potential to produce profits is greater. Thus this geographical flexibility actually serves the transnationals in gaining a greater control over the workers. For it produces competition between nations and localities which, in their desire to attract industries and so to create employment, are willing to sacrifice their own control over wages, working conditions, and environmental standards, even if this goes at the expense of the workers and the environment.[3] For whether they like it or not, they have to accommodate themselves to the wishes of the transnational corporations which are only prepared to establish production units in places with cheap wages, weak unions, lax regulations, etc. If they fail to do so, they are "out."[4]

[3] F. Wilfred, Human Rights or the Rights of the Poor. Redeeming the Human Rights from Contemporary Inversions, *Vidyajyoti. Journal of Theological Reflection*, 62 (1998) 734–752; here 738–739. For the relation between globalization and ecology, see L. Rasmussen, Global Ecojustice, *Mission Studies* 16 (1999) 123–134.

[4] The transnational corporations are supported in their policies by "the governments of the strongest industrial countries [the so-called G 7 countries] who have long been actively responsible for creating and steering international institutions in the direction of more and more power to the capitalist markets and less and less power to the political institutions that could regulate markets towards social and ecological goals. Since the 80s the G 7 countries with their dominating voting power in the undemocratic IMF, World Bank and GATT [the present WTO] pushed the whole world more and more into the Structural Adjustment Programmes (SAPs) which mean money stability for the capital owners and social degradation for the working and socially dependent majorities. The instrument to blackmail the countries is the overindebtedness of the national budgets. Starting with the scandalous debt crisis in the South this cancer has reached nearly all countries... These SAPs are now harming more and more impoverished groups of people in Europe. The same policies are being promoted in the US—even more so by the growing influence of the Republicans. And the recent swing back to the LDP in Japan and their attempts to save corrupt banks with tax money shows the same basic philosophy: privatise the gains and socialise the losses." Duchrow 37–38. For a concrete example of how the SAPS cripple African countries, and particularly their educational and health sectors, see F. Fox, Forgive us our debts, *The Month* July–August 1997, 262–267. See also L. Lado T. and A. Brice Adanhounme, Globalization and socio-cultural mutations: A black african perspective, *Hekima Review* no. 21 (May 1999) 58–67. An important statement on this matter was issued by the "Religious Working Group on the World Bank and the IMF": Moral Imperatives for Addressing Structural Adjustment and Economic Reform

Thus, whereas globalism presents itself as the solution for humankind and its problems in that it transcends spatial barriers and so brings people together in the "global village," in fact, it leads to the establishment of new barriers in that it includes those who are ready to adapt to the new rules of the financial markets while excluding those who cannot comply. And even those who do comply, do not have their situations in their own hands. Although they are now a part of the so-called global free market, they are not free at all, but bound, hands and feet, by the conditions imposed by the transnational corporations which are free to control the market for their own profit at the expense of poor and the weak.[5] And if they, despite their long days of hard work under often very unfavorable circumstances, do not make any progress, they are blamed all the same and called lazy, non-enterprising, inefficient, etc.[6] For, as the prosperity theology which has been developed in support of the neo-liberal ideology of global capitalism proclaims to the world, God blesses those who believe in God and are well adapted to the system. When they are enterprising and work hard, they will prosper in this life and the next.[7]

Measures, *SEDOS Bulletin* 29 (1997) 244–247. Recently, due also to the action Jubilee 2000, supported by pope John Paul II, the G 7 countries decided to cancel some of the debts of some of the most poor countries, but much more remains to be done, if justice is to be achieved.

5 See e.g. M. Amaladoss, Christian Vision of a New Society, *SEDOS Bulletin* 31 (1999) 288–294.

6 Yet, without their work the world economy would not function. In fact, they create economic growth without themselves sharing in the growing prosperity. See J. Breman and A. Das, *Down and Out. Labouring under global capitalism*, Amsterdam 2000.

7 This prosperity theology is quite prominent in Pentecostal churches and the charismatic movement. See C. de Oliveira Ribeiro, Has Liberation Theology Died? Reflections on the Relationship between Community Life and the Globalization of the Economic System, *The Ecumenical Review* 51 (1999) 304–314. For a "catholic" justification of neo-liberal global capitalism, see M. Novak, *The Catholic Ethic and the Spirit of Capitalism*, New York 1993. He hails the capitalist catholicity which is including those "currently excluded within the beneficent circle of [its] fruitful practices" (153). Certainly, in India, for example, most children are no longer wandering about without clothes; there are less people suffering from chronic diseases; more children are going to school, albeit irregularly. Statistical figures, however, can easily make us forget the millions of people who remain excluded and kept there thanks to the economic policies of global capitalism which

A sober analysis of globalism shows that it increases the gap between rich and poor and hence its claim of being the salvation for humankind and bringing peace to all people is a false one. Yet, the majority of the people in the rich countries continue believing in it. It is for them like a new faith, a new religion whose central tenet is making money, making profit, and which gathers around it, as Anthony Sampson observes, "the sorts of accretions of reverence and ritual" normally associated with religion. And he continues: "...everywhere the same screens display the same magic numbers, subjugating a hundred different cultures and traditions to the same universal homage to its language, proclaiming with total faith the first commandment: that money makes the world go round."[8] Thus, captivated by the universal religion of money, they are unable to discover how this religion blinds their eyes to reality so that they cannot see the miserable state of millions of people all over the world who have to live below the poverty line, and how it blocks their ears so that they cannot hear the cries of the weak, the marginalised, and the exploited.

It is evident then that the master narrative of neo-liberal globalism which professes to enhance the freedom of people through its policy of free trade, of free flow of capital, of free markets, shows in a certain way the same totalitarian traits which it abhors and condemns in the narrative of communism. Its pretense to have all the answers prevents its defenders from listening to other views and to be open to alternatives. This leads to a situation in which not only the narratives of individuals and of minority groups are in danger of being overpowered and suffocated by the dominant global narrative, but a situation whereby globalism forces itself and its policies upon those who wish to remain attached to their own traditions and culture, and to maintain their own identity. For insofar as the global neo-liberal narrative is the only right one, the others are by definition wrong. This, in turn, legitimates the position of those who occupy places of authority and power within its system, and gives them the right to use force against those who think differently by

---

allows some benefits to trickle down to the down and out, but is first and foremost not directed toward a more just redistribution of wealth but rather toward the accumulation of ever greater profits in the hands of the rich and powerful.

[8] A. Sampson, *The Midas Touch: Money, People and Power from West to East*, New York 1990, 17; quoted by Duchrow 39–40.

withdrawing certain economic privileges, by imposing trade embargoes, by supporting military dictatorships or guerilla movements, whatever suits them best, or even by waging war whenever this is considered necessary to secure the availability of those natural resources and so-called strategic raw materials needed for the realisation of the aims of globalism and so for the upholding of their own positions of power in the world.[9]

Because of its totalitarian claims, the narrative of global neo-liberal capitalism cannot possibly enter into a meaningful and enriching dialogue with other narratives, especially not when they question its pretensions. On the contrary, being a narrative which, out of a feeling of superiority, wants to establish its hegemony over the whole world, neo-liberal globalism speaks a language of power, mostly of economic and/or political power, but also, if deemed necessary to defend its interests, of military power. This has led to a situation where the attempts of peoples and nations to recover their threatened identity by a return to their religio-cultural traditions, to their "fundamentals," has rather unfortunately been drawn into the sphere of international power politics. In fact, all too often, their legitimate quest for their identity is being abused by their religious and political leaders. At first, they may have been genuinely interested in the welfare of the people and the eradication of injustice and oppression. However, once in power, they were able to manipulate the people's national and/or religious sentiments and to turn their quest for identity into an instrument to try and enlarge their power, even by violent means, both within their own country and against their own people, and in the world at large. The fact that this "fundamentalism" violates the very "fundamentals" of their religion is either not seen by them, convinced as they are that their views are the only right ones, or, if seen, brushed aside because whatever they do is justified by the goal they want to reach: to free the world of the powers of evil, as they see them. The other side of the coin is that this violent fundamentalism, which receives wide publicity in the media, offers the

[9] "...some western corporations did not and will not hesitate to finance civil wars here and there in Africa, their only god being their business. The implication of ELF (a French petroleum company) in the recent civil war in Congo-Brazzaville is but one example of such mechanisms of destabilization of African countries, which have condemned millions of people to the misery of refugee camps." Lado and Brice Adanhounme 59. Their example could be multiplied by many more.

defenders of the new global order, after the loss of communism as their enemy, an easy opportunity to rally all their power and might against the new enemy: fundamentalism. The fact that this leads to the discrediting of all forms of "fundamentalism," even those that concern the return of people to their cultural and religious roots in order to recover their threatened or lost identity, is taken in stride.

All these negative and destructive consequences of the grand master narrative of neo-liberal globalism explain why today more and more voices are heard that increasingly call for a profound change of mentality. Even Western financial and political leaders call for "a globalism with a human face." Thus they admit that the present globalism does not have a human face or, at least, that, if it has, it needs to be improved by a greater concern for the human persons involved, especially the labourers. Their interests are often at the bottom of neo-liberalism's list of priorities which is topped by the interest in making the greatest possible profit. Pope John Paul II, in his social teaching, speaks of the need for what is called "the third way."[10] It is a way which tries to find a balance between the good of the individual person and the common good of society; between individual freedom and our solidarity with one another, between the independence of the human person and the need to recognise the interdependence of all. In this way all that is good in liberalism with its stress on the individual and his or her rights is brought together with all that is good in socialism with its stress on human solidarity and the common responsibility of all for the good of all.

For this reason, one might think that the failure of the master narrative of neo-liberal globalism might open new possibilities for the Christian narrative to fill up the gaps left by it.[11] Unfortunately, the reality is not that simple. For the Christian narrative, as it is presented by the churches and their leaders today, has lost its power to attract people. It speaks a religious language that has largely become unintelligible to the people of today. Its words and expressions do no longer mean anything to them. These words do not touch the human heart; they do not

[10] For a survey of recent papal teaching, see J.T. Pawlikowski, Papal teaching on Economic Justice: Change and Continuity, *New Theology Review* 10, 4 (November 1997) 60–77; D. Hollenbach, Christian Social Ethics after the Cold War, *Theological Studies* 53 (1992) 75–95.

[11] For this and what follows, see A. Jansen, Franciscus: een verhaal voor de eenentwintigste eeuw?, *FL* 82 (1999) 211–220. See also Duchrow 39–40.

put it on fire. The reason for this failure lies in the fact that, during the last centuries, Christianity was presented as a "closed" narrative. It had clear answers to all the questions, answers, moreover, which were sanctioned by the church's sacral power. These seemingly clear answers, repeated over and over again in spite of profound cultural changes,[12] have squeezed all life out of the Christian narrative. Only stale wine remains.[13]

The question, then, which remains, is: how today, when people have become suspicious of past and present masternarratives, to give new

[12] "One of the major reasons... for the loss of vitality of the Church in many of the former 'Christian' nations can be attributed to the failure of the Christian communities in these cultures to keep phase with the cultural changes so that they would have remained relevant and meaningful to their context." In other words, they have forgotten that "inculturation is an ongoing process valid for *all* churches, since culture itself is dynamic and changing." J. Kavunkal, Mission as Inculturation, *Vidyajyoti. Journal of Theological Reflection* 63 (1999) 860–869, here 863.

[13] As a result many young people, dissatisfied with the present Christian narrative, start looking elsewhere. They have this possibility thanks to globalism and its transcendence of spatial and temporal barriers. For this enables them to get to know and experience other cultures and religious traditions and to select from them whatever they consider meaningful for themselves in their own situation. This "syncretistic" search can lead people to a deeper and richer understanding of the mystery of God, the Ultimate Reality, which cannot adequately and exhaustively be expressed in any particular religion, as all religions are historically determined and hence bound by time and place. Religions therefore are not mutually exclusive, but complementary. As such, they have to collaborate with each other in helping people to penetrate in an ever more adequate and profound way into the mystery of God and the plans which God has with humankind and with the world. Thus, through their collaboration, they are able to provide a common moral and spiritual foundation for people's involvement in building a just and peaceful world. See Amaladoss 294; also: H. Küng and K-J Kuschel (eds) *A Global Ethic*, London 1993. There exists, however, a danger for this "syncretistic" search. Instead of leading to a deeper understanding of the divine mystery, it often results in people making a God in their own image and to their own liking. This God answers their own private needs at that particular moment but is likely to be disposed of, as happens with most goods in our consumerist world, when this God no longer serves their purposes. See Cavanaugh 188. Moreover, as people are mostly looking for an answer to their own private needs because they feel powerless to solve the global problems of poverty and hunger, violence and war, their newly won image of God often does not challenge them to become involved in the transformation of the sinful social and political structures. See Mary Grey, I B 7, note 34.

vitality to the Christian narrative? Or how to free the Christian narrative from its closed character and to make it an open, inviting narrative, which can offer the "fragmented" people of today a coherent vision from which they can draw meaning, so that they do not wander directionless through this world but know where to go and what they hope to achieve? It is here that Francis' narrative in which his vision, his dream of paradise, occupies a central place, can play its role insofar as it presents a radical alternative to the master narrative of neo-liberal global capitalism and its ills. Basic to the Franciscan alternative are the six virtues of *The Salutation of the Virtues* which form a complete antithesis to the "values" of neo-liberal globalism.

Whereas globalism is based on the power that money brings, and creates a profound division between the rich and the poor, Francis emphasizes that people should mutually serve one another and so become one great sister- and brotherhood. Whereas globalism preaches competition and ruthlessly excludes those who cannot come along, ever more widening the gap between the rich and the poor, Francis proclaims poverty and humility as acts of liberating solidarity with the poor and marginalized, by which those who were left out are taken in and made to share in the goods of creation which equally belong to all. Whereas globalism forces itself and its policies upon others, not concerned about their needs but only about its own economic interests, Francis wishes lovingly to listen to the others and their needs because it is in and through them that the Lord appeals to him to become engaged in God's mission to build a world where there are no needy any longer. Whereas globalism imposes a monoculture on the world and suffocates minority groups who wish to maintain their own cultures and traditions, Francis wishes to be subject and submissive to all people in the world and to respect them and their culture and to form one universal sister- and brotherhood. Whereas globalism is ready to use violence and even to go to war against those who, in its eyes, endanger its interests, Francis wishes to live in peace even among those who are considered enemies. In short, whereas globalism as it manifests itself in the present context, is oppressive, exploitative and divisive, the six foundational virtues which Francis recommends, are, by their very nature liberative, empowering and unifying. Whereas globalism keeps millions of people all over the world in bondage within its sinful structures, Francis' six holy virtues are able to confound these evil structures and to set the people free, as they were originally meant to be when God created them and placed them in paradise.

Francis and his brothers developed this great universal vision in the course of many years. Every time they met a new situation on their journey through the world, they sat down, analysed the situation and tried to find an answer in accordance with the ideal they had set for themselves: an alternative society that would be fair and just, that would not exclude anyone but accept all people as sisters and brothers, especially the poor and the lepers and the beggars by the wayside. Thus the Franciscan vision was a dynamic and open one, always critically yet constructively interacting with the new situations, the new challenges it had to face. It was this dynamic, open vision which Francis and his first brothers shared with those who joined the brotherhood. As we have pointed out on more than one occasion, they were not always prepared to accept the challenge of such a dynamic and open vision, and sought safety and security by accommodating themselves within existing social structures. No longer alert to their transforming mission within society, they were satisfied to settle down and live comfortably in conformity with accepted cultural standards. In their hands, the Franciscan narrative lost its countercultural character. It was no longer the inspiring source of an antithetical society of which their world was so much in need.

On the other hand, however, we see how, throughout history, the Franciscan narrative continued to touch the hearts and minds of people who, in a critical interaction with their world, wanted to reform their world and to build an alternative society, in which, in line with Francis' ideals, people would share with each other the goods of creation and so realise in deeds the greeting of peace which the Lord gave to Francis. In this context, it is often said that no religious order in the church has known as many reform movements as the Franciscan order. And even today we witness how the Franciscan narrative of solidarity with the poor and marginalised, of non-violence and peace, of universal sister- and brotherhood, of respect for other cultures and religions, of reverence for Mother Earth, because of its dynamic and open character, is able to inspire people and to move them to become actively involved in the peace movement, the lobby against the sale of arms, the human rights movement, the dialogue with other religions, especialy Islam, the ecological movement, etc.

It is remarkable that among these people there are many lay people and even people of other religious traditions or of no religious tradition at all. They are attracted by the way in which Francis built an alternative society not based on power and might which divide people, but on mutual service and solidarity which bring people together, and not only people, but even wild beasts and animals. In their own way all these people, scattered all over the world, confound the evil in the world and express their faith in the power of goodness and love to bring back paradise, even if only on a small scale or in some remote, insignificant place, or for a brief span of time. These instances are worthwhile to be celebrated, just as Francis celebrated them in his *The Salutation of the Virtues* which confound vices and sins. For they keep the hope alive in us and enable us to awaken and set free in us the creative and liberating energy that empowers us to remain committed, even in this time of globalization and its many adverse effects on people and the world, to Francis' universal vision of a new world, of Paradise Restored.

Bibliography

R. Armstrong, 'Prophetic Implications of the Admonitions,' *Laurentianum* 26 (1985) 396–464.

____. *St. Francis of Assisi. Writings for a Gospel Life*, New York, 1994.

R. Armstrong - I. Brady, *Francis and Clare. The Complete Works*, New York, 1982.

____, W. Hellmann, W. Short (eds), *Francis of Assisi: Early Documents, Vol. I: The Saint*, New York, 1999.

O. v. Asseldonk, 'Verso un cuore puro con la pura, semplice e vera pace dello spirito (RegNB 17,15),' *Laurentianum* 33 (1992) 481–531.

I.M. Boccali, *Opuscula S. Francisci et Scripta S. Clarae Assisiensium*, Assisi, 1978.

____. *Concordantiae verbales opusculorum S. Francisci et S. Clarae Assisiensium*, Assisi, 1995.

J. Bumke, *Höfische Kultur, Literatur und Gesellschaft im hohem Mittelalter*, 2 vol. München, 1986.

F. Cardini, 'The Warrior and the Knight,' in *The Medieval World*, ed. J. Le Goff, London, 1990.

____. 'I musulmani nel giudizio dei crociati all'inizio del Duecento,' *Archivio Storico Italiano* 146 (1988) 371–388.

C. Cargnoni, 'Umiltà, umiliazione,' *Dizionario Francescano*, Padoa, 1983, 1870–1902

Th. Desbonnets, *De l'intuition à l'institution*, Paris, 1983. English translation: *From Intuition to Institution: The Franciscans*, Chicago, 1988.

S. v. Dijk, *The Ordinal of the Papal Court from Innocent III to Boniface VIII and Related Documents*, completed by J. Hazelden Walker, Fribourg, 1975.

W. Egger, "Verbum in corde - cor ad Deum," Analyse und Interpretation von RegNB XXII,' *Laurentianum* 23 (1982) 286–311.

K. Esser, *Das Testament des heiligen Franziskus von Assisi. Eine Untersuchung über seine Echtheit und seine Bedeutung*, Münster,1949.

____. *Die Opuscula des hl. Franziskus von Assisi*, Grottaferrata, 1976.

____. *Opuscula Sancti Patris Francisci Assisiensis*, Grottaferrata, 1978.

D. Flood, *The Birth of a Movement*, Chicago, 1975.

'The Domestication of the Franciscan Movement,' *Franziskanische Studien* 60 (1978) 311–327.

____. 'A Brief Survey of Early Franciscan History,' *Haversack* 1,5 (May–June 1978), 2–14.

____. 'Franciscans and Money,' *Haversack* 4,2 (December 1980) 12–21.

____. 'Die wirtschaftliche Grundlage der franziskanischen Bewegung in ihrer Entstehungszeit,' *Wissenschaft und Weisheit* 44 (1981) 184–204.

____. 'Peace in Assisi in the Early Thirteenth Century,' *Franziskanische Studien* 64 (1982) 67–89. Reprinted in *Franciscan Digest* 1,1 (May 1991) 1–20.

____. 'Assisi's Rules and People's Needs: The Initial Determination of the Franciscan Mission,' *Franziskanische Studien* 66 (1984) 91–104. Reprinted in *Franciscan Digest* 2,2 (June 1992) 69–89.

____. 'The Testament as Recall,' *Haversack* 11,1 (October 1987) 18–19.

____. 'The Confusion of Evil: Franciscan Nonviolence,' *Haversack* 11,3 (February 1988) 3–5

____. 'The Politics of "Quo Elongati,"' *Laurentianum* 29 (1988) 370–385. Reprinted in *Franciscan Digest* 3,1 (June 1993) 39–55.

____. *Francis of Assisi and the Franciscan Movement*, Manila, 1989.

____. *Poverty's Condition. A Reading of the Sacrum Commercium*, Chicago 1990.

____. *Work for Everyone. Francis of Assisi and the Ethic of Service*, Quezon City, 1997

G.P. Freeman, *Gelukkig wie in Jezus' voetspoor gaat*, Utrecht, 1981.

____. 'Der Wolf, Franziskus und Gubbio. Eine synchrone Lesung von Fioretti 21,' *Wissenschaft und Weisheit* 48 (1985) 122–150.

____. '"Usquequo gravi corde?" Zur Deutung der 1. Ermahnung des Franziskus,' *Laurentianum* 29 (1988) 386–415.

____. 'De zieke die zich niet bekeert,' *Franciscaans Leven* 81 (1998) 3–11. English translation: 'The Sick Man Who Does Not Repent,' *Franciscan Digest* 9,1 (March 1999) 1–10.

____. 'Het woord van de vader,' *Franciscaans Leven* 81 (1998) 99–106. English translation: 'The Word of the Father,' *Franciscan Digest* 9,1 (March 1999) 19–27.

____. 'Kinderen van de hemelse vader,' *Franciscaans Leven* 81 (1998) 251–258.

English translation: Children of the Heavenly Father. *Franciscan Digest* 10,1 (March 2000) 15–23.

G.P.Freeman - H. Sevenhoven, *De nalatenschap van een arme*, Utrecht, 1989. English translation: 'The legacy of a Poor Man,' *Franciscan Digest* 3,1 (June 1993) 1–18; 3,2 (December 1993) 80–96; 4,1 (June 1994) 34–63; 4,2 (December 1994) 63–83; 6,1 (April 1996) 1–26.

E. Gilson, 'La Sagesse de Saint François,' *Les Amis de Saint François*, 6, 22 (1939) 7–15.

E. v.d. Goorbergh, 'Het officie van het lijden van de Heer,' *Franciscaans Leven* 72 (1989) 70–83; English translation: 'The Office of the Passion of our Lord,' *Franciscan Digest* 8,1 (June 1998) 48–60.

E. v.d. Goorbergh - Th. Zweerman, *Was Getekend: Franciscus van Assisi*, Assen, 1998.

M.A. Habig (ed.) *St. Francis of Assisi. Writings and Early Biographies. English Omnibus of the Sources for the Life of St. Francis*, Chicago, 1972.

L. Hardick - E. Grau, *Die Schriften des heiligen Franziskus von Assisi*, Werl, 1980.

J. Hoeberichts, 'The Admonitions of Saint Francis: Words of Life and Salvation. The Fifth Admonition,' *FIA Contact*, 5, 4 (1984) 22–31

____. 'Ministry to the Friars in the Writings of Francis and the Early Biographers,' *FIA Contact* 6,4 (November1985) 2–9.

____. 'Een bevrijdingstheologisch perspectief op Franciscus en zijn keuze voor de armen,' *Franciscaans Leven* 72 (1989) 219–233. English translation: 'Francis and His Option for the Poor from a Liberation-theological Perspective,' *Franciscan Digest* 6,1 (April 1996) 27–43.

____. *Franciscus en de Islam*, Assen, 1994. English translation: *Francis and Islam*, Quincy, IL., 1997.

____. 'Eucharist and Priesthood according to Francis, with special reference to the First Admonition, *Franciscan Digest* 7,2 (December 1997) 13–27.

B. Holter, *"Zum besonderen Dienst bestellt." Die Sicht des Priesteramtes bei Franz von Assisi und die Spuren seines Diakonats in den "Opuscula"*, Werl, 1992.

L. Izzo, 'Semplicità,' *Dizionario Francescano*, Padova, 1983, 1687–1706.

A. Jansen, 'Woorden van heil van Franciscus. Kommentaar op de 27e Vermaning,' *Franciscaans Leven* 64 (1981) 163–186. English translation: 'Words of Salvation of Saint Francis. A Commentary on Admonition 27,' *Franciscan Digest* 4,2 (December 1994) 1–24.

____. 'The Story of the True Joy. An Autobiographical Reading,' *Franziskanische Studien* 63 (1981) 271–288. Reprinted in *Franciscan Digest* 2,2 (June 1992) 1–27.

'Lofzang op de deugden I,' *Franciscaans Leven* 75 (1992) 60–74.

'Lofzang op de deugden II,' *Franciscaans Leven* 75 (1992) 167–182.

____. 'Mijn juk is zoet,' *Franciscaans Leven* 81 (1998) 107–116. English translation: 'My Yoke is Sweet,' *Franciscan Digest* 9,1 (March 1999) 28–38.

____. 'Franciscus: een verhaal voor de eenentwintigste eeuw?' *Franciscaans Leven* 82 (1999) 211–219.

M.A. Lavilla Martin, La sumisión a toda criatura por Dios, propuesta por Francisco de Asís.

Un pasaje de la historia exegética de 1 Pt 2,13, *Antonianum* 74 (1999) 463–499.

P. v. Leeuwen - S. Verheij, *Woorden van heil van een kleine mens*, Utrecht, 1986.

L. Lehmann, *Tiefe und Weite. Der universale Grundzug in den Gebeten des Franziskus von Assisi*, Werl, 1984.

____. 'Der Mensch Franziskus im Licht seiner Briefe,' *Wissenschaft und Weisheit* (46 (1983) 108–138. English translation: 'The Man Francis in the Light of his Letters,' *Franciscan* 2,2 (June 1992) 29–67.

____. 'Grundzüge franziskanischen Missionsverständnisses nach Regula non bullata 16,' *Franziskanische Studien* 66 (1984) 68–81. English translation: 'Main Features of the Franciscan Understanding of Mission according to the Rule of 1221,' *FrancDigest* 2,1 (January 1992) 1–20.

S. Lopez, 'Obbedienza, comando, autorità,' *Dizionario Francescano*, Padova, 1983, 1111–1132.

A. v. Lotringen - I. Nije Bijvank, 'Liefde en vernedering. De ridderlijke idealen van Franciscus en Lancelot,' *Franciscaans Leven* 72 (1989) 112–126.

A. MacIntyre, *After Virtue: A Study in Moral Theory*, London, 1985.

C. Maier, *Preaching the Crusades. Mendicant Friars and the Cross in the Thirteenth Century*, Cambridge, 1994.

R. Manselli, *St. Francis of Assisi*, Chicago, 1988.

A. Matanic, 'Virtù,' *Dizionario Francescano*, Padova, 1983, 1979–1988.

G. Miccoli, 'Francis of Assisi's Christian Proposal,' *Greyfriars Review* 3,2 (August 1989) 127–172.

N. Nguyên-Van-Khanh, *Le Christ dans la pensée de Saint François d'Assise d'après ses écrits*, Paris, 1989. English translation: *The Teacher of his Heart*, St. Bonaventure, New York, 1994.

H. Nolthenius, *Een man uit het dal van Spoleto: Franciscus tussen zijn tijdgenoten*, Amsterdam, 1988.

R. Reijsbergen, *Omkeer van een verdwaalde mens. Poging tot een maatschappijhistorische interpretatie van de Lofzang op de deugden van Franciscus van Assisi*, Den Haag, 1989.

A. Rotzetter, *Die Funktion der franziskanischen Bewegung in der Kirche*, Schwyz, 1977.

____, W.C. Van Dijk, T. Matura, *Franz von Assisi. Ein Anfang und was davon bleibt.* Zürich, 1981. English translation: *Gospel Living Francis of Assisi Yesterday and Today*, St. Bonaventure, New York, 1994.

O. Schmucki, 'La 'Lettera a tutto l'Ordine' di San Francesco,' *L'Italia Francescana* 55 (1980) 245–286; English translation 'St. Francis's Letter to the Entire order,' *Greyfriars Review* 3,1 (April 1989) 1–33.

O. Schmucki - Th. Jansen, 'Nachhall zu einem Geburtszentenar,' *Collectanea Franciscana* 56 (1986) 246.

K.V. Selge, 'Franz von Assisi und die Römische Kirche,' *Zeitschrift für Theologie und Kirche* 67 (1970) 129–161.

H. Sevenhoven, 'Hoe gehoorzaamheid liefde wordt,' *Franciscaans Leven* 67 (1984) 222–232. English translation: 'How Obedience Turns into Love,' *Franciscan Digest* 7,2 (December 1997) 1–12.

____. 'Oorspronkelijk en ontroerend. Franciscus' omgang met de dieren,' *Franciscaans Leven* 75 (1992) 193–201

'Het theater van de deugden,' *Franciscaans Leven* 82 (1999) 99–105.

W. Short, 'Hagiographical method in reading Franciscan sources: stories of Francis and creatures in Thomas of Celano's "Vita Prima" (21:58–61),' *Laurentianum* 29 (1988) 462–495.

R.D. Sorrell, 'Tradition and innovation in Saint Francis of Assisi's sermon to the birds,' *Franciscan Studies* 43 (1983) 396–407.

____. *St. Francis of Assisi and Nature. Tradition and Innovation in Western Christian Attitudes toward the Environment*, Oxford, 1988.

M. Steiner, 'El "Saludo a las virtutes" de S. Francisco de Asis,' *Selecciones de Franciscanismo* 16, 1 (1987) 129–140.

L. Temperini, 'Amore di Dio, amore del prossimo,' *Dizionario Francescano*, Padova, 1983, 55–76.

S. Verhey, *Der Mensch unter der Herrschaft Gottes. Versuch einer Theologie des Menschen nach dem hl. Franziskus von Assisi*, Düsseldorf, 1960.

____. 'De oorspronkelijke onschuld. Franciscus spreekt met de vogels en de andere dieren,' *Franciscaans Leven* 61 (1978) 16–30.

W. Viviani, *L'ermeneutica di Francesco d'Assisi. Indagine alla luce di Gv 13–17 nei suoi scritti*. Roma, 1983.

H. de Vos, 'Uw lieve Zoon, Heer en Leraar,' *Franciscaans Leven* 80 (1997) 261–269; English translation: 'Your Beloved Son, Lord and Teacher. A Short Reflection on Francis' Office of the Passion,' *Franciscan Digest* 8,1 (June1998) 38–47.

____. *De psalmen van Franciscus van Assisi. Een weg naar innerlijke vrede*, Utrecht, 1999.

Z. Zafarana, 'La predicazione francescana,' *Francescanesimo e vita religiosa dei laici nel 200*, Assisi, 1981, 203–250.

Th. Zweerman, 'Mystik bei Franziskus von Assisi. Unter besonderer Berücksichtigung der "Salutatio Virtutum,"' in *Mystik in den franziskanischen Orden*, ed. J-B. Freyer, Kevelaer, 1993.